REGULATION INSIDE GOVERNMENT

# Regulation inside Government

## WASTE-WATCHERS, QUALITY POLICE, AND SLEAZE-BUSTERS

CHRISTOPHER HOOD
COLIN SCOTT
OLIVER JAMES
GEORGE JONES
and
TONY TRAVERS

OXFORD

UNIVERSITY PRESS

# OXFORD
### UNIVERSITY PRESS

Great Clarendon Street, Oxford OX2 6DP

Oxford University Press is a department of the University of Oxford.
It furthers the University's objective of excellence in research, scholarship,
and education by publishing worldwide in

Oxford New York

Athens Auckland Bangkok Bogotá Buenos Aires Calcutta
Cape Town Chennai Dar es Salaam Delhi Florence Hong Kong Istanbul Karachi
Kuala Lumpur Madrid Melbourne Mexico City Mumbai
Nairobi Paris São Paulo Singapore Taipei Tokyo Toronto Warsaw

with associated companies in Berlin Ibadan

Oxford is a registered trade mark of Oxford University Press
in the UK and in certain other countries

published in the United States
by Oxford University Press Inc., New York

British Library Cataloguing in Publication Data

Data available

Library of Congress Cataloging in Publication Data

Regulation inside government: waste watchers, quality police, and
sleaze-busters / Christopher Hood . . . [et al.].
Includes bibliographical references.
1. Public administration—Great Britain.   2. Public utilities—
Great Britain—Management.   3. Great Britain—Politics and
government.   I. Hood, Christopher, 1947– .
JN318.R44   1999  352.3′5′0941—dc21   98-54456

ISBN 0-19-828099-8

1 3 5 7 9 10 8 6 4 2

Typeset in Sabon
by Best-set Typesetter Ltd., Hong Kong

Printed in Great Britain
on acid-free paper by
Biddles Ltd., Guildford and King's Lynn

# PREFACE

All theory, said Nietzsche, is autobiography, and such theory as this book contains is heavily shaped by our own experience of regulation over the public sector in Britain in the 1990s. The book began as a casual conversation between two of us (Christopher Hood and Tony Travers) five years ago. That discussion turned—as casual conversations can do—into several years of hard work for five people under the aegis of the ESRC's 1995–7 Whitehall programme (whose financial assistance we gratefully acknowledge). The original conversation was about the development of regulation inside government, something that seemed to be a *leitmotiv* of UK public management in the 1990s, but was at that time attracting much less attention from academics than regulation of business or other aspects of the so-called New Public Management. This book summarizes what we found out about the changing world of regulators inside government.

The book is a genuinely collaborative effort. If it is a horse designed by a committee, the humps are not there by accident, because the book is the product of much group discussion—including many conversations that were far from casual—of the patterns we were observing and how to tell the story. For the record, Chapters 1–4 and 9–10 were primarily drafted by Christopher Hood and Oliver James with substantial help from Colin Scott; Chapter 5 was drafted by George Jones with the help of Oliver James; Chapters 6 and 8 were drafted by Colin Scott with the help of Oliver James; and Chapter 7 by Tony Travers with Oliver James. Christopher Hood, Colin Scott, and Oliver James took the lead in developing the analytic framework of the book and Christopher Hood acted as overall editor.

We have many debts to acknowledge. The book would not have been possible without the contribution of the eighty-odd people we interviewed—many of them regulators and some of them at the receiving end of the process—who gave generously of their time in sharing with us their insights and perspectives on regulation inside government. We do not have space to mention them all by name and many were serving civil servants who by convention remain anonymous in such cases (for the same reason, we have not identified individuals in person when we quote from interviews). We must also thank the body of public-service regulators whom we assembled for a collective ESRC-sponsored seminar at LSE in 1997 to discuss the phenomenon as a group. We are grateful to those who commented on our work as it developed, including the participants at another ESRC-sponsored seminar at LSE in 1996 to explore concepts of regulation in government, and the various conferences at which we presented our ideas (including the 1996 American Political Science Association and Political Studies Association conferences, the 1995 and 1997 Socio-Legal Studies Association conference, the 1997 European Group for Public Administration conference, the European University Institute's 1997 seminar on the New European Agencies, and the special ESRC conference on 'Whither Whitehall' in London in 1997). In particular, we thank those who read drafts of chapters including Kenneth Armstrong, Damian Chalmers, David Downes, Peter Grabosky, Richard Harding, Simon Hix, Imelda Maher, Jill Peay, Genevra Richardson, Paul Rock, John Stewart, and Joanne Scott. We are also especially heavily indebted to Andrew Dunsire, Martin Loughlin, and John Braithwaite who read the whole draft and offered valuable comments. We are grateful to Cliff Nicholson for helping as to track down material on District Audit, and to Martin Lodge, Lene Lindgreen, Steve John, and Helena Tunstall for research assistance during the project. We are also grateful to Gillian Hood for proof-reading and indexing.

Some of the chapters in the book draw on work published elsewhere, including Christopher Hood's 'Control over Bureaucracy: Cultural Theory and Institutional Variety' in the *Journal of Public Policy* 1996, Christopher Hood and Colin Scott's 'Bureaucratic Regulation and New Public Management in the United Kingdom: Mirror-Image Developments' in the *Journal of Law and Society* 1996, and Richard Parry, Christopher Hood, and Oliver James's 'Reinventing the Treasury: Economic Rationalism or an Econocrat's Fallacy of Control?' in *Public Administration* 1997. Part of the argument in Chapter 10 appeared in an article by all of us in *Public Money and Management* in 1998.

In addition to the ESRC's support, we are grateful for support from the LSE staff research fund and from STICERD, which funded our work on EU regulation of the activities of member governments. The ideas in this book also began to take shape in a sabbatical year taken by Christopher Hood in 1994–5 and spent in four different places: Manchester University's Government Department, Humboldt University Berlin, the University of Copenhagen, and Nuffield College Oxford. Those sojourns were generously supported by a Leverhulme Senior Research Fellowship and by a D. N. Chester Senior Research Fellowship at Nuffield College, and produced a valuable opportunity to think about the phenomenon of regulation in government and try out some preliminary ideas. Colin Scott also had the opportunity to test and develop some of the ideas within a lively community of regulation specialists as a Visiting Fellow in the Law and Reshaping Australian Institutions programmes of the Research School of Social Sciences, Australian National University, during 1996–7, with financial help from the Society of Public Teachers of Law.

*London School of Economics*
*July 1998*

# CONTENTS

# LIST OF FIGURES

# LIST OF TABLES

# PART ONE

## Introducing and Analysing Regulation inside Government

# 1

# A Regulatory State inside the State?

> The more strictly we are watched, the better we behave.
>
> Jeremy Bentham, unpublished MS quoted by
> Bahmueller, *The National Charity Company*

We are said to live in the age of the 'regulatory State' (Majone 1994; Loughlin and Scott 1997; McGowan and Wallace 1997). That phrase suggests modern states are placing more emphasis on the use of authority, rules and standard-setting, partially displacing an earlier emphasis on public ownership, public subsidies, and directly provided services. The expanding part of modern government, the argument goes, is *regulation*—a much used word rarely defined with precision, but broadly denoting the use of public authority (often in the hands of specialized agencies) to set and apply rules and standards. The regulation of business, and especially regulation of the privatized utilities (where the shift from a 'public-bureaucracy state' to a 'regulatory state' in the UK seems most dramatic and controversial), has attracted much attention from both policy-makers and academics.[1] Much has been written about problems like the accountability of regulators, how compliance cost should be factored into regulatory policy, the proper balance between formula-driven and discretionary approaches to regulation, the relative advantages of collegiate and single-headed authority structures for regulatory bodies, and specialization versus inclusiveness in the jurisdiction of regulators.

Less commonly discussed are analogous processes of 'regulation' *within* the public sector. We are not accustomed to think of government as 'regulating' itself. The word regulation is not generally used to denote the various ways in which public organizations are

---

[1] Examples include Hancher and Moran (1989) and Ogus (1994) on general regulation; and a host of works on utilities regulation, including Foster (1992), Veljanovski (1991; 1993), and Prosser (1997).

shaped by rules and standards emanating from arm's-length authorities. In fact, there is no generic word for the sum of such activities applied to government in the same way as for the private sector. Only a minority of constitutional lawyers and political scientists have recognized regulation inside government as a key part of accountability regimes,[2] and none has explored it systematically. Yet regulation in government merits attention as a matter of some political and constitutional significance. It is conventionally argued that the orthodox constitutional checks on executive government—the courts and elected members[3] of the legislature—face inbuilt dilemmas and limitations as control and checking mechanisms, particularly in an era of expanded government.[4] Regulation in government, coming somewhere between these two orthodox 'separation of powers' checking devices, accordingly has a quasi-constitutional importance. But this regulatory world has only been imperfectly mapped, its working has been explored only in isolated parts rather than as a general phenomenon, and it is only beginning to be discussed as an overall system.

Against that background, this book argues there is a range of regulation processes inside government. Just as a business firm is exposed to a set of different regulators—auditors, inspectors, licensing bodies, competition and fair-trading authorities—so a typical public organization faces a collection of waste-watchers, quality police, sleaze-busters, and other 'regulators'. Some of those oversight organizations, in the UK at least, are common to the public and private sectors (for instance data-protection and safety-at-work regulators). But many are specific to public bodies, in the form of distinctive systems of audit, grievance-handling, standard-setting, inspection, and evaluation.

This book reports what we learned about the regulation of UK government during a two-year exploration. We had two main aims. One was to reveal the overall scope and scale of regulation inside British government: how much of it went on, through what institutional forms, where it had expanded, and where it had shrunk in

---

[2] For example see Jennings (1959: 194–5); Day and Klein (1987); Harden (1995); Scott (1996a); Daintith (1997).

[3] Plus the members of the House of Lords, in the British case.

[4] Hence the burgeoning literature on 'agency' problems facing legislatures and the choices they face in monitoring government, e.g. between 'police-patrol' and 'fire-alarm' approaches (McCubbins and Schwartz 1984).

recent decades. The other aim was to discover, mainly through in-depth interviews with a selection of 'regulators' and their clients,[5] how the process of regulation in government worked—how standards were set and enforced, how conflict and cooperation among the various actors played out, how regulation of the public sector had altered with the complex of changes conventionally summed up as New Public Management (Ferlie *et al.* 1996).

The rest of the book discusses what we discovered, and its significance for the understanding of contemporary bureaucracy and regulation. Three main themes run through the book. First, the sum of regulation inside UK government amounted to a surprisingly large enterprise, approaching if not exceeding the scale of regulation of private business. It was an 'industry' which seemed to have grown topsy-like, with no overall rationalization or consistent practice. It was not so much a world within a world as several unrelated worlds. And it was itself regulated at best patchily, little exposed to the kinds of disciplines it imposed on those it regulated.

Second, regulation of government seemed in many of its domains to have increased in formality, complexity, intensity, and specialization over the last two decades. Patricia Day and Rudolf Klein (1990: 4) speak of an 'age of inspection' in the social services. Michael Power (1997) speaks of the development of an 'audit society' obsessed with constant checking and verification. Geoff Mulgan (1995) and Paul Hoggett (1996) have identified a formalization of controls over government, contrary to the stereotype that New Public Management involved 'bonfires' of government manuals and rule-books. Martin Loughlin (1996: 30) sees contemporary developments in public management as a resurgent triumph of the administrative doctrines of the utilitarian philosopher Jeremy Bentham. Certainly, one of Bentham's doctrines for good government (as summed up in the epigraph to this chapter, and applied by Bentham's disciple Edwin Chadwick to administrative design in the nineteenth century) was strict central inspection, linked to

---

[5] Senior figures were interviewed in regulator and regulatee organizations, including heads of audit and ombudsmen offices, senior officials in inspectorates, senior civil servants, local-authority chief executives, heads of local authority services, and teachers. The interviews were conducted under Chatham House rules, so quotations are not attributed. Interviewees are identified in the text by codes corresponding to the type of interview. The codes are explained in Appendix I, which also gives an anonymized list of interviewees.

'tabular-comparison' of the performance of different elements of the public service on common scales and the use of lay members of the public as well as professionals and the judiciary as inspectors of public services (cf. Foucault 1977: 195–228 and Hume 1981: 51). These Benthamite and Chadwickian themes were much in evidence for some public service developments in the 1980s and 1990s, though other Benthamite management principles were much less so,[6] and, as we shall show later, even the 'strict-inspection' theme was applied much more to some services than others.

At first sight such developments seem paradoxical, since conventional wisdom holds that UK public management from the late 1970s underwent a management revolution intended to cut down excessive rules hampering the ability of managers to 'add value' (Moore 1995) to public services and make management in government more like that of business. So was some red-tape equivalent of the law of conservation of matter playing out in government bureaucracy, with operating rules being displaced from one set of activities only to appear in another? Paul Light (1993: 14) has distinguished different forms of accountability in government, in particular contrasting 'compliance accountability' (in which managers are subject to detailed rules, with some sort of sanction for non-compliance) with 'performance accountability' (in which managers are subject to incentives to reach goals), and much of the rhetoric of New Public Management stressed the relative importance of the latter, emphasizing a change from tactical to strategic prescription, direct to indirect command, detailed instruction to freedom within constraints. Even on that characterization, new regimes of performance regulation can be expected to emerge in parallel with new managerial freedoms, and 'compliance' regulation (over procedures, for instance on merit-hiring or complaint-handling) can take new, often enhanced, forms in a more managerial public service. So in some domains at least, aspects of regulation in government seemed to be moving in the opposite direction from that of operational management,[7] with the extra

---

[6] Such as 'local-consideration-consulting' and 'habit-respecting'.

[7] Such a development would be consistent with Hoggett's (1996) finding that changes in UK public management have produced increasingly formal controls (contrary to the stereotype of cutting down red tape) and with Power's (1997) argument that the search for auditability has produced a formalization of self-regulation.

'freedom to manage' that was given with one hand being checked by more regulation imposed by the other hand.

There is no conventional term of art that labels such a dynamic in public management. We use the term 'mirror image' to sum it up (drawing a rough analogy with processes like mirror-image dancing where as one partner moves to the right the other moves to the left and vice versa), but this metaphor has its limitations. Part of the process may be closer to the Marx Brothers' famous mirror-scene in *Duck Soup* (1933) (where Chico and Harpo, both dressed as Groucho, act as if mirroring Groucho, to avoid detection) than to a true mirror-image. Readers might prefer to think of the process in terms of 'reversed polarity' (particularly since we shall be linking it up to a culture switch in Chapter 9). This mirror-image theme seems to sum up some of the developments we observed, but there were major exceptions to it, particularly in regulation of local government by central government and of regulation of member states by the EU. We explore the mirror-image theme further in Parts Two and Three.

Our third theme is that regulation in government varied substantially in how close 'regulators' were to those they oversaw. Some regulators came from the same professional-social backgrounds as their 'clients', as with many of the overseers of the civil service. 'Poacher' and 'gamekeeper' came from the same world and their roles might be reversed over the course of a working lifetime. In other cases regulators came from different professional-social backgrounds, for example civil servants regulating local-authority bureaucracies. Doctrine about best practice in internal regulation was variegated and largely implicit. Sometimes it was asserted: 'former poachers make the best gamekeepers', or at least that familiar doctrine was reflected in practice, as in the long tradition of drawing the Comptroller and Auditor-General (the Head of the National Audit Office) from the ranks of the top civil service. But often, and increasingly in recent years, the opposite principle was favoured, with reactions against cosy inbred professional communities inside public services such as education and the growing controversy over police investigating police over allegations of wrongdoing. The Benthamite theme of lay inspectors of public services became highly favoured as a counterweight to 'incestuous' professional relations in the 1990s, harking back to an older tradition of oversight of public bodies by local notables, such as prison visitors. The doctrine implied by such developments was that effective regulation needed to be socially distant from the regulated. As will be shown later, many regulator organizations inside government were in fact hybrid, part-close and part-distant. But in many cases (there were exceptions) we found the more distant such regulators were from their 'clients' in professional-social backgrounds, the more regulatory they tended to be in the sense of more formal and more rule-bound.

The chapters which follow pursue these themes. The rest of this introductory chapter does three things. First, it explores in more detail what is meant by regulation in government. How can the domain of such regulation be defined? What are its boundaries and what are the fuzzy cases at the edges? Second, it looks at regulation inside government against the broader repertoire of processes for controlling public bureaucracies and institutions. What is the basic tool kit or inventory available for such activities? Third, it lays out the 'route plan' for the rest of the book.

## 1. WHAT IS 'REGULATION' INSIDE GOVERNMENT?

Our focus is on regulation of government—the way regulation works inside and over government at the bureaucratic level. Such regulation is conceived as the range of ways in which the activities of public bureaucracies are subject to influence from other public agencies that come between the orthodox constitutional checking mechanisms referred to earlier (the courts and the members of the legislature), operate at arm's length from the direct line of command and are endowed with some sort of authority over their charges. It thus has three basic dimensions that are schematically portrayed in Figure 1.1:

- one bureaucracy aims to shape the activities of another;
- there is some degree of organizational separation between the 'regulating' bureaucracy and the 'regulatee';
- the 'regulator' has some kind of official mandate to scrutinize the behaviour of the 'regulatee' and seek to change it.

All those elements need to be present to count as 'regulation' in the sense used in this book.

Many different agencies and units come within that general

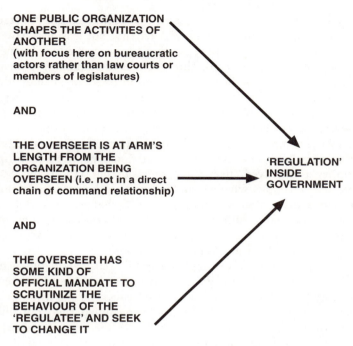

**ONE PUBLIC ORGANIZATION SHAPES THE ACTIVITIES OF ANOTHER** (with focus here on bureaucratic actors rather than law courts or members of legislatures)

**AND**

**THE OVERSEER IS AT ARM'S LENGTH FROM THE ORGANIZATION BEING OVERSEEN** (i.e. not in a direct chain of command relationship)

**AND**

**THE OVERSEER HAS SOME KIND OF OFFICIAL MANDATE TO SCRUTINIZE THE BEHAVIOUR OF THE 'REGULATEE' AND SEEK TO CHANGE IT**

**'REGULATION' INSIDE GOVERNMENT**

FIG. 1.1. Features of 'regulation' inside government

definition. As will be shown in the next two chapters, regulators of government in that sense use a range of methods to shape the behaviour of their charges, running from the role of official whistle-blower, able to do no more than draw public attention to lapses or problems, to the role of 'terminator', able to close down an organization deemed to be failing (or, in the case of local-authority auditors appointed by the Audit Commission, to impose financial surcharges and disqualifications from office on local councillors and officials). Some regulators, as noted already, are more sharply separated from their charges than others. And the mandates possessed by such regulators vary too. Some have statutory authority, some are established by Order in Council, many have no formal mandate other than what is assumed to be the policy of the government of the day.[8]

---

[8] See Appendix III.

Not only is regulation of government as conceived above hetero-geneous in terms of institutions and activity, but it is also hard to define with precision where regulation begins and ends. To mean anything, it needs to exclude direct 'chain-of-command' manage-ment relationships, as in the organization chart of an individual organization and the controls chief executives deploy. So internal audit or review does not count as regulation for our purposes, because it is not conducted by another organization operating at arm's length (though it may well work as part of an overall regula-tory system). It also needs to exclude relationships where no formal authority is involved, like pure advice-giving (Hood and Scott 1996). For example, whatever influence might be exercised among top mandarins by 'Sir Humphreyesque' exchanges over clubland lunches, represents a different sort of social control (though that too may be a key part of the culture within which regulation operates, as will be argued later in the book).

Inevitably, there are overlaps and grey areas raised by such a conception of regulation. While direct oversight of public bureau-cracies by legislators (but not of their bureaucratic agents), and the oversight exercised by the law courts are excluded, there are ambi-guities on the margin, as will be shown in the next chapter. For example, are Britain's seventy-odd administrative tribunals to be counted as specialized administrative courts or bureaucratic regu-lators? Similarly, the distinction between internal chain of com-mand structures and external regulation can be blurred. Some heads of public organizations can view arm's-length regulators the way others see management consultants, as a welcome tool for influencing their own organizations and bringing extra pressure to bear on problematic individuals or units within their domains.[9] Like regulation of business, regulation of government often works in conjunction with 'allies' inside departments or agencies, in that the concerns of the regulator are often reflected in a set of special units within departments (like safety committees), and often with allies in the outside world too, such as the 'humanity lobbies' in the case of prison inspection. The border between regulation and ad-vice can also be problematic. Organizations which ostensibly have no power but to advise (like the National Consumer Council) may

---

[9] Cf. Laughlin and Broadbent (1996), who cite examples of school head teachers regarding outside inspections as a 'free MOT' (the term used in Britain for annual roadworthiness checks on vehicles) and opportunities 'to pull staff up'.

still have have *de facto* regulatory influence. And, just as for business regulation, elements of self-regulation are often intertwined with formal regulation of government. Moreover, while the notion of regulation in government starts from the oversight of one public bureaucracy by another, private actors often figure in that process, as with the private accountancy firms appointed to conduct local-authority audits by the Audit Commission (and thus able to wield powers of disqualification and surcharge) or the private-sector teams used for many school inspections. So the relatively fuzzy boundaries of regulation in government need to be recognized when measuring their scale and growth, as the next chapter shows. A single-figure estimate of the size of such regulation is much less meaningful than a range with maximum and minimum values.

Even if it is blurred at the edges, regulation inside government is a phenomenon familiar to every public servant. Over a working life—perhaps even a working day—public managers or officials are exposed to multiple regulatory influences, in the form of demands or pressures from an army of outside waste-watchers, quality police, and sleaze-busters rather than from their immediate bosses in the chain of command. Parts of this regulatory landscape inside government have been intensively discussed by scholars, notably in studies of public audit bodies (Buttery *et al.* 1985; Glynn 1985; Bowerman 1994), ombudsmen and complaint-handlers (Lewis and Birkinshaw 1993; Seneviratne 1994; Citizen's Charter Complaints Task Force 1995), professional inspectorates (Hartley 1972; Rhodes 1981), and particular parts of central government, especially Treasury control of expenditure (Heclo and Wildavsky 1974; Thain and Wright 1996). We do not claim to be the first to have discovered the phenomenon of regulation inside government, and we do not aim to replicate such specialized studies. Our account differs from those more specific investigations in two ways.

First, it attempts to look at regulation inside government in the round, exploring the 'archipelago' as a whole, rather than only particular islands within it. Regulation of business by government is often highly compartmentalized, and firms often complain that their multiple regulators work in isolation from one another. But for business regulation there are institutionalized pressures for government to take a synoptic look across all types of regulators to assess the overall scale of activity and the burden it imposes on the private sector, to investigate best practice and suggest general guidelines for operation. Periodic government-wide assaults on the burden of regulatory requirements and red tape imposed on business are a regular feature of the policy process in Britain: indeed this role became institutionalized in the form of a new agency to oversee government departments, which was established in the mid-1980s as part of a 'deregulation initiative' and has subsequently been relaunched and renamed on several occasions (Froud *et al.* 1998). But there has been no equivalent synoptic look at regulation inside government, in the form of either official or academic inquiries.

Second, this book aims to take what may be loosely called a generic 'regulation' perspective on a range of activities and organizations involved in oversight and monitoring of public bureaucracies. Rather than examining each particular overseer in the specific professional or statutory language applied to its own domain—audit-speak, inspection-speak, ombudsman-speak—our aim is to look comparatively across the whole set of organizations, not just at bureaucratic scale and growth but also at the analytic issues that face any regulator, such as how the regulator relates to the regulatee, what methods are used to shape behaviour and gain compliance, and how much discretion regulators have. We are not the first to have conceived all forms of oversight of public bureaucracies by other public bureaucracies as regulation, but this study is the first systematic book-length account of regulation inside government. In the USA James Q. Wilson and Patricia Rachal (1977: 3) two decades ago posed the important question, 'Can the government regulate itself?', highlighting circumstances 'when the end in view requires that one government agency modify the behaviour of another'. But though they suggested special difficulties that may apply to regulation inside government, Wilson and Rachal did not develop this important perspective through systematic inquiry. Cybernetics-based explorations of the regulation of bureaucracies (notably Dunsire 1978) view all systems of control in government in a common analytic frame, and there are isolated examples of applying perspectives originally developed for business regulation to regulation within government, on which we draw in Chapter 3. Such work includes 'reading-across' the theory of principal and agent from the literature on industrial regulation to the organization and provision of public services (Barrow 1996) and the discussion of regulation within quasi-markets for public-service provision, notably in health care or education (Le Grand and

Bartlett 1993). Recognizing the importance of such insights, this book aims to develop the regulation perspective further and to deploy it systematically.

## 2. REGULATION IN GOVERNMENT AND THE CONTROL-OF-BUREAUCRACY PROBLEM

Regulation inside government needs to be set in the broader context of control over bureaucracy. There are many possible ways of classifying the different processes or mechanisms that can be used to keep public bureaucracy under control. As a first step, we can distinguish self-conscious oversight (termed 'comptrol' by one of us in earlier work (Hood 1986)) from the various forms of 'inspector-free' control over bureaucracy (Beck Jørgensen and Larsen 1987), in which a system is held within limits without overt controllers in the form of official overseers—the bureaucratic equivalents of Adam Smith's hidden hand. Nor need those 'hidden hands' necessarily be the exchange process of a market: from an anthropological perspective, Mary Douglas (1985: 3) describes culture as 'a general regulatory mechanism for human behaviour'. The distinction between 'comptrol' and 'inspector-free control' is important, because the main lesson of cybernetic analysis for bureaucracy is that a system can be under control without having identifiable overseers and that in any complex system control cannot be effected by simple steering alone, but must in large measure consist of self-controlling mechanisms (cf. Beer 1965; Dunsire 1978; Brans and Rossbach 1997). Theorists of law and administration steeped in cybernetic analysis (notably Teubner 1987) have noted the risk that 'command and control' styles of regulatory intervention can produce unintended side effects or even reverse effects through functional disruption of the system being regulated (Sieber 1981). But the problem of excessive or overlegalistic intervention has been much less discussed for regulation of government than for regulation of society at large (for an exception see Loughlin 1996).

Oversight or comptrol is the point of departure for our investigation of regulation inside government. But, as we will see in later chapters, that regulation often takes place against a background of other types of control over bureaucracy and is frequently linked with the inspector-free ways of keeping bureaucracies under control. Three of the latter types of control (derived by one of us (Hood 1996*a*; 1998*a*) from cultural theory) are competition, mutuality, and contrived randomness. These types can be considered as alternatives to comptrol in one sense, but in practice are often linked to formal oversight. They are summarized diagrammatically in Figure 1.2.

*Competition* is one important inspector-free control over public bureaucracy, but formal overseers often aim to promote competition within and among bureaucracies. Competition among civil servants for promotion is claimed by Murray Horn (1995: 114–15 and 121–2) to be a central element in keeping traditional forms of public bureaucracy under control, since it puts the onus on bureau-

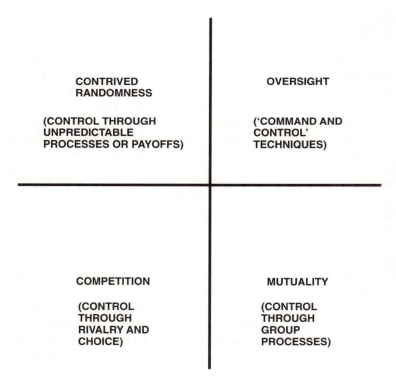

CONTRIVED
RANDOMNESS

(CONTROL THROUGH
UNPREDICTABLE
PROCESSES OR PAYOFFS)

OVERSIGHT

('COMMAND AND
CONTROL'
TECHNIQUES)

COMPETITION

(CONTROL
THROUGH
RIVALRY AND
CHOICE)

MUTUALITY

(CONTROL
THROUGH
GROUP
PROCESSES)

Fɪɢ. 1.2. 'Oversight' and three other 'inspector-free' types of control over public management

crats to show that their activities serve the wider objectives of their superiors or government as a whole rather than placing the onus on the top political executive to find evidence about the quality of bureaucratic performance. Even though 'career service' is said to be weakening as a feature of the British civil service, aspiring senior mandarins still vie to be recruited (with over fifty applicants in 1995 for every fast-stream Grade 7 vacancy), and those who succeed must then compete for promotion, attention from Ministers, medals, and decorations, and even for key jobs in quangos or private firms after they leave the civil service. Competition among departments, agencies, and other units for 'turf', budgets, and the policy limelight is also commonly argued to be a key element in maintaining external control over bureaucracy (cf. Niskanen 1971), contrary to the doctrine that competition within the public service is wasteful and disruptive. For those of a 'public-choice' persuasion, a gram of competition in bureaucracy may be viewed as worth a tonne of regulation through oversight.

*Mutuality* in its pure form works in exactly the opposite way from regulation through oversight, because it denotes ways that individuals are controlled through the influence of a group. In a classic study more than two decades ago Hugh Heclo and Aaron Wildavsky (1974) saw mutuality, not formal oversight from Ministers or Parliament, as the central regulatory process governing the behaviour of the top civil service in Britain. They portrayed a small 'village world', with the villagers intent on pursuing reputation among their peers over the course of decades and in turn rating their colleagues:

The number of people involved is at most a few hundred, and they change but slowly. They all know or have heard of one another, and they all enjoy rating one another. . . . The ratings work by slow accretion. It is difficult to get a high rating and equally difficult to lose one. But over the years events reveal to colleagues that some . . . are bright and others dull; some strong, others weak; some trustworthy and others not. (Ibid. 14–15)

In a variant of this interpretation Christopher Foster (1996, 1998) sees the ethical questions that are dealt with by administrative law courts or statutory codes in other countries as having been traditionally regulated in Britain by 'conversations' between Ministers and senior civil servants outside a chain-of-command structure. Sometimes mutuality is built into formal structures of consultation or group decision-making, through board or collegial structures. 'Government by committee' (in Wheare's (1955) classic phrase) is pervasive in Britain, with individual action restrained by group decision-making and the climates of expectations and mutual obligations that those committee structures generate.

A final type of inspector-free control is *contrived randomness*. It acts as a check on behaviour by making outcomes and operating conditions unpredictable. Opportunities for joining with colleagues or clients to organize 'scams' or corrupt anti-system conspiracies at any level will be substantially hindered if you cannot predict for the short- or medium-term future what job you will be doing, what part of the organization or of the country you will be working in, or who your colleagues, subordinates, superiors, or clients will be (cf. Rose-Ackerman 1978: 183–6; Bentham 1983: 281; Burnheim 1985: 167). Contrived randomness figures large in the operation of imperial bureaucracy, tax bureaucracy, and large field structures in many kinds of organization, including churches and multinational corporations. In such a structure key employees are posted unpredictably around the system (to prevent them 'going native') in a way that prevents people in the organization from knowing in detail what their next posting is likely to be or with whom they will be working in the near future. Just as the Chinese imperial bureaucracy involved a convention of no more than a three-year tenure in any one position, with no certainty about where the next position would be, the UK civil service has a tradition of limited-term postings which is matched by similar conventions in organizations like the military, the tax bureaucracies, and the security services. Taken to extremes such practices turn public organization into something less like a predictable slot-machine than a gaming machine, making it difficult to predict in detail where the chips will fall at any one time (see Hood 1976: 160–3).

As noted above, at one level these three forms can be seen as inspector-free substitutes for control by oversight, and we shall explore changes in the overall 'mix' of controls in Part Three, arguing that control through an increased emphasis on oversight has accompanied heavier stress on competition in the UK public service over the past two decades. But at another level oversight can be mixed with the three inspector-free types of control to produce hybrid forms. Indeed, such compounds are commonplace in regulation of UK government, to the point that control by pure oversight appears to be more unusual than the hybrid forms. Oversight is frequently linked with competition and mutuality and sometimes even with randomness, and we will encounter such hybrids later in the book. An example of oversight linked with competition is the way that overseers of government (like the Audit Commission in its assessment of comparative local-authority performance on a range of services) often encourage their charges to compete for high ratings in a 'saints and sinners' table. An example of oversight linked with mutuality is the system of rating UK universities for teaching and research quality by panels of assessors drawn from the world of university teaching and research, and linked with funding and quality control by government overseers. An example of oversight linked with randomness is the way the Prisons Inspectorate combines a programme of visits arranged in advance with a series of unannounced spot checks on prisons (said by several of our interviewees to be far more effective than the visits announced in advance).

In short, we discovered not only that comptrol or oversight within government comprises a variety of forms, but also that oversight mixes with other inspector-free modes of control to produce a range of hybrids. Nor do the compound forms consist only of simple pairwise hybrids. Sometimes we find three or more of the types combined, as in the case of prison regulation, as mentioned above, which not only combines randomness with oversight (in the form of unannounced snap inspections by the Prisons Inspectorate), but also elements of competition between state-run and contracted-out prisons. Chapter 3 examines variations in ways of working more closely, and the cases described in Part Two indicate a range of different dynamics and styles. To borrow a phrase from Oscar Wilde,[10] regulation within government is seldom pure and never simple.

## 3. THE PLAN OF THE BOOK

The next chapter surveys the overall scale, growth, and variety of regulation of UK government. It reveals an 'industry' containing well over a hundred 'firms', employing more than 10,000 people

---

[10] *The Importance of Being Earnest*, Act 1.

full time, costing the UK taxpayer about £2bn. per year (if we include indirect as well as direct costs) in the mid-1990s, and growing substantially in staff and spending at a time when public bureaucracy as a whole had been radically downsized. Chapter 3 focuses on the operation of regulation inside government. Does it resemble business regulation, or are the two forms of regulation 'alike in all unimportant respects' (to borrow a phrase from Graham Allison (1984))? Developing the analysis of methods of operation briefly sketched out in the last section, the chapter argues that operating styles cut across different institutions within the world of government regulators, that there are important common features between regulation of government and regulation of business, and that the social distance between regulator and regulatee seems to be linked to operating styles, in the sense that formality in regulation is often associated with social distance.

After we have looked at the overall scale and growth of regulation in government and surveyed the analytic issues that it raises, Part Two examines how regulation worked in five selected domains of UK government activity that we investigated in the mid-1990s, with a chapter devoted to each. In the light of the themes discussed in Chapter 3, it looks at the regulation of local government by central government, the regulation of central and local government by the European Union, and the regulation of central government by itself. Cutting across those categories, it examines regulation in two major public services, schools and prisons, both of which provoked major controversy in the 1990s and represent modes of regulation of government which differ widely on some of the dimensions discussed in this chapter. This second part of the book suggests that the Benthamite or Chadwickian theme of 'strict inspection' referred to earlier was applied more strongly to local government and other parts of the public sector than to the core of Whitehall. It suggests that in some cases the outcome of regulatory changes was less the mirror-image process described earlier (with more emphasis on performance accountability and correspondingly less on compliance accountability) than a double whammy, with increased emphasis on both compliance and performance controls. And it demonstrates the variety of regulation styles in government, from ostensible 'reign of terror' regulation in the case of schools to the more light-rein style of much regulation in Whitehall.

The final part of the book turns from the examination of particular public services and parts of government to the overall picture. Chapter 9 examines how far an analysis of regulation in government modifies the conventional picture of New Public Management. Following the mirror-image analysis discussed in this chapter, it links the notion of a mirror image to a cultural switch among some of the broad mechanisms available for keeping bureaucracy under control that were discussed earlier in this chapter, arguing that competition and oversight have received increased emphasis as control mechanisms, while relatively less emphasis was laid on mutuality and contrived randomness. It suggests that the mirror image is by no means the only pattern to be observed, but that it has appeared over much of the landscape of British public services. Early in the century the Fabian luminaries Sidney and Beatrice Webb (1920) argued the British civil service should be divided into two, with half acting as inspectors and overseers and the others as 'doers' engaged in executive work. This long-forgotten Fabian vision has been partly revived with the separation of execution, delivery, and implementation activity from policy and monitoring activity in public bureaucracy, together with increasing preoccupation with 'the proper conduct of public business' in appointments and financial management. In short, a version of the regulatory state may be developing inside government.

The final chapter discusses the issues of policy and institutional design that this development raises. It considers how regulation inside government might itself be regulated, examining four possible 'deficits'—of competition, mutuality, oversight, and randomness—in the system as it has evolved. It explores possible ways of remedying those deficits, such as ways of transferring information and good practice and taking stock of developments among the separate tables of regulation in government and the case for assessing and reporting compliance costs—a key element of debate over business regulation—for public-sector regulation. If regulation of government is to be part of the solution to the operation of public services rather than part of the problem, such policy issues merit attention.

# Running the Ruler over Regulation inside Government

There are so many hobgoblins in the mist for the civil service, whether it is the PAC or the National Audit Office or their own senior department or the Cabinet Office, the Citizen's Charter Unit. There are so many people bearing down on them . . . brandishing regulations.

John Ford, contributing to 'Inside the New Civil Service', BBC Radio 4, 13 January 1994

Having set the scene in the last chapter, we now explore the overall size, shape, and growth of regulation (in the sense of arm's-length oversight) in UK government. This phenomenon cannot be measured to three places of decimals, but we can identify some general characteristics and orders of magnitude. This chapter aims to demonstrate three things about regulation in government. First, such regulation—taking all its different forms together—is big business. For example, UK government invests far more resources in regulating itself than it does to regulating the much discussed privatized utilities. Second, regulation of government is a growing business. Over two decades in which UK government substantially reduced the number of its direct employees—with more than one civil servant in four disappearing from the payroll between 1976 and 1996—regulation of government expanded dramatically. Third, regulation inside government is diverse in several senses. It is multi-organizational, not monolithic, in that it consists of a variety of organizations, pursuing various and sometimes conflicting goals, with no sense of belonging to any overall 'policy community' (cf. Day and Klein 1987, 1990). It is diverse in the way it is organized and how it operates. There is no single model or agreed best-practice approach. These features raise questions of policy and institutional design, which we will pursue further in the final chapter.

## 1. REGULATION INSIDE GOVERNMENT IS BIG BUSINESS

Just how much regulation exists inside government is one of those how-many-angels-can-dance-on-the-head-of-a-pin questions that keep academics in employment. The exact number depends not just on how we define regulator (as we saw in the last chapter), but also government or public sector. There are no standard international definitions of any of those terms, and there are inevitably grey areas at the margins where definitions become problematic. Indeed, as in any field, the most interesting cases tend to be found at the margins. But we can confidently say that, within a range of definitions, regulation inside UK government is big business. It is an activity that contains scores of separate organizations, directly employs thousands of people, and costs hundreds of millions of pounds to run. When we start to add in estimates for the compliance side of the operation, it becomes larger still.

As explained in Chapter 1, regulation in government is broadly conceived as arm's-length oversight involving the setting or monitoring of standards, and based on some element of authority. It is in principle distinguishable from simple advice and from line management through a direct chain of command. Units which play an oversight role within their own organizations might be considered regulators on an extended definition, and frequently figure in overall regulatory systems, as we will see in Part Two, but we exclude them from our general count here. For this purpose, we focus on bodies organizationally distinct from their regulatory clients.

When it comes to the 'regulatees', we can define the public sector in several different ways, including legal power, state ownership, or public financing. Table 2.1 focuses on ownership and financing to map out some of the different domains of state activity in a fairly conventional way. Boxes 1A and 1B identify a core public sector comprising bodies (like central-government departments and local authorities) that are both owned by the state and largely funded from general taxation. Beyond that core is a mixed sector (boxes 2A, 2B, 2C, 3A, and 3B), which also consists of several parts. One is a mixed public/private sector (boxes 2A, 2B, and 2C), consisting of state-owned bodies mainly financed from sources other than general taxation (like user fees or revolving funds), and bodies

TABLE 2.1. *'Regulation' within different components of the public sector*

| Components of the public sector | Mainly financed from general tax funds | Mainly financed from other sources |
|---|---|---|
| Publicly owned central-government bodies | *1A. Core public sector: central government*<br>Example: departments, executive agencies, NDPBs<br>*Main regulators*<br>NAO, PCA, central agencies, specialist overseers (e.g. HM Inspectorate of Prisons) | *2A. Mixed public/private sector*<br>Example: some remaining nationalized industries<br>*Main regulators*<br>Sponsoring departments |
| Publicly owned local public bodies | *1B. Core public sector: local public bodies*<br>Example: local authorities, NHS Trusts<br>*Main regulators*<br>Audit Commission, LG ombudsmen, specialist overseers (e.g. OFSTED) & funder-regulators (e.g. FEFCE) | *2B. Mixed public/private sector*<br>Example: local-authority trading bodies<br>*Main regulators*<br>Sponsoring units, plus regulators of local public bodies |
| Charities and not-for-profit companies in private or independent ownership | *2C. Mixed public/private sector*<br>Example: most HE institutions & housing associations, TECs<br>*Main regulators*<br>Special-purpose overseers and funder-regulators (e.g. Housing Corporation) | *3A. Mixed private/public sector*<br>Example: some HE institutions & housing associations, most charities<br>*Main regulators*<br>Charity regulators (e.g. Charity Commission) |
| Privately owned for-profit bodies | *3B. Mixed private/public sector*<br>Example: contracting companies like EDS<br>*Main regulators*<br>Regulators of subsidized industries (e.g. Rail Regulator) | *4A. Core private sector: industry-specific regimes*<br>Example: utilities, fishing<br>*Main regulators*<br>Specialist overseers (e.g. OFTEL)<br>*4B. Core private sector: economy-wide regimes*<br>Example: general manufacturing<br>*Main regulators*<br>Generic overseers (e.g. HSE) |

which are independently or privately owned (not for profit), but mainly financed from general taxation.[1] But another part of the mixed sector is less public on both of the dimensions of Table 2.1 (boxes 3A and 3B). This mixed private/public sector includes independently owned not-for-profit bodies funded largely from sources other than general taxation (for example many housing associations), and private for-profit firms largely funded from a public source (like contracting firms or franchisees making most of their income from services to government).[2] Beyond the mixed sector comes the sector which is formally private on both of the dimensions of Table 2.1, involving privately owned, for-profit, firms which are mainly funded from private sources (boxes 4A and 4B).

If, following this categorization, we conceive of the public sector as comprising central government, local public bodies, and the more public part of the mixed sector (Table 2.1, 1A to 2C), then on the definition of regulators given above, we found in those sectors a minimum of 135 separate regulators in total,[3] directly employing around 14,000 staff, and costing £770m. to run in 1995[4]—just over 30p in every £100 UK government spent at that time, if we take out the biggest transfer payments in the form of debt interest and cyclical social security (Treasury 1996a: 22 and 25). Table 2.1 also indicates the main regulators of each part of the public sector,

[1] The few remaining nationalized industries are in this sector, along with Training and Enterprise Councils (TECs) and some higher-education institutions and housing associations.

[2] Most HE institutions are placed in box 2C because they are Corporations under the Education Reform Act 1988 or constituted under Royal Charter, Acts of Parliament, or a body of statutes under the authority of the Privy Council or are private trusts or Companies Act companies. A few HE bodies are in box 3A because they receive most of their funding from the private sector. FE colleges are placed in box 1B because they are independent corporate bodies under the 1992 Further Education Act and receive the majority of their funding from public sources. TECs are in box 2C because they are private companies by share or guarantee that in England receive 90% of funding from the taxpayer (NAO 1995: 5). Housing associations are in boxes 2C and 3A. They are constituted as charitable trusts, companies (limited by guarantee or with not for profit shareholding), or industrial and provident societies which can be charitable or non-charitable. The amount of public funding varies, though development support and housing benefit amount to substantial sources of finance in many cases.

[3] Appendix II lists those 135 organizations and gives some basic information about their costs, staffing, legal basis, and operation.

[4] Where an organization performed other major functions, only the part of its budget and staffing relating to regulation was included.

placing those regulators within the segment of the public sector with which they predominantly dealt, though many of them operate in more than one category.[5]

The size of regulation inside government would increase if we adopted a less conventional definition of public sector than suggested above. If we adopted the juridical approach favoured by EU institutions and conceived of some public utilities (like gas, water, and railways) as public bodies in the sense of possessing special and exclusive rights even though in private ownership, at least half a dozen regulators of privatized utilities would enter our population, adding costs of about £33m. per year. If we were further to consider Britain's seventy-odd administrative tribunals as regulators (rather than specialized administrative law courts) in the same sense as ombudsmen, the population would jump to over 200.[6]

We excluded both categories from the conservative or minimal view of regulation used for the general count described above, though in both cases it is a line-ball judgement (and our general conclusions about the scale and growth of the phenomenon do not hang on that judgement). But if we moved away from that minimal view, at least two other groups of regulators might be added to our population. Were we to add the EU regulators of British government (discussed in Chapter 8), our specimens would include the European Court of Auditors and several parts of the Directorates-General in the European Commission, comprising at least 600 staff in total and expenditure of more than £60m. (of which the UK-attributable component, as one of the larger EU States, would be substantial). In addition, there was a set of mainly private-sector regulators which also oversaw the public sector, for which the public-sector proportion would need to be estimated. Some organizations in this group were generic or issue-based regulators, like the Health and Safety Executive (HSE), the UK's risk-at-work bureaucracy whose regulatory empire includes public and private bodies alike. Others were industry-specific regulators whose clientele includes both public and private organizations. The twenty-odd

---

[5] e.g. NAO had an interest in many local public bodies because of their funding by central government. However NAO's main focus is on central government so it was classed as a regulator of bodies in box 1A.

[6] We included the Council on Tribunals, as the regulator and standard-setter for tribunals, but there is no equivalent formal regulator of ombudsmen, and ombudsmen (particularly the PCA) go beyond casework on occasion to enunciate more general standards. See n. 21 below.

bodies in this group cost over £1bn. per year to run, and it is hard to make a precise assessment of the resources they devoted to the core public sector (Table 2.1, boxes 1A to 2C). But £250m. per year on top of the total given above would be a conservative estimate.

Another potential addition is the world of local-level regulators of public-sector bodies. In this book, we concentrate on national-level regulation in government (though the different nations within the UK had different arrangements, to be discussed below), but a number of public-sector regulators operated at local-government level. As we shall see in Part Two, local authorities as well as national-level bodies regulated schools and social services, and though there are no national-level data for the scale of those activities, figures quoted to us suggest a UK total of least 1,000 staff and costs of more than £30m. a year. To that need to be added local regulators of services provided by central government, of which the main example was the 130-odd local boards of prison visitors (discussed in Chapter 6), comprising 1,700 part-time visitors and costing approximately £1m. per year (Cabinet Office 1995*b*: 25 and 33). More substantial is the realm of local regulators who oversee public and private bodies, notably local Environmental Health and Trading Standards officers, adding close to another 20,000-odd staff and almost £500m. of running costs, of which at least 3,500 people and £170m. could be attributed to regulating the public sector.

As this discussion shows, any single estimate of the scale of regulation inside government can be of only limited meaning. It is better to think of the phenomenon as a set of concentric circles (like an archery target or dartboard), ranging from a minimal core at the centre to a maximum at the edges. Our estimate of the number of regulator organizations in the national public sector runs from about 130 to over 200 and our estimate of the direct running costs from about £700m. at the low end to about £1bn. at the top end. But even on the most restrictive and conventional definition of the UK public sector, and a view of tribunals as court-like rather than regulators, the scale of investment in regulation of government is close to the total of private-sector regulation and (as noted earlier) far greater than that of regulation in the much discussed utilities sectors.[7] If we add in estimates of the scale of government

---

[7] For the same year, the gross expenditure of specialized regulators of privatized utilities (OFTEL, OFWAT, OFFER, and OFGAS) was just under £33m. (NAO

regulation at the local level, the direct running costs would approach £1bn. even on a conservative calculation, and the army of regulators would number almost 20,000.

Regulating government is thus a sizeable operation. The number of employees in this industry is similar to those working in the funeral services business or for licensed taxi firms in Britain (Office for National Statistics 1996: 5–6)—although most public-sector regulators are much less visible to the population at large than undertakers and taxi-drivers because the general public rarely deals with auditors and inspectors. And the indicators of scale discussed above themselves only describe the *direct* costs of such regulation. But as with all regulation, such costs amount to only a part—in some cases, a trivial part—of the overall picture, because much of the cost comes in the form of compliance costs. Compliance costs are what it costs regulatees to meet the requirements of those who regulate them. As anyone who has ever had to fill out an income tax form can testify, those costs—'invisible' in the public accounts, because the work is not done by public employees nor paid for from the public budget—can be very substantial.

The notion of compliance costs is familiar in the business world (especially since the introduction of initiatives in the mid-1980s designed to reduce the regulatory burden on business), but little attention has been paid to these costs in the public sector, and we return to this issue in the final chapter. Estimating compliance costs is difficult, because they raise complex counterfactual questions of what organizations would do in the absence of any regulation, and because regulatees have an incentive to overstate (and regulators to understate) such costs. In the public sector estimates are particularly problematic, since on one view we might reckon almost all public spending as compliance costs. But that is not a very illuminating conclusion: a narrower and more tractable definition of compliance costs for our purposes[8] is what it costs the regulatee to interact with the regulator, including the costs of dealing with

1996: 3 and 30). Even if the expenditure of the Monopolies and Mergers Commission and the Office of Fair Trading (which were heavily involved in regulating privatized utilities) is included expenditure on regulators was only 0.1% of the industries' £51bn. turnover.

    [8] As well as one closer to what regulatees tend to complain about (Hogwood *et al.* 1998: 12).

requests for information, consulting the regulator, setting up, and acting as guide on visits and inspections.

Costs of compliance in this sense were not routinely logged across government, but we found some pointers to their magnitude in local authorities. For one inner London borough, we estimated the 'narrow' compliance costs of dealing with central government departments, inspectorates, ombudsmen, and local audit bodies as not less than £1.85m. per year. If that figure is extrapolated to all local authorities in England using Treasury and CIPFA analyses of spending profiles (Treasury 1996a: 4; CIPFA 1996), the total compliance costs for local government of dealing with their regulators would amount to not less than £173m. for England as a whole, or about 30p in every £100 spent by local government. Figures from the former Department of the Environment (DOE 1996) suggest the costs to local government in England of providing information required by its central-government regulators would run to at least £30m. per year. OFSTED inspection of secondary schools has been estimated to cost each school around £20,000 in expenses directly connected to the inspection, and those costs rise further if, as in some cases, the LEA mounts a 'mock' inspection before the OFSTED visitation (IEE1, IEE2).[9] One ombudsman put the total compliance costs for the bodies within his jurisdiction as at least the same as the direct costs of his office. Putting such pieces of information together, it seems safe to conclude that compliance costs even in the narrow sense used above make the total cost of regulation inside UK government at least double the sum directly spent on the main regulatory bureaucracies.

We found regulators of government for the most part made no attempt to assess the costs to their clients of complying with their demands, and in almost all cases saw those costs as negligible—a 'Nelson's-eye' practice which few private-sector regulators would be able to pursue with impunity. And many of the newer systems of regulation over the UK public sector relied on what Ian Ayres and John Braithwaite (1992: ch. 4) term 'enforced self-regulation'—that is, requiring regulated organizations to set up machinery for internal review (as with teaching-quality assessment in higher education or clinical audit in health care (NAO 1995)), with the external regulator operating only at the top of the bureaucratic pyramid.

---

[9] These labels denote interview sources; for the key, see Appendix I.

Such practice—seen by Michael Power (1997) as central to the audit explosion that has developed in the UK—amounts to a development of what in US parlance is known as 'unfunded mandates'— that is, obligations being imposed by one part of government on another with no provision of resources to carry out those obligations.[10]

## 2. REGULATION INSIDE GOVERNMENT IS A GROWTH SECTOR

Regulation in UK government is not only a big business; it is also a booming one. Over the past two decades, it seems to have grown steadily, both in direct spending and in 'body count'. Using the minimal view of the scale of national-level regulation in government (as discussed above), Table 2.2 compares numbers of regulators in 1976 and 1995 in the different parts of the public sector

TABLE 2.2. *National-level regulators of UK government, 1976–1995*

| Regulators | No. of bodies, 1976 | No. of bodies, 1995 | Percentage increase, 1976–95 | Estimated factor of growth in expenditure, 1976–95 |
|---|---|---|---|---|
| 1. Core public sector (Table 2.1, box 1A): central government | 48 | 54 | 14 | 2 |
| 2. Core public sector (Table 2.1, box 1B): local public bodies | 57 | 67 | 18 | Between 2 and 3 |
| 3. Mixed public/private sector (Table 2.1, boxes 2A, 2B, and 2C) | 5 | 14 | 180 | 4 |
| Total | 110 | 135 | 22 | Between 2 and 3 |

[10] As is shown in Ch. 8, some EU oversight of expenditure involved funding for member States to engage in fraud-control activities, but that is unusual: most EU oversight depended heavily on 'enforced self-regulation'.

identified in Table 2.1. It indicates growth in all sectors, with stronger growth in body count in local government and (most dramatically) the mixed public/private sector than in central government. Overall, the number of regulator organizations overseeing government seems to have risen by more than one-fifth over those two decades.

Not only did regulator organizations grow in number, they also substantially increased their claims on the public budget. Indeed, spending on such regulators seems to have grown more than the body count of such organizations. In an era when governments aspired to be leaner and meaner in the name of efficiency, regulators as a group showed no signs of becoming leaner: because they were the instruments chosen for making the rest of the public service leaner and meaner. We estimate there was a doubling of expenditure by central-government regulators and increases by a factor of at least two in local government and four in the mixed sector.[11] The latter in part reflects a general growth of spending in the mixed sector and more centralized funding regimes. Taking the parts of regulation in government whose costs are most easily identifiable over two decades we found growth in real-terms spending in four out of five types, as shown in Table 2.3. Spending on public audit bodies at least doubled; it increased by a factor of three for inspectorates and grew at least fourfold in some other cases. Only central-agency regulators exhibited a stable level of spending.

Northcote Parkinson (1961) built his famous 'law' of work expansion by observing the apparent puzzle that in the early twentieth century the number of clerks in the British Admiralty grew as the number of warships decreased. Something similar seems to have happened in regulation inside government in the last two decades. The staffing increases shown for regulators in Table 2.3 contrast sharply with what happened to employment in the public sector as a whole. Overall civil-service numbers fell by more than 30 per cent between 1976 and 1995, with white-collar 'non-industrial' civil-service staffing dropping by 16 per cent (Cabinet Office 1995: 47). Local-authority numbers fell by 21 per cent over the same period (DOE 1996: 57). But total staffing in public-sector regulators went

---

[11] Expenditure on local-government regulation may have increased by as much as three times: the growth factor of two is a conservative estimate.

TABLE 2.3. Direct investment in public-sector regulation, 1976 and 1995

| Regulators | 1. No. of bodies, 1976 | 2. No. of bodies, 1995 | 3. Change in no. of bodies (%), 1976–95 | 4. Estimated % change in average staffing, 1976–95[a] | 5. Estimated % change in average real terms spending, 1976–95 | 6. Estimated factor of growth in total real spending, 1976–95[b] |
|---|---|---|---|---|---|---|
| A. Public audit bodies | 4 | 4 | 0 | 60 | 130 | 2 |
| B. Inspectorates and equivalents | 23 | 27 | 17 | 75 | 100 | 3 |
| C. Ombudsmen and equivalents | 9 | 17 | 78 | 150 | 200 | 4 |
| D. Central agency regulators | 13 | 18 | 38 | 0 | 0 | 1 |
| E. Funder-cum-regulators | 6 | 14 | 133 | 10 | 100 | 4 |
| F. Departmental regulators of agencies | 29 | 26 | –10 | n.a. | n.a. | n.a. |
| G. Central regulators of local public bodies and the NHS | 26 | 29 | 11 | n.a. | n.a. | n.a. |
| All regulators in government | 110 | 135 | 22 | 60 | 106 | 2.5 |

[a] Figures for staffing (col. 4) and expenditure (col. 5) change are an average for bodies which existed throughout the period 1976–95 estimated from available data (which were available for all public audit bodies, three-quarters of ombudsmen and central-agency regulators, and one-third of inspectorates and funding bodies). A reliable estimate of the average size of change for central-government regulators and central-local and NHS regulators was not possible so the average for all regulators in government excluded these types.

[b] Total expenditure growth 1976–95 includes changes shown in col. 5 but additionally spending on new bodies. A reliable estimate of the factor of growth for other central-government and central-local and NHS regulators was not possible from available data so the total for all regulators in government excluded these types.

dramatically in the other direction, with estimated growth of 90 per cent between 1976 and 1995.[12] Some of that growth came from long-established regulatory bodies acquiring extra staff (with an average increase of 60 per cent, as shown in Table 2.3), and some from the creation of new regulators. Overall investment, in terms of expenditure on regulators, at least doubled.[13] Four out of the five types of regulator for which we could calculate spending over time showed average real growth rates between three and six times higher than the real growth in general government expenditure between 1976 and 1995.[14]

There are some exceptions to this general 'Parkinsonian' picture of growth. Central-government investment in oversight of national- ized industries shrank as the privatization juggernaut reduced those industries to a small rump—though the regulatory regimes for many of the privatized utilities are much more elaborate and resource-intensive than those operating during the nationalization era (for example, total civil-service staff involved in the oversight of telecoms more than quintupled between 1980 and the mid-1990s). Regulation of government departments by central executive agen- cies also shrank in direct spending and employment, with a 10 per cent decline in the body count between 1976 and 1995. The biggest decline was the running-down of what had been a large middle- level administrative machine (once involving more than 1,500 staff, variously located in the Treasury, the Civil Service Department, and a number of successor units after the CSD was abolished in 1981) concerned with detailed oversight of pay and grading across depart- ments. This system was replaced by a mixture of overall running- cost controls and general personnel guidelines involving around 500 people at the centre (Civil Service Dept. 1980: 14–17; Cabinet Office 1995).

But while that aspect of regulation inside government shrank, there was compensating growth elsewhere. As civil-service depart- ments spun off what had previously been directly managed execu- tive operations into arm's-length executive agencies from the late

[12] This figure is also a conservative assumption, assuming a minimum of stable staffing in the 'other central government' and 'central-local public bodies and NHS' regulators.

[13] This figure assumes, at a minimum, stability in expenditure by other central- government and central-local public bodies and NHS regulators.

[14] Over that period general government expenditure grew in real terms from £215,800m. to £289,700m. (in 1994–5 prices), a rise of 34% (Treasury 1996a: 8).

1980s, management relationships were replaced by regulatory oversight from the executive agencies' 'parent departments'—oversight regimes which seemed in many cases to involve substantial second-guessing and 'bean-counting', to the point that some civil-service observers argued that what had intended to be a reform to empower agency managers had instead empowered departmental regulators. The Trosa report (1994: 36) quoted an agency chief executive declaring, 'There is a whole bureaucracy [in the parent department] set up to monitor us' and interviewees made similar comments to us. For example, an agency chief executive said, 'After the initial enthusiasm for [agency] freedoms, central bodies . . . clawed back power by placing new sets of requirements on agencies' (IT6). In interviews with executive officers, Hogwood *et al.* (1998: 15) also reported criticisms to the effect that 'everything is so regimented and regulated . . . we are not left to get on with it.'

An analogous process appears to have happened in the National Health Service, with the replacement of a nominally monolithic nationally managed organization by quasi-independent public hospital trusts heavily regulated by central government. Similarly, quangos (special-purpose public bodies outside central-government departments) were subject to increasing regulatory oversight since 1976, and the partial or complete replacement of local-authority responsibility for provision of services like education was reflected in a growth (133 per cent in body-count terms) of regulator-funders like the Further Education Funding Councils for England and Wales. These bodies, part of a new breed of funder-cum-regulator set up in the 1980s and 1990s, combined standard-setting functions with control of the purse strings for a particular service. They formed part of an ostensible mirror-image development in administrative structure over the 1980s and 1990s, that were briefly discussed in Chapter 1 and will be further explored in Chapter 9.

However, as noted earlier, regulators' body count and administrative inputs are only part of the iceberg of regulatory compliance. And compliance obligations can change (usually in the direction of imposing much greater costs on regulatees) without any substantial change in the regulators' visible costs.[15] Changes in regulatory

[15] e.g. in 1996 the Office of Public Service decreed that by 2000 all organizations employing civil servants should be recognized as 'Investors in People' (Cabinet Office 1996*a*). One executive agency Chief Executive estimated it would cost his

compliance costs within government are hard to estimate even in approximate terms, but from interview and other evidence it seems likely they rose at least as fast as direct administrative costs over the two decades to the mid-1990s.

## 3. REGULATION INSIDE GOVERNMENT IS DIVERSE

Regulation inside government may be a large and growing industry, but it is also a highly diverse one. There was no single focal point for the 130-plus organizations discussed earlier and listed in the appendix at the end of the book. There was no overall 'policy community' for regulation in government and no central point in Whitehall capable of, or responsible for, overseeing, or gauging its size and growth. One of the regulators of government was a Cabinet Office unit (formerly called the Deregulation Unit, subsequently retuned to a later version of political correctness under the title of 'Better Regulation Unit') concerned with the promotion of common practices in business regulation and looking at business regulation in the round across the highly compartmentalized boundaries of the public service. But there was no corresponding unit for regulation inside government, even though, as shown earlier, such regulation was similar to business regulation in scale and density. Some public-sector regulators formed self-conscious policy communities on a national or even international scale. There was a 'club' for the growing population of ombudsmen, and the same went for public auditors and (to a lesser extent, and of more recent creation) for professional inspectorates. And the Audit Commission has links with a number of the professional inspectorates, on which we comment in Chapter 5. But for the most part we found little evidence of community among regulators of government. By and large they did not meet one another in a regular way, did not see themselves as engaged in similar operations or use any generic word (certainly not regulator[16]) to describe what they did, and there were no mechanisms for encouraging or ensuring consistency of practice

---

organization £60 per person to obtain that recognition, and if those figures were extrapolated to all executive agencies, this decision would cost more than £20m. for all executive agencies (IT6; Cabinet Office 1997).

[16] There are exceptions; for one, see Collier (1996).

or standards across the disparate organizations involved.[17] Indeed, the regulation industry within government was itself wholly unregulated as an *industry*.[18]

Looking at regulation within government from the perspective of those at the receiving end, we found all parts of the public sector faced multiple, not single, regulators, and that those multiple regulators tended to work independently and with little awareness of the activities of their counterparts. Both for central and local government there was a plethora of different regulators pursuing efficiency and value for money in one form or another—public auditors like the NAO and the Audit Commission, value-for-money scrutineers in central agencies like the Treasury and Cabinet Office (which had at least three separate units operating in that domain at the time of our study) overseeing central departments and agencies, and for local government a number of professional inspectorates as well (cf. Day and Klein 1990). To that we can add the efficiency-chasing activities of those organizations which combined regulation with allocation of funding for specific policy domains like housing and education, which overlap with the work of the various auditors and inspectors (see Cabinet Office and Treasury 1996: 39). Even the two main public audit bodies (the National Audit Office and the Audit Commission for England and Wales) in some cases appear to work the same bureaucratic territory. According to Mary Bowerman (1994: 49), the overlap between the two bodies amounted to 7 per cent of NAO's value-for-money domain and 47 per cent of the Audit Commission's, in the early 1990s. In fact the structure of regulation for efficiency in government seemed to reflect an implicit belief that duplication, overlap, and unrationalized proliferation of separate units making costly demands on their regulatory charges promoted value for money—yet for service-delivery organizations those same organizations commonly argued the opposite. We shall be coming back to the 'do as I say, not as I do' problem of regulation inside government later in the book.

[17] When we ran a seminar for some of the main regulators of UK government in London in early 1997, we found that most of them had never met one another. In contrast to the USA the UK is not normally seen as a 'government of strangers' (Heclo 1977), but many of its regulators appear to be strangers to one another.
[18] Though individual parts had regulators of a sort—invariably mixed with sponsorships—such as the parliamentary select committees overseeing the work of the NAO and PCA.

However, regulatory diversity does not end with multiple units pursuing the same general values. Different regulators often represent competing administrative values, like cost minimization versus probity, humanity, or security. In central government, as we show in Chapter 6, prison governors were faced with the pressure to improve the humanity of their prison regimes from HM Inspectorate of Prisons and countervailing pressures to increase security by regulators inside the Prison Service. Central-government officials more generally were exposed to Treasury pressures for efficiency conceived as cost minimization, and rival pressures to extend 'due process' values in their work, notably by the Parliamentary Commissioner for Administration (PCA).[19] For example, *The Ombudsman in Your Files*, an official guide to good administrative procedure produced by the Cabinet Office and PCA in 1995, encouraged civil servants to 'admit that you have made a mistake, apologize and offer appropriate redress; and deal with complaints positively' (Cabinet Office 1995: 24). But the conception of good practice coming from the waste-watching regulators in the Treasury, close neighbours to the Cabinet Office in Whitehall, stressed cost minimization as the major concern.[20] Similarly cross-cutting regulatory pressures bear on local-authority chief executives: one complained to us, 'You have regulators that don't talk to each other . . . government departments don't seem to talk to each other . . . we notice this particularly with the different formats they want us to use when presenting information to them' (IEE8). Another commented 'I'm obsessed by what the District Auditor is saying, and what OFSTED is saying about our schools, what Social Services Inspectorate might say and where we are in the league

---

[19] The PCA investigates cases of alleged maladministration, oversaw the non-statutory 'open-government' code which preceded the Freedom of Information legislation being prepared at the time of writing, and produces thematic reports outlining principles of good administrative procedure. The PCA in 1996 put on record his view that downsizing public bureaucracies would be likely to lead to 'more, not less, maladministration', because automation of administrative procedures would not fully compensate for staff cutbacks (Parliamentary Commissioner for Administration 1996: 2).

[20] e.g. a Treasury 'Dear Accounting Officer' letter from 1992 stated that as a guiding principle: 'In general a lump sum settlement amounting to more than 50% of the loss claimed is unlikely to be justified; and a lower figure might well be more appropriate. Departments should remember that by definition the complainant has no legal entitlement to any compensation at all' (1992 DAO (GEN) 15/92, in HC 112: Appendix A, xxx).The letter was redrafted in 1996 in the light of criticism from the Select Committee for the PCA.

tables, but the system isn't coordinated and it's hard to cultivate a good relationship with all of them at once' (IEE11).

In addition to diversity in the general sense of proliferating multi-organizational form, competition, and overlap, regulation inside UK government was diverse in at least five other senses. It was *functionally* diverse, since there were distinct regulatory 'families' overseeing government activities in different dimensions and using different tool kits. It was *territorially* diverse, since regulation of government varied according to the different nations within the UK. It was *sectorally* diverse, since the style and scale of regulation were not the same for the core of central government as for local government or the outer reaches of the public sector. It was *institutionally* diverse, since the way regulators in government were set up (in independence from their charges and the extent to which their operations are rule-bound or formula-driven) was far from uniform. And it was *presentationally* diverse (for want of a better word), since the extent to which different regulators were (or aimed to be) in the limelight varied greatly from one to another.

First, regulators were functionally diverse since they could be separated into different families of organizations with different functional domains. Seven relatively distinct types of internal regulator are identified in Table 2.4, together with an indication of their staffing and running costs at the time of our inquiry.[21] We have already referred to most of these seven types. *Public audit bodies*' main responsibilities are to monitor and enforce probity and efficiency values (in practice, involving wide-ranging policy analysis): they operated to some extent in all parts of the public sector, but did not function as the first-line auditors of government contractors, nationalized industries, and some other 'fringe' organizations in the public sector. *Professional Inspectorates* oversee specific services, mainly but not exclusively operated by local public bodies, monitoring performance and often enforcing standards in a specialized domain. The UK does not share the French tradition of having an *inspection générale* attached to (almost) every domain of public service, but its government structure incorporates more than a score of specialized inspectorates employing well over 2,000 people. *Ombudsmen*, an institution imported by the UK from

---

[21] Some information about each organization is given in Appendix III.

TABLE 2.4. *Regulators in the UK public sector by type: number, staffing, and own expenditure, 1994–1995*[a]

| Regulators | | Number | Staff 1994–5 | Own expenditure 1994–5 (£m.) |
|---|---|---|---|---|
| A: Public audit bodies | Central | 2 | 2,228 | 139 |
| | Local | 2 | | |
| | Mixed | 0 | | |
| B: Inspectorates and equivalents | Central | 2 | 2,338 | 180 |
| | Local | 23 | | |
| | Mixed | 2 | | |
| C: Ombudsmen and equivalents | Central | 6 | 536 | 24 |
| | Local | 9 | | |
| | Mixed | 2 | | |
| D: Central agency regulators | Central | 18 | 1,205 | 37 |
| | Local | 0 | | |
| | Mixed | 0 | | |
| E: Funder regulators | Central | 0 | 1,140 | 42 |
| | Local | 8 | | |
| | Mixed | 6 | | |
| F: Departmental regulators of agencies | Central | 26 | 1,000 | 46 |
| | Local | 0 | | |
| | Mixed | 0 | | |
| G: Central regulators of local public bodies and the NHS | Central | 0 | 5,700 | 302 |
| | Local | 29 | | |
| | Mixed | 0 | | |
| Total | | 135 | 14,147 | 770 |

[a] Regulators were allocated to one of the three parts of the public sector in the same way as for Table 2.2.

Sweden over thirty years ago, now operate in every part of the public sector and have spread over to the private sector. Their main role is in individual grievance-handling, but has extended in some cases to the explication of general principles of 'good' administrative procedure. *Central agency regulators* are located in the central agencies of government (mainly the Treasury and Cabinet Office) and set, monitor, and/or enforce rules for the conduct of central government, for example on the use of staff or expenditure. *Funder-cum-regulators* (which experienced a notable 'population explosion' over the last decade or so, as noted earlier) set, monitor, and enforce conditions for the provision of public services by local public bodies which are also partly or wholly funded by these regulators, often using a mixture of audit and inspection techniques. *Departmental regulators of agencies* are those sections of core departments which regulate organizations within their department's domain, setting standards and monitoring behaviour both of executive agencies (civil-service organizations notionally operating at 'arm's length' of Ministerial departments) and public bodies outside the civil service. For example, the much discussed 'Of-type' regulators of the privatized utilities (like OFTEL), which were not part of our population because they regulate private business, not government, were constituted as non-Ministerial departments and subject to monitoring and oversight from the relevant Ministerial department. The final category, *Central regulators of local public bodies and the NHS*, contains two groups. One consists of central-government department regulators exercising what in traditional French parlance was called *tutelle* of local authorities, setting rules, and monitoring behaviour (and exercising a funder-regulator role for this class of bodies). In each of the four main parts of the UK (two kingdoms, a principality and a province) there was a different 'lead department' with primary responsibility for regulating local authorities, but there were several other major players in each case, exposing local authorities to a variety of sources of imperative instruction and guidance (cf. Griffith 1966). The second part, central NHS regulators, are organizations which set, monitor, and enforce standards for health-service bodies. This regulatory activity grew in salience as the UK's National Health Service changed from a structure ostensibly managed as a single organization to a 'holding company' or pluriform pattern.

Second, regulatory arrangements were territorially diverse. Most regulatory arrangements were split between either three or four bodies covering different parts of the UK. Table 2.5 summarizes the situation at the time of our study. The most territorially differentiated group of regulators includes most inspectorates, funder-regulators, and central regulators of local public bodies and the NHS. Ombudsmen and public audit bodies were also differentiated and institutionally complex. For example England and Wales

TABLE 2.5. *Territorial diversity of regulators in government: differentiation between England, Scotland, Wales, and Northern Ireland*

| Degree of territorial differentiation | Characteristics of differentiation and types of regulator with examples |
| --- | --- |
| UK-wide bodies | Most 'central agency' regulators (e.g. Commissioner for Public Appointments, HM Treasury) |
| UK-wide arrangements except for *one* other body | Scotland—Some inspectorates (e.g. HM Inspectorate of Prisons, HM Inspectorate of Prisons Scotland), Scottish Prisons Complaints Commission<br>Northern Ireland (NI)—A few central agency regulators (e.g. Civil Service Commissioners); some ombudsmen (e.g. Parliamentary Commissioner for Administration, NI Parliamentary Commissioner for Administration)<br>England; Wales—none |
| UK-wide arrangements except for *two* other bodies | Scotland and NI—All public audit bodies, except audit of expenditure on law and order in NI (conducted by NIAO as an agent of NAO); most central government regulators and most central regulators of local public bodies and the NHS (e.g. DETR, Scottish Office Development Department, Department of the Environment (NI))<br>England and Scotland; England and Wales, England and NI; Scotland and Wales; Wales and NI—none |
| Separate bodies for England, Scotland, Wales, and Northern Ireland | Some inspectorates (e.g. OFSTED, HM Inspectors of Schools Scotland, Office of HM Chief Inspector of Schools in Wales, NI Education and Training Inspectorate); some central government regulators; some central-local public bodies regulators in sectors where Scottish departments, Welsh Office and NI departments all had responsibilities (e.g. education); most ombudsmen (e.g. Commission for Local Administration (CLA) in England, CLA Wales, CLA Scotland, NI Commissioner for Complaints); most funder-regulators (e.g. Housing Corporation, Scottish Homes, Housing for Wales, Northern Ireland Housing Executive) |

and Scotland had quasi-independent commissions overseeing local-authority audit (the Audit Commission for England and Wales and Accounts Commission for Scotland) while local-authority accounts in Northern Ireland were audited by sections of a government department. Northern Ireland (from 1997) had a single public audit body including NHS audit, but central and local audit was split elsewhere in the UK, and suggestions that they might be unified tended to be met with the response that such a step would be constitutionally unthinkable. The only bodies in our population with UK-wide coverage were the central agencies, and it seems unlikely (particularly with the advent of a Scottish Parliament and Welsh Assembly) that territorial diversity will decline; the opposite pattern seems more likely.

Third, regulation was sectorally diverse since the proportionate size of investment in regulation was higher in local government and the outer reaches of the public sector than in the core of central government. Of the 135 organizations included in the most conservative count of regulators within the UK public sector (as described above), with approximately 14,000 staff and expenditure of close to £800m., over 60 per cent of the regulator organizations, over 75 per cent of the staff, and over 80 per cent of the spending was devoted to the oversight of organizations outside the core of central government. Local government appeared to be more heavily regulated in that way than central government, with nearly three times the number of staff employed by regulators of local government compared to regulators of central government, and direct regulatory spending by local-government regulators amounting to roughly twice the proportion of total spending being overseen (0.5 as against 0.2) compared to central government. The larger investment in regulation of local rather than central government is consistent with the theme of 'relational distance' which the next chapter discusses.

Fourth, not only did the relative density of regulation vary across sectors of government, but the way regulation was set up varied from one part of the public sector to another. Some regulators were more independent than others, in distance from their charges or from the general policy process. Some were more regulatory than others, in the formality and extensiveness of the regulatory process. We postpone to the next chapter a discussion of variations in formality and operating styles. But it can be noted at this point that regulation varies in a variety of institutional and behavioural dimensions, such as how far regulators are external to the bodies they oversee (as opposed to being part of those bodies), how far regulation is conducted separately from other functions (as opposed to being brigaded with functions such as management, allocation of funds, or policy advice), how far operating rules are formal and explicit, and how far regulation consists of all aspects of setting standards, monitoring, and enforcement or only some of them.

Finally, regulators were presentationally diverse, in the extent to which they are in the public eye, or seek to be. Some internal regulators, like the Chief Inspector of Schools for England, were almost household names, with high media exposure, and public auditors' waste-watching *exposés* (notably stories of policy and administrative mismanagement produced by the National Audit Office and the tables of saints and sinners produced by the Audit Commission ranking different local authorities according to different performance criteria) attracted much media attention. Other regulators, like the Inspectorate of Fire Services or the Magistrates' Courts Inspectorate, hardly figured in public debates, emerging into the limelight only occasionally or not at all. When we explored the media profile for ten regulators whose activities are analysed in more detail in Part Two in six UK national newspapers and one news magazine, we found that the most media-salient body (OFSTED, the schools inspection agency for England) attracted more than 100 times more mentions than the least media-salient body (the Fire Services Inspectorate). The National Audit Office and Audit Commission also figured prominently.

Some—no doubt most—of this hundredfold variation may be explained by general political contentiousness and inherent 'newsworthiness' of the bodies. But regulators inside government also varied considerably in the extent to which they aimed to be in the public eye and to use general exposure to pursue their aims. Some treated media exposure, at least implicitly, as an indicator of good performance, and many adopted strategies of media management, attempting to use public exposure as a lever to draw attention to their efforts and put extra pressure on those they were 'naming and blaming' to change their ways. But there were other regulators who took the opposite line, preferring to 'do good by stealth' and stay out of the spotlight.

## 4. CONCLUSION

Regulation inside government is a complex and apparently growing industry, in spite, or perhaps because, of recent preoccupations with rolling back bureaucracy and empowering managers. Its scale cannot be measured with precision, but even on the most conservative view of its scope it involved at the time of our study direct costs approaching £1bn. per year and an army of regulators many times larger than that of the regulators of the much discussed privatized utilities, both in absolute terms and relative to turnover. Indeed, the overall scale of regulation inside government seems to be similar to the *entire* investment in regulation of private business in the UK. More important perhaps, yet even more difficult to assess, is the scale of indirect costs of this activity—compliance costs mandated on to other parts of the public sector, which are likely to dwarf the direct costs of the regulators themselves.

Even without taking account of compliance costs, regulation inside government grew substantially in the UK public sector in staffing and spending terms over the two decades up to the mid-1990s. There seems to have been a reversal of a pattern observable from the late nineteenth century to the 1970s, when few new regulators of government were created and the staffing and spending of public-sector regulators grew proportionately less than general public expenditure and staffing (Normanton 1966; Rhodes 1981). Indeed, were the patterns of regulator growth and civil-service downsizing continued at the 1975–95 rate indefinitely, we should find by the later 2000s the civil service had become like the abattoir industry in the 1990s, with more than two regulators for every 'doer', and over ten regulator organizations for every major government department. Such an outcome seems unlikely, but the projection brings out the remarkable combination of regulator growth and civil-service staff cutbacks over the last two decades of the twentieth century.

In Chapter 3 we turn our attention from scale, growth, and institutional variety to an exploration of how internal regulators work in government. Did they behave like business regulators? To what extent can we 'read across' themes that have been developed in describing and accounting for the behaviour of business regulators, or were the two spheres of regulation fundamentally dissimilar? How distinct were regulators of government from their clients, and how did that affect the way they work?

# 3

# Regulation in Government: Tools, Characteristics, and Behaviour

> Thus, all else constant, a policeman is more lenient toward someone close to him—a relative, friend, neighbour, or fellow policeman.
>
> D. Black, *The Behaviour of Law*

This chapter explores three interrelated themes: the tools and approaches regulators used to do their job; the extent to which regulation of government resembled regulation of business; and the extent to which regulatory behaviour and style were related to the social distance between the regulators and those they regulate. It argues that, while there was no single style of regulation in government, the tools and approaches used by the regulators cut across the different institutional types identified in the last chapter. It also claims there were important parallels between regulation of government and regulation of business; and that the way regulators behave tended to be linked to the 'relational distance' between regulator and regulatee.

## 1. TOOLS AND APPROACHES

Chapter 2 identified seven main institutional types of regulators inside government—public auditors, professional inspectorates, ombudsmen, central-agency regulators, funder-regulators, departmental regulators of agencies, and central-government regulators of local authorities, and the NHS. Many of those we interviewed from each of these seven types saw their form of regulation inside government as *sui generis* and unrelated to any other, but when we looked in detail at documentary accounts of the operation of a sample of twenty-eight regulators inside government (comprising specimens drawn from each of the seven institutional types), we found methods of working were not rigidly aligned with institutional type. Different methods could be used within a single organization, while organizations in different regulator 'families' often used essentially similar instruments.

There is no generally accepted framework for characterizing the tools or instrumentalities of regulation, in contrast to institutional types of regulator.[1] Chapter 1 contrasted pure comptrol or oversight with three generic inspector-free types of control over bureaucracy, namely competition, mutuality, and contrived randomness, and noted that many forms of regulation in government involve hybrids of these generic types (namely oversight linked with competition, oversight linked with mutuality, and oversight linked with randomness). Oversight linked with competition (in the form of quasi-markets and league tables comparing public service providers across a set of published performance indicators) has been a marked feature of reforms in the institutional structure of public health care and education, though it seems to have been less applied to the central core of government in Whitehall. Oversight linked with mutuality is also a common hybrid, particularly in the use of peer group review teams for quality assessments (like NHS clinical audits or university research assessment exercises) and also in career structures in which professionals may switch between overseer and regulatee roles in the course of a career, as in the inspection of fire, police, or prison services. Oversight linked with randomness as a recipe for regulation inside government seems to be the exception rather than the rule, but it is far from unknown. A number of oversight systems make it difficult for regulatees to predict when they will be assessed or by whom (sometimes neither), and overseers sometimes aim to be inscrutable, choosing to make unpredictability part of their tool kit.

Any of these social bases of control—pure and hybrid—can also be analysed as elements of 'viable'-control systems in a cybernetic (control theory) perspective. Control in such a perspective must by definition contain some method of setting standards (a 'director'), some way of gathering information about whatever is being controlled (a 'detector'), and some way of modifying behaviour (an

---

[1] For accounts of differences in regulatory regimes, see Carson (1970); Hawkins and Thomas (1984); Grabosky and Braithwaite (1986); Baldwin (1987); Rowan-Robinson *et al.* (1990); Black (1995).

'effector') if the system swings off limits (Dunsire 1978: 59–60; Hood 1983). What instruments did regulators in government use as directors, detectors, and effectors?

For the director element of the control process, we found wide variation among overseers within government. As will be shown later, standards for regulation inside government seemed to vary widely in *explicitness*—how far they were spelt out in advance of case decisions and how far they were formula-bounded, in the sense of being expressed in precise and measurable targets rather than ambiguous mutually contradictory values to be balanced off against one another. They also varied in *reflexivity*—how far they were imposed uniformly from the top or were part of a self-regulation process in which regulatee organizations were free to set their own standards within some zone of acceptability; and in *stability*—how far the targets were stable over time, or volatile as political and other circumstances change. As will be shown later, it was rare for regulators inside government to combine high degrees of explicitness, reflexivity, and stability in the standards they apply.

For detection, most of the regulators we surveyed obtained their information by one or more of five overlapping methods—inspection, audit, certification, authorization, and adjudication or mediation. *Inspection* involves visits to the worksite for direct observation of the organization's operations, to check whether the buildings, staff, and equipment on the books exist in reality and function effectively. *Audit*, originating in the investigation of financial regularity and accurate bookkeeping but increasingly extending to other domains, involves compulsory examination of documentary records to assess performance. *Certification* means an official declaration of the fitness or quality of some individual, organization, or object. Widely used in business regulation (for instance, in certificates of airworthiness or roadworthiness) and overlapping with audit (since auditors issue certificates), certification procedures have often been applied to the regulation of the public service, for instance in quality-of-service awards, police efficiency certificates, and much of the work of the professional inspectorate. *Authorization* means the regulator gains information through its role as an overseer with powers to approve particular acts, since its permission is needed for a particular course of action to be valid, in the same way that real-estate developers must seek permission from the

local planning authority for their projects. *Adjudication* or mediation means the regulator gains information through a process of
conflict by the assessment of complaints and disputes. Inspection
tends to be an active form of detection (Hood 1983), in that the
regulator takes the initiative in making visits, while adjudication
and authorization tend to be passive in that regulators work mainly
by responding to complaints or requests. But audit and many forms
of certification tend to be interactive, since the regulators work by
requiring their charges to produce documents and submissions to
which they then react over a scrutiny cycle. In practice these detector forms overlap, and many regulators inside government used
more than one of these mechanisms, though few seemed to use
more than two.

The third analytic component of a control system in a cybernetic
perspective—ways of changing behaviour—varied widely too.
As noted earlier, some regulators of government (such as school
inspectors, overseers of contracted-out prisons, and central
departments applying compulsory competitive tendering regimes)
possessed the 'nuclear weapon' of power to recommend the closure
of public organizations. One, the Audit Commission's Auditors,
also had heavy artillery in the form of the ability to certify expenditure as illegal, rendering individuals presiding over such spending liable to be surcharged for large sums.[2] Others had powers of
formal censure of individuals or organizations (such as the ability
of the Police Inspectorate to deny an efficiency certificate to a police
force), and in some cases might operate as the first stage in processes of litigation (like police complaints authorities and the Prisons
Ombudsman). Many (like the National Audit Office) had substantial ability to 'shame' their errant charges by naming and blaming
them in ways that could be expected to hurt their careers, and a
number had the power to hit regulatee organizations (but not
individuals) in the pocket by decisions that could be expected
directly or indirectly to affect budgetary allocations. Others had
lighter weapons, consisting only of honorific certificates (like the

---

[2] Under sect. 20 of the 1982 Local Government Act, the auditor can directly
certify that a sum is due from a person on the basis of 'wilful misconduct', rendering
him/her liable to automatic disqualification for office for five years. Under sect. 19
of the Act, auditors can apply to the court for a declaration that an item of account
is contrary to law, and the court can order the person responsible to pay back some
or all of the money spent, and may also disqualify him/her from office for a period.

'Chartermark' for good public service) that might or might not be valued, the power of moral suasion, or simply the ability to 'blow the whistle' on their charges by bringing their shortcomings into public debate.

We can combine the analysis of the social basis of control over bureaucracy with the three generic components of any control system to conceive of twelve basic ways regulators (whether of government or business) might go about doing their job. Table 3.1 summarizes such an analysis.

As the table indicates, *oversight* in its pure form can be linked with a style of standard-setting that entrenches non-negotiable targets or rules based on acknowledged expertise or authority (for example in rules for probity or regularity in public audit); with an information-gathering style that works 'subpoena-style' by imposing obligations to provide documents or answer questions, and with an approach to behaviour modification focusing on the imposition of authority through some graded set of sanctions. *Competition* can be linked with a style of standard-setting that involves a struggle among rival standards (with rival regulators propounding different standards, and regulatees having to work out the appropriate balance for themselves among the competing demands being placed on them, as in the case of security and humanity regulators of prisons noted in the last chapter); with information-gathering through incentives rather than directives (that is, where there is an expected or possible pay-off for providing information, for example in complaints made in the hope of securing redress or 'whistle-blowers' aiming to settle scores with their bosses or colleagues); and with a style of behaviour modification that relies on the desire to outpoint potential competitors (for example, by occupying a higher position in a 'league' than rivals).

*Mutuality* can be linked with a style of standard-setting involving participation among those affected to arrive at targets or goals (for example, through close consultation with regulatees, or even effective veto rights); with a style of information-gathering that relies on exchanges through networking across a group (information volunteered on a basis of reciprocity, for instance among fellow-professionals); and behaviour modification through mutual influence and persuasion within a community. Finally, *contrived randomness* can be linked with a style of standard-setting that is unpredictable and disorganized (with no certainty as to what

TABLE 3.1. *A regulator's tool kit: twelve instrumentalities*

| *Social basis of control* | Analytic components of control system | | |
|---|---|---|---|
| | Standard-setting (director) | Information-gathering (detector) | Behaviour modification (effector) |
| Oversight | (1) Hierarchical ordering | (2) Subpoena-style | (3) Response to authority |
| | *Example*: entrenched non-negotiable rules | *Example*: obligatory returns | *Example*: ability to prosecute or confer/withhold licences or certificates |
| Competition | (4) Developing through 'natural selection' | (5) Incentive-style | (6) Quest to be/stay high in a league |
| | *Example*: tension between contradictory demands | *Example*: yardstick competition | *Example*: ratings leagues or prizes for top performers |
| Mutuality | (7) Participative | (8) Network-style | (9) Exposure to mutual influence or persuasion |
| | *Example*: standards agreed by consultation with regulatees | *Example*: exchange of information among professionals | *Example*: convincing case in debate/discussion |
| Contrived Randomness | (10) Unpredictable/ disorganized | (11) Lottery-style | (12) Pay-offs of action unpredictable |
| | *Example*: volatile or inscrutable standards | *Example*: random selection or unannounced visits | *Example*: limitation of opportunism by uncertainty about future regime or career direction |

standards will be applied at any one time, or through what procedures); with an approach to gathering information that relies heavily on processes of chance (unpredictable questions, visits out of the blue); with an approach to behaviour modification that works through making the pay-offs of action unpredictable.

These twelve forms, it must be stressed, are ideal types, not a taxonomy of observations. But some regulators in government approximated to the ideal types in their operating styles. For instance, public auditors' traditional 'regularity' oversight (but not value-for-money audit) approximates to the oversight mode depicted in Table 3.1, in that standards are relatively 'given' and non-negotiable, information is 'requisitioned', either through direct access to the organization's books or by inspection of the work of other auditors (supplemented to some degree by information obtained from confessions, whistle-blowing, and complaints, for example through MPs' letters to the Comptroller and Auditor-General or management concerns about dishonesty among employees), and behaviour is modified by sanctions running from informal advice through 'management letters'[3] to qualification of accounts, public shaming, and in some cases more severe sanctions.

On the other hand, much of the oversight exercised within Whitehall by the family of central agencies (and regulation of professionals within the public sector more generally), seems traditionally to have involved something closer to the mutuality mode. Standards have tended to be softer and more negotiable, information has been gained as much through professional exchange as formal requisitioning (albeit supplemented with formal returns, often irksome to small departments[4] or newcomers to the bureaucracy), and behaviour modification by clublike persuasion rather than formal graded sanctions. However, as will be argued in the next chapter, this traditional style seems to have changed to some degree, if only because the advent of 140-odd executive agencies made the older clublike form of regulation more difficult to sustain.

Moreover, within 'central-agency oversight', some features of traditional Treasury expenditure control approximated in some ways to the contrived randomness mode, with objectives uncertain and often impenetrable, information elicited by an unpredictable

---

[3] Letters addressed to those responsible for the management of the body being audited; see Hollingsworth *et al.* (1998: 93–4).
[4] Cf. Hogwood *et al.* (1998: 15).

process of *ad hoc* questioning triggered by requests for authorization (in which questions might tail off quickly or might lead to a major inquiry), and opportunistic behaviour to beat the system limited by inability to predict the consequences of action because of the vagaries of the expenditure-control and promotion-posting systems in producing unforeseen developments (new spending control systems introduced every few years with different detailed rules, career structures that made it hard for players to predict whether or when their paths will next cross or whether today's ally will be tomorrow's enemy, or vice versa).

Perhaps the closest approximation to the competition mode is the system of regulation for higher education which emerged along with the formal ending of the 'binary divide' between polytechnics and universities (the former externally regulated, the latter largely self-regulated) in the 1990s, with contradictory pressures entrenched in different regulators of research and teaching excellence, information provided by HE institutions to regulators in the hope of maintaining or improving their reputation and funding, and an approach to behaviour modification which relied heavily on rating institutions and arraying them in a league, linked with differential funding according to ratings.

However, most regulators inside government used operating methods that spread across these 'ideal types' and mixed and matched among them. For example, many of our regulators whose main information-gathering instrument was the subpoena-style return (Table 3.1, type 2) also made use of incentive-type information-gathering (type 5) by developing a complaint-handling facility, either directly or through links with other grievance-handling regulators. Similarly, some regulators who operated with standards that were relatively given and non-negotiable (type 1), like the Parliamentary Commissioner for Administration, sought to supplement them with codes of practice on which the regulatees were consulted, introducing elements of type 7 into the standard-setting process.

We drew three general conclusions from our analysis of operating methods of regulators inside government. First, the regulators ranged across the instruments depicted in Table 3.1, and were less distinctive from one another in basic operating methods than their compartmentalization into different institutional families might lead one to suppose. For example, the regulation of Whitehall departments by central agencies, the operation of many of the professional inspectorates, and the value-for-money work of the public auditors seemed to share a similar cluster of methods with the regulation of professional services (Table 3.1, types 7, 8, and 9, with elements of type 6 for behaviour-modification). Similarly, the operation of many of the funder-regulators (like the Further Education Funding Council for England) and the central departments regulating local public bodies involved a similar combination of methods (in the form of types 1, 2, and 3, with elements of types 5 and 6). If different institutions make use of similar methods, they may have more to gain from exchanging information and ideas about best practice than current arrangements permit. We return to this issue in Chapter 10.

Second, units within the same institutional family frequently employed different operating methods. As has already been noted, public audit bodies used something approximating to the ideal-type oversight style for fiscal or regularity audit (types 1, 2, and 3), but other forms—closer to mutuality or competition—in their value-for-money audit work (types 7, 8, and 9). Moreover, different public audit bodies engaged in value-for-money audit used different instruments. The Audit Commission laid emphasis on type 6—the ordering of local authorities in much publicized leagues of saints and sinners—in a way eschewed for central departments by the National Audit Office, which tended to avoid interdepartmental comparison and chose to put the spotlight on departments and agencies *seriatim*. And as already noted, the ultimate behaviour-modification sanction available to local-authority (regularity) auditors—the initiation of court proceedings to surcharge councillors and bureaucrats—had no parallel for the National Health Service or for central-government departments.

Third (to anticipate the discussion in the next section), the range of methods employed by regulators inside government suggests there may be so much variation within this 'world' as to make it doubtful whether there are strong generic differences between regulation inside government and regulation of business (which is also highly diverse) which outweigh the differences within each regulatory domain. For example, regulators of the privatized utilities (like OFTEL, OFWAT, OFGAS) and several funder-regulators within the public sector shared an emphasis on types 1, 2, and 3 mixed with types 5 and 6. If there is a difference between the two sectors, it seems more likely to lie in the mix of the range of instruments depicted in Table 1.2 rather than the basic ingredients.

Moreover, we found many regulators inside government resembled their private-sector cousins in some important operating methods. In many cases they could choose what weapons to select from their armoury to shape the behaviour of their clients, and, except in cases of gross malfeasance they tended to start with low-key or informal ways of responding to a perceived problem, escalating to heavy bombardment only if a softly-softly approach failed to bring the desired responses. In explaining this 'ladder-of-sanctions' approach to us (Table 3.1, type 3), regulators often drew an analogy with a football referee who begins with 'yellow card' warnings before sending players off the field, and in several cases we found more than one level of yellow card. Not only did regulators of government appear to be as diverse as regulators of business in the way they worked, but they also had general concerns which resembled those of business regulators. We explore this issue further in the next section, and 'hierarchy of sanctions' is a recurring theme in Part Two.

## 2. REGULATION OF GOVERNMENT AND REGULATION OF BUSINESS: 'ALIKE IN ALL UNIMPORTANT RESPECTS'?

In a well-known essay, Graham Allison (1984) argued management in government and business were 'alike in all unimportant respects'. For Allison, superficial similarities between the two forms of management were outweighed by more fundamental differences. Can the same be said about the regulation of government and the regulation of business?

Some of our interviewees among regulators of government thought so. As noted in Chapter 2, for the most part they did not use the word regulation to describe what they did. Since they tended to associate the word exclusively with the activity of the quasi-independent bodies like OFTEL which set prices and trading conditions for the privatized utilities, it had an alien ring for them and they were quick to point out differences between the way they worked and the *modus operandi* of OFTEL-type regulators. Reflecting this view, one of the ombudsmen said, 'I don't feel that I'm a regulator in the OFTEL sense because I cannot just intervene, I can only react' (I5).

In addition to such perceptions, there are other reasons that might be invoked to support a view of regulation in government as 'alike in all unimportant respects' to business regulation. Some tools available to business regulators cannot be used by regulators of government, and vice versa. As noted in Chapter 1, Wilson and Rachal (1977) argued that a major difference between regulation of government and regulation of business was that regulators of government, unlike their business-regulation cousins, are not in general able to prosecute their erring charges for non-compliance—a factor likely, in Wilson and Rachal's view, to mean it is harder to regulate government than business firms because of the lack of decisive sanctions available directly to the regulator and the need to haggle politically over any enforcement action. Moreover, it could be argued that state ownership of the regulatee bodies may make possible regulatory responses different from those available when regulation and ownership are separated; that funding can be linked to regulation in government in ways not available to most business regulators; and that regulation in government can rely on career pressures to induce compliance, while in business regulation such pressures may commonly have the opposite effect, with the search for profits pulling against incentives to follow regulatory codes.

Each of these arguments seems to have some force—but only up to a point. Even the perception that regulation of government is different from regulation of business seems to be far from universal. Many of the regulators in government we talked to saw important parallels between at least parts of their work and that of business regulators. Perhaps not surprisingly, in view of the similarity of the methods they use (as noted in the last section), funder-regulators were the most comfortable with the comparison, and one commented, 'Yes, I recently bumped into [one of the regulators of the privatized utilities] at a conference and got chatting; the resemblance between our jobs was striking' (I30). And those working in the organizations being overseen—like local government chief executives (IEE11), school head teachers (IEE1), prison governors (IEE3)—tended to recognize themselves fairly readily as regulatees, 'subject to a set of bodies setting down requirements for what we do', in the words of a chief executive of a central-government executive agency (IT5). It therefore seems that perceptions about the parallels between regulation of business and government varied, but in government those on the receiving end of the process were more likely to recognize it as regulation than those who were dishing it out. Indeed, regulatory denial by the latter group may go with a 'Nelson's-eye' approach to the compliance costs of regulation in government, an issue touched on in the last chapter and to which we return at the end of the book.

Of the other arguments noted above for viewing regulation of government as 'alike in all unimportant respects' to regulation of business, the most telling one at first sight is Wilson and Rachal's suggestion that it is the lack of prosecutorial powers that makes regulation of government different from business regulation. It is true that prosecutions are rarely available to regulators inside government (especially for central government). A few have powers to instigate action against individual officials for illegal behaviour (notably Auditors pursuing local councillors for unlawful expenditure, often in politically charged circumstances, HSE in its role of safety regulator spanning the public and private sectors, and regulators concerned with corruption). In addition, powers of legal compulsion are sometimes invoked by central departments in the regulation of local authorities, for instance in enforcement of Compulsory Competitive Tendering requirements; and the same goes for EU regulators securing compliance with Community norms by member states, to be discussed further in Chapter 8.

However, the rarity of prosecution as a weapon in the hands of regulators in government needs to be considered against the fact that many regulators of business rarely invoke their prosecutorial powers in practice (as has been revealed in a number of studies, including those by Cranston (1979) and Grabosky and Braithwaite (1986)). It also needs to be noted that some key business regulators (for example, those overseeing the privatized utilities) lack powers of criminal prosecution; and that enforcement of business regulation itself often operates through the medium of elected politicians, for example in the discretion vested in Ministers to act on or disregard recommendations by the UK's Monopolies and Mergers Commission. And even though regulators within government typically did not have access to prosecutorial powers, it is not the case that they invariably lacked teeth in the sanctions which they could bring to bear. After all, in some circumstances a mere adverse comment (for example by the Civil Service Commissioner) might do considerable damage to politicians' reputations through the 'ripple effect' produced through the media and Parliament. Moreover, as has already been noted, some regulators in government have access to sanctions as draconian as those possessed by their private-sector counterparts, such as the ability to recommend closure of an institution (notably in the case of schools declared to be 'failing') and consequently to generate an atmosphere of fear among regulatees unusual in business regulation.

The notion that regulation in government is different from business regulation because government as owner of the institutions being regulated has courses of action available to it that are not available to business regulators, seems even less convincing as a general proposition. According to property rights theory in institutional economics, an owner, through control of the residual uses of assets, can undertake direct *ad hoc* interventions not open to an arm's-length regulator—which might include selective dismissal of top-level staff, keeping an organization going (when a regulator can only decide to close it down), or reallocating people or capital to specific new uses (cf. Coase 1960; Schmid 1978; Alchian 1987). But in practice regulation in government very rarely seems to rely on ownership power *stricto sensu*. That is because the powers of 'ownership' in public organizations are typically divided up and fenced in by procedural restrictions (indeed, a recent report on the reform of New Zealand bureaucracy (Schick 1996) found ownership was typically subordinated to other considerations in government). It is rare to find a regulator, even at the core of Whitehall, directly wielding all the powers available to an owner in abstract theory. Perhaps the closest form is the regulation of executive agencies by their departmental owners, with command over residual uses of assets not otherwise prescribed by contract or regulation. But for the most part regulators in government command ownership powers only indirectly, through ability to make recommendations to Ministers or other sources of ownership of public organization. Moreover, given the diversity of the public service in the UK—divided as it is among the civil service, local government, police forces, statutory corporations, and a range of other independent public bodies—there can only be said to be common ownership of the various institutions in a general 'state theory' sense, but not in law or practice. For example, local authorities are not owned by central departments in any meaningful sense, having power rooted in statute.

Consequently, most regulators in government—just like regulators of business—oversee organizations whose behaviour they must attempt to shape by means other than direct powers of ownership, for example by encouraging competition among producers or providing consumers with information to improve the quality of their choices, as in the case of league tables giving comparative ratings of local authority and school performance. If the owner needs to employ techniques commonly used by regulators in business, we must conclude either that the power of ownership does not mean much for public bureaucracies, or that regulators have largely to rely on other sources of control.

More plausible is the idea that regulation in government differs from business regulation because government can shape the behaviour of its own institutions by controlling their spending directly. In principle, the allocation of funds to public bureaucracies provides extra levers for a regulator to influence a regulatee, through extra resources for good performers, taking funds away from bad performers, or by shaping financial incentives to fit with regulatory objectives (as in the case of fundholding budgets for GPs, introduced in 1992 after decades of unsuccessful attempts to contain the NHS drugs bill by persuading doctors to take account of costs in their decisions over prescribing). And as noted in the last chapter there is a class of funder-regulators, for example, in housing and education, where oversight and financial allocation are deliberately linked. But it has to be noted that direct linking of oversight and funding is more the exception than the rule. Many regulators of government are carefully detached from the bodies formally responsible for funding, and while their reports can provide ammunition for funding bodies, they cannot themselves determine how, when, or even whether the fiscal weapon is to be used. Even in funder-regulator organizations, we commonly find 'Chinese walls' between the regulatory and financial allocation components. And on the other hand, linking funding and regulation is far from unknown in business regulation. It is pervasive in agriculture under the CAP regime, where subsidy and regulation are closely interwoven; and price-control regulation over monopolies or near-monopolies, as in the case of the RPI-$x$ regimes for the UK's privatized utilities, can sometimes amount to the same thing as the use of funding as a regulatory tool, for instance in compensating water companies for complying with EU environmental standards. Indeed, the reviews carried out by OFGAS, OFTEL, OFFER, and OFWAT prior to changes in price controls (NAO 1996: 24–7) have noticeable similarities to value-for-money studies undertaken by public auditors in that they are closely concerned with the efficiency of the organizations being overseen in comparison with the business sector as a whole. Even for funding the 'alike in all unimportant respects' thesis is hard to press very far.

A final argument noted above is that regulation in government is distinctive because it can work by manipulating public servants' careers in a way not available within business regulation, where business executives criticized by a regulator may have their career prospects enhanced if the transgression reflects behaviour which puts the interests of the firm above those of the regulator. But for the same reason that regulators within government seldom in practice deploy all or even any of the state's theoretical powers of 'ownership' over the organizations being overseen, those regulators are rarely in a position to shape career advancement of their regulatees directly. Indeed, it may commonly work the other way round, particularly in central government, where top-level regulatees (politicians and mandarins) may often be able to exert influence over the selection or reselection of their regulators. It is true that the handling of challenges from regulators can be an important test of executive careers in government, and poor reports from inspectors can damage the standing of those in charge of services or organizations (like prison governors or head teachers), but such features are not unique to the regulation of government. After all, the chief engineer of a motor company whose new car encounters damning criticism from safety regulators is unlikely to have undimmed future career prospects in the industry, and the same applies *a fortiori* to professionals in private practice who can be disciplined, barred, or 'struck off' by their statutory regulators. It may be more accurate to see regulation of government as generally characterized by a compliance culture, particularly in the 'Whitehall village' where regulators and regulatees have traditionally been drawn from a common career corps. But the effect seems as likely to blunt the edge of regulation (since regulator and regulatee can change places over a career) as to sharpen it. Moreover, compliance cultures in regulation are neither unique to the public sector nor universal in a public-sector context. At least one of the public-sector regulators we talked to faced the problem that formal disciplinary action had an effect which was the reverse of that intended, being treated as a badge of glory by those 'at the sharp end' of the service. Many found that getting their charges to adopt their recommendations was often a far from straightforward or instant affair, often requiring repeated action over a long period. And even the theory of the effect of a common career corps producing a compliance culture in the public service may be undermined by structural changes fragmenting the different 'businesses' involved and by the 'audit-explosion' risk that more formal regulatory regimes may turn formerly responsible self-regulating professionals into cheating regulatees looking for loopholes to exploit (Power 1994; 1997).

Rather than clear-cut differences between public- and private-sector regulation, it seems safer to conclude that there is a spectrum of types and cultures in both cases, albeit with differences of mix and emphasis. Section 1 discussed the variety in tools used by different public-sector regulators. In both business and government regulation, we can find examples of regulators who work in a blaze of publicity and others who stay out of the limelight, and in both sectors self-regulation frequently figures large as a regulatory strategy. Indeed, several of the types of business regulator identified by Grabosky and Braithwaite (1986) have counterparts in regulation within government. Auditors of local government resemble their 'benign big guns', having powerful sanctions which they seldom use. Ombudsmen and adjudicators correspond to their 'conciliators', making little use of their more formal endorsement powers, and many central-agency regulators also resemble conciliators.

If there is any general difference of emphasis between public- and private-sector regulation, our analysis suggested regulators within government were less likely to work in a 'token enforcement style' (the commonest approach to business regulation found by Grabosky and Braithwaite (1986: 226)) and there seemed to be few equivalents to Grabosky and Braithwaite's 'modest enforcers' which use formal powers sparingly. Regulators inside government seemed more likely to work through non-discretionary application of rules than their business-regulation counterparts, and consensual styles were a marked feature of some fields of regulation within government. Examples included central government value-for-money audit (but not regularity audit), regulation within Whitehall (even including the regulatory regimes for executive agencies), and some regulation of professionals by special inspectorates. But when it came to regulation of local authorities by central departments or of the outer reaches of the public sector, regulation in government tended to be less consensual, and less likely to involve the regulatees in the standard-setting process. One way of explaining that variation in style is the notion of relational distance in regulation, to which we turn in the next section.

## 3. RELATIONAL DISTANCE: 'US' AND 'THEM' IN REGULATORY FORMALITY

One theme in the business-regulation literature that we singled out for particular attention is that of 'relational distance'. The term was coined by Black (1976: 40), observing: 'People vary in the degree to which they participate in one another's lives. This defines their intimacy, or relational distance.'[5] The higher the RD, the greater the social distance. Black claimed RD both shapes the conditions in which law is used to order social relations (law was most likely to come into play as a regulatory instrument at intermediate levels of RD rather than very high or low levels), and also law enforcement (the harshness of enforcement varying with the RD between regulator and regulated). RD might also be expected to be crucial to regulatory operation for the perspective of grid/group cultural theory (Thompson *et al.* 1990) since it represents social cohesion and the differentiation of one group from another, which is one of the fundamental coordinates of human organization for cultural theory.

Grabosky and Braithwaite (1986: 207) applied Black's idea of RD to Australian business regulation, arguing: 'one would predict that the greater the relational distance between regulator and regulatee, the greater the tendency to use formal sanctions.' They explored four main hypotheses along these lines and claimed to find compelling support for the RD hypothesis, using prosecutions as their main indicator of formality.

[5] For Black (1995: 41) RD could be measured in several ways, including 'the scope, frequency, and length of interaction between people, the age of their relationship, and the nature and number of links between them in a social network.'

Even for business regulation, that method might be challenged,[6] but in any case it cannot be readily applied to regulation in government. Since, as noted in the last section, prosecution is only available to a handful of regulators in government, there is no single uniform regulatory action for which interval level data can be collected. Indeed, formality in governmental action is a slippery concept. For example, the incidence of official sanctions is not necessarily the same as a disposition to follow 'rule and rote'. A regulatory system could combine low use of sanctions with high 'ruliness' if the latter has a sufficiently deterrent effect—a combination which Grabosky and Braithwaite's analysis of formality does not allow for.

The chapters in Part Two provide a qualitative discussion of the effect of RD on regulatory operation in five different regulatory domains. But for a general analysis we devised a qualitative index of formality from an examination of the main methods used by forty-two regulators across government (between a quarter and a third of the total population discussed in the last chapter). Like Grabosky and Braithwaite, this analysis fused formality into a single dimension. On this index, regulatory methods in which standard-setting was non-participatory, regulatory behaviour was rule-bound and heavy reliance was laid on formal reporting and sanctioning (approximating to the oversight method discussed in Section 1 above) scored higher on formality than participatory, discretionary regulation with cooperative methods for gathering information and modifying behaviour (the 'mutuality' method discussed earlier). The regulators' view of regulatees was also used as an indicator of formality: regulators who saw their charges as 'amoral calculators' (predisposed to non-compliance for 'low' reasons unless constrained by regulatory carrots and sticks) were scored as higher on formality than those who saw their charges as 'moral citizens', inclined to comply unless principled reasons intervened (cf. Kagan and Scholz 1984).

The forty-two regulators were ranked on formality in these

---

[6] e.g. Grabosky and Braithwaite (1986: 204) did not look at the number of companies agencies deal with or the number of potential offences, claiming offences are potentially infinite in every case. This simplifying assumption excludes crucial questions about variations in compliance culture and it seems difficult to dismiss the idea that, all other things being equal, the number of prosecutions might be expected to relate to the number of companies being regulated.

terms, and put into three groups, corresponding to high, medium, and low formality (these groupings, it should be stressed, refer to formality in this sense relative to the other regulators in the study, i.e. relative rather than absolute formality). Four hypotheses were then explored about the relationship between formality of regulation in government and RD. The forty-two regulators were ranked and put into three categories on four RD scales (to be described below), and the relationship between the ranking of the regulators on each of the four RD scales and their ranking on the formality scale was then explored using a simple proportional reduction in error test (tau-b) for ordinal data calculated from the bivariate tables.

The four hypotheses about the effect of RD on regulatory formality can be termed the 'experience' hypothesis, the 'contact-frequency' hypothesis, the 'client-homogeneity' hypothesis, and the 'size' hypothesis. The *experience* hypothesis is that regulatory formality can be expected to be higher in regulators scoring high on RD in the sense of a low proportion of staff with experience of working in a regulatee organization. The *contact-frequency* hypothesis is that regulatory formality can be expected to be inversely related to the frequency of contact between regulator and regulatee. The *client-dispersal* hypothesis is that regulatory formality can be expected to be higher where regulatory clients are located in many different policy sectors than where they are homogeneous. Finally, the *size* hypothesis is that regulatory formality can be expected to be higher the larger the number of regulatee clients involved. These four hypotheses correspond loosely to those examined by Grabosky and Braithwaite.[7]

The analysis produced at least moderate support for all four hypotheses, particularly for experience and contact frequency. The size hypothesis was weakly to moderately confirmed (tau-b = +0.26), in contrast to the clear support found by Grabosky and Braithwaite in their study. Outside the world of public auditors (with many clients and fairly formal methods of working), there

---

[7] Two of Grabosky and Braithwaite's hypotheses (the analogues of our experience and contact-frequency hypotheses) come directly from Black's conception of RD, but two go beyond Black (the analogues of our client-dispersal and number-of-clients hypotheses) by positing a link between RD and the number of companies and industrial sectors, on the grounds that the smaller the clientele and sectoral 'spread' the easier contact between regulator and regulatee is likely to be.

seemed to be no clear relationship between formality and the number of regulatees. In the case of the client-dispersal hypothesis (for which Grabosky and Braithwaite found less evidence than for the size hypothesis), we found moderate support (tau-b = +0.31). Auditors and ombudsmen are examples of regulators scoring fairly high on formality which deal with clients drawn across a wide range of policy sectors, while funder-regulators and professional inspectorates are cases of regulators scoring lower on formality and tending to be concentrated on single policy sectors.

The contact-frequency and experience hypotheses were more strongly confirmed. In the former case, we found moderate support (tau-b = −0.32), as did Grabosky and Braithwaite.[8] For example, inspectorates with frequent full inspections of their clients seemed to have less formal relationships with their charges than bodies with less frequent contacts in that form. The RD/formality hypothesis which had the strongest support from this analysis is the experience hypothesis (tau-b = +0.36).[9] For example, several professional inspectorates (including fire, police, probation, prisons, and social services) scored low or medium on formality and had a large proportion of staff drawn from the sectors they inspected. By contrast public auditors, ombudsmen, and funder-regulators scored higher on the formality scale and had a smaller proportion of staff with experience of working for the regulatees. Table 3.2 arrays the regulators according to the experience hypothesis. Almost half the cases fall within boxes on the diagonal from bottom left to top right (fully consistent with the experience hypothesis), nineteen cases are partly consistent with the experience hypothesis, and only four regulators appear in the top left and bottom right boxes of the table, strongly inconsistent with the hypothesis.[10]

This analysis suggests that while size may not be everything when it comes to explaining regulatory formality, shared experience and familiarity do seem to count in aggregate. There are exceptions, to be discussed in Part Two, and the relationship between RD and

[8] Though in their analysis the relationship disappeared when the size of regulated firm was controlled for.

[9] By contrast, Grabosky and Braithwaite found only weak support for their variant of the experience hypothesis, and the relationship disappeared altogether when they controlled for agency size.

[10] Of these four two are now regulators of privatized industries (railways and nuclear installations) and the other two are small organizations (HMMCSI and the Prisons Ombudsman).

TABLE 3.2. *Evaluation of the 'experience' hypothesis: formality (row) and proportion of staff without experience in a regulatee organization (column)*

| Proportion of staff without experience in regulatee organization | Relative formality | | |
|---|---|---|---|
| | Low | Medium | Upper third |
| High | (N = 2) 5%<br>HM Railways Inspectorate (HSE), Nuclear Installations Inspectorate (HSE) | (N = 6) 14%<br>OFSTED, Office of HM Chief Inspector of Schools in Wales, Audit Commission, Accounts Commission (Scotland), PCA and Health Services Commissioner, Northern Ireland PCA and Commissioner for Complaints | (N = 6) 14%<br>NAO, Northern Ireland Audit Office, Commissions for Local Administration (3). Police Complaints Authority |
| Medium | (N = 5) 12%<br>HM Inspectors of Schools Scotland, HM Inspectorates of Constabulary (2), HM Inspectorates of Prisons (2) | (N = 3) 7%<br>Higher Education Funding Council for England, Higher Education Funding Council for Wales, Housing Corporation | (N = 7) 17%<br>Housing Assn. Tenants Ombudsman, Housing Assn. Ombudsman for Scotland, Funding Agency for schools, Scottish HE Funding Council, Further Education FEFC England (excl. inspectorate), FEFC for Wales, FE Funding Division (Scotland) |
| Low | (N = 10) 24%<br>The Adjudicator's Office, HM Insp. of Anatomy, HM Insp. of Probation, HM Insp. of Fire Services (2), HE Quality Council, Social Services Insp. (2), Social Work Services Insp. (Scotland), Social Service Insp. NI | (N = 1) 2%<br>NI Education and Training Inspectorate | (N = 2) 5%<br>HM Magistrates' Courts Service Inspectorate, Prisons Ombudsman |

formality becomes more problematic when we disaggregate incidence of sanctions and rule-following as dimensions of formality
(considered together in the analysis above). Equally, it seems to
show up more strongly when we consider incidence of sanctions
alone. That conclusion is borne out by a further examination of the
experience and contact-frequency hypotheses within the OFSTED
system of contracted-out inspection of secondary schools in England from 1993 to mid-1997 (3,599 inspections in total) which we
report in Chapter 7. The OFSTED system involves inspection teams
varying in background and experience, and thus allows us to examine the link between regulatory formality and different types of
inspection team (varying in their RD scores) within a single regulatory system. As will be shown in Chapter 7, that analysis revealed
strong support for both the experience and contact-frequency
hypotheses.

We conclude from this analysis that RD often seems to be important in shaping the way regulation in government works, and that
shared experience seems if anything to have a stronger association
with the formality of regulatory behaviour than Grabosky and
Braithwaite found for business regulation in Australia. RD, far
from lending enchantment to the view, seems to be associated with
formality in general and for punitiveness in particular (in the
OFSTED schools-inspection case). Accordingly, one of the key
questions for institutional design of regulation in government is
how close or distant the regulator–regulatee relationship should be.
That design issue was handled very differently for the core of
central government in Whitehall, which in general was exposed to
regulators with low RD relative to their charges, than for local
authorities and other parts of the public sector.

## 4. CONCLUSION

It must be stressed that this analysis only indicates *association*
between RD and regulatory formality, and does not say anything
about the form and direction of any causal link. Such qualitative
issues are considered in Part Two. Moreover, there are certainly
exceptions to the association between high RD and formality,
either in the sense of rule-following or punitiveness, and we will
discuss some of those cases in Part Two. Nevertheless, this analysis

offers some support for presumptions about the institutional design of regulation in government to which we turn in Chapter 10. Whether or not former poachers make the best gamekeepers, experience in working in a regulated organization does often seem to go with a distinctive style of operation. Why then do 'experienced hands' figure in only some types of regulation in government, but not others? At the end of the book we consider the case for building a degree of RD into regulation of central government similar to that typically applying to regulation of local government and mixed public/private bodies.

This chapter has argued that generic regulatory methods and styles cut across the private and public sectors. Given the variety of methods employed by regulators inside government, and the way many of them are carefully distanced from directly wielding government's 'ownership' powers over its own organization, it seems difficult to follow Allison in concluding regulation of business and government are 'alike in unimportant respects'. Indeed, the regulation of local government and of the mixed public/private sector seems to have more in common with business regulation than with the regulation of central government in the use of formal powers and publicity. And the association between RD and regulatory formality seems just as strong for regulation inside government as it is for business regulation.

While regulators inside government did not generally use prosecutions against their regulatee clients, a number of them had powerful sanctions at their disposal—or at least the power to recommend such sanctions to Ministers. Moreover, many of them (especially those operating in low-RD modes) had better access to information than applies to many business regulators or to EU regulators of member state bureaucracies. And that suggests Wilson and Rachal's (1977: 4) claim that, 'in general it is easier for a public agency to change the behaviour of a private organization than of another public agency', may be too simple. Wilson and Rachal's hypothesis flowed from their argument that regulators within government share the authoritative power of the State with those they regulate and can only secure enforcement by appealing to political superiors (ibid. 10). While this idea seems plausible for regulators whose RD relative to their clients is low (notably where central civil service units regulate central-government departments), it is less so for EU regulation of member states, and central-government regulation of local authorities and other parts of the public sector.

The chapters which follow in Part Two explore the themes set out here (and in the last two chapters), in five different domains of regulation inside government. We do not present each case according to a mechanical formula, but rather try to bring out its special characteristics. Nevertheless, RD between regulator and regulatee, the methods or instruments deployed by the regulator (in particular the 'ladder of sanctions' available), and the extent to which arm's-length regulatory development represents some sort of mirror image of a more managerial approach to service delivery in government, are themes that figure large in the next five chapters.

# PART TWO

Five Domains of Regulation inside Government

# Regulating 'Village Life' in Central Government

When we speak of family life in the Treasury or village life in Whitehall we are talking about people unified by coherent patterns of praxis . . . people whose common kinship and culture separates them from outsiders.

H. Heclo and A. Wildavsky,
*The Private Government of Public Money*

It used to be 'my word is my bond'. Now there are more what you might call 'uncouth businessmen' in the civil service, and you have to write things down.

Senior Official, Cabinet Office, March 1996

## 1. THE 'OLD VILLAGE'

Earlier chapters have referred to mutuality as an alternative to oversight for regulating bureaucracy in the broadest sense, and noted Heclo and Wildavsky's (1974) classic study identifying peer-group interaction as the central mechanism in the governance of the higher civil service in Britain. For Heclo and Wildavsky what kept the high office-holders of government under control was not so much enacted rules and judicial or legislative oversight as a 'village culture' of common experience, shared values, and continuous mutual assessment of ability and trustworthiness over a career normally lasting over thirty years and mostly spent in a square mile of central London. With some exceptions, the regulatory systems at the top of the structure had all the characteristics of the mutuality style noted in the last chapter—participative standard-setting, network-style information-gathering, and behaviour modification through persuasion and mutual influence.

A version of the same mutuality culture might have been detected in the upper reaches of many other professions in the 1970s, such as academia (cf. Bourdieu 1988; Becher 1989), health care, and even the financial world, where a tradition of unwritten rules and self-regulation tended to go with an exclusive social basis and elite socialization processes.[1] Sociologically the pervasiveness of mutuality as a style of governance in the professions may have been a product of public-school culture and may also relate to a society where (Ireland excluded—and even that might be debated) the middle class had not been torn apart by civil war or political upheavals of equal force to those witnessed in many of the continental European states in the first half of the twentieth century.

This culture was linked to a relatively non-litigious judicial environment, a pattern of high compliance with light-rein regulation, a lack of elaboration of formal or legal codes for the public service, and a structure in which the relational distance (RD) between regulator and regulatee (discussed in Chapter 3) was kept low for those regulatory organizations that did exist. Again, such features were by no means unique to central government in the 'old public management', but they were perhaps more marked for Whitehall and Westminster than for other domains of the public service. Unlike local government (discussed in the next chapter), there was traditionally no statute for the civil service, which for the most part was formally regulated under the Crown's prerogative power;[2] and the *ultra vires* doctrine traditionally used by the courts to keep local government in check had less force in central government, since many of its organizations were not constituted by statute, and much of its legal power derived from royal prerogative rather than statute. Before UK membership of the EU, no 'foreign' regulator oversaw Whitehall's activities, and the three main traditional regulators of central government were all characterized by low RD.

---

[1] e.g. Ian Hay Davidson, former chief executive of the Lloyd's insurance market, described the old regime at Lloyd's in the 1970s as a 'world of unwritten rules' traditionally observed on the basis of socialization (*Sunday Times* 17 June 1984: 67).

[2] As Mackenzie and Grove (1957: 13) put it, 'The framework of regulation is law, but it is law made by the Crown and not by Parliament, and it retains something of the patriarchal and domestic spirit in which the medieval king regulated his household.' Civil servants are subject to particular statutes, like the Prevention of Corruption Act 1906, the Official Secrets Acts, and (as employees of public bodies) the Corrupt Practices Act 1889, but there is no general statute establishing the entitlements and obligations of civil servants, in contrast to most continental European countries.

They were the central public audit body (the Exchequer and Audit Department, created in 1866 and replaced by the National Audit Office in 1983), traditionally headed by a former senior 'mandarin' who knew the conventions for doing business in Whitehall; the Civil Service Commissioners established in 1855 to oversee the merit principle in civil service appointments and traditionally headed by a senior career civil servant; and the Treasury (to which was added the Civil Service Department after 1970 and its various successor units after 1981) as the main regulator of the way central departments were managed, for staffing, pay, spending, and procurement.

The traditional picture of a village world regulated in a relatively informal way through largely unwritten rules, a compliance culture and low RD between regulator and regulatee still appeared to capture much of the style of regulation within Whitehall a quarter of a century after Heclo and Wildavsky's study. The civil-service culture (described in a Cabinet Office seminar by a Grade 2 with experience of working in Washington as 'a constant search for consensus over rules that no one ever quite specifies') had evidently not changed overnight. Indeed, the creation of a Senior Civil Service in 1996 (establishing a civil-service-wide corps comprising Grades 1–5 on common terms and conditions) seems to have been intended to preserve or recreate some of the features of the village, notably 'common citizenship, mobility between posts and common professional civil service skills' (I20)—the traditional model of a cohesive go-anywhere corps dominated by generalists.[3] Several of our interviewees said they worked across central government largely on the basis of trust in non-legalistic collegial relationships (I14),[4] and one Permanent Secretary declared he had no sense of any audit explosion impacting on his work (I20), in sharp contrast to what some of the other players at the fringe of the Whitehall village have perceived, for example in the comments made by Next Steps executive agency heads in Sylvie Trosa's (1994) report on executive agencies about the weight of the regulatory yoke imposed on them by their

---

[3] Though the experience of 'Senior Executive Service' systems elsewhere, as in Australia and New Zealand, suggests it may not be easy to develop a truly go-anywhere corps, particularly if pressures for delayering and lateral entry rise (see Schick 1996: 50).

[4] e.g. the head of an executive NDPB said: 'My relationship with the Department relies on trust. If something happens, I tell them about it before they find out' (IP3).

parent departments, echoed in Hogwood *et al.*'s (1998) more recent work on agencies' perceptions of pathologies of accountability.

However, Heclo and Wildavsky's village world had not been completely preserved in aspic, nor had it been totally bypassed by the regulatory explosion it had visited on other parts of the public service. If, as some assert (Dunleavy 1991), the topmost Whitehall mandarins responded to importunate political demands for a managerial transformation of the public service by outsourcing, 'agencifying' and creating quangos for executive work, retaining a high-status and collegial niche for themselves in policy advice, resource allocation, information exchange, regulating and reorganizing everyone else, the effect of those strategies created pressures for new types or styles of regulation from which even the centre of the old village cannot be entirely immune.

The old-village regulatory structure depicted above began to change from the late 1960s with the separation of civil-service management from the Treasury in 1970 when the Civil Service Department was created. A further regulator, the Parliamentary Commissioner for Administration (PCA), appeared in 1967 to check 'maladministration' and was originally headed by an ex-senior mandarin in the same style as the Comptroller and Auditor-General. Over the following two decades about a dozen more regulators of central government were added to the set and some of the existing regulators substantially changed their styles of operation. Even though the density and growth of regulation were less for central government than for local government (as shown in Chapter 2),[5] and the 'reign of terror' aspects of some regulation applied to local services (such as compulsory competitive tendering regulations requiring local public servants to compete for their own jobs or the prospect of school closure following 'failure' at review) were more muted at central government level, Whitehall's villagers faced some 20 per cent more regulators in the mid-1990s than they did at the time of Heclo and Wildavsky's study in the 1970s, and a number of the old regulators were working in ways that would be new to a time-traveller from the 1970s. This chapter traces changes in the regulation of central government, though we leave discussion of EU regulation of UK government until Chapter 8. The story

[5] It will be recalled from Ch. 2 that we identified over sixty bodies regulating central government in the mid-1990s, spending two or three times as much in real terms as their counterparts of two decades before.

includes cases of deregulation as well as regulatory growth and attempts to 're-engineer' regulation through increased codification and enhanced relational distance.

## 2. RESHAPING THE PUBLIC SERVICE: DEREGULATION AND REREGULATION

The reshaping of central government in the New Public Management era of the 1980s and 1990s had at least three effects for regulation inside government. First, the advent of 140-odd executive agencies whose heads were recruited on special contracts by open advertisement and the move to increase 'lateral entry' to the higher reaches of the public service brought in more outsiders, potentially weakening the traditional mutuality system of a high-compliance culture and largely unwritten rules learned by a long process of socialization by career bureaucrats. Second, a population explosion in the number of separately managed organizational units in Whitehall, from twenty to thirty major departments and about the same number of non-Ministerial departments in the late 1970s (cf. Hood and Dunsire 1981) to nearly 200 departments and agencies two decades later, put pressure on traditional methods of regulating staff and spending through central authorization systems. Third, the same process, of establishing executive agencies and powerful quangos headed by people on limited-term contracts alongside traditional Ministerial departments staffed by people on indefinite contracts, created the potential for a substantial increase in the patronage available to Ministers and top civil servants. Each of these three changes had implications for the traditional style of regulation inside government and had produced a new mix of deregulation and reregulation.

### (a) *More incomers in the village*

Whitehall's village saw an influx of incomers from outside the career civil service taking up senior positions. By the mid-1990s just under a third of all Grade 1–3 vacancies were open to external competition rather than being filled by career civil servants in the traditional style, with about half of those competitions leading to an external appointment (see Civil Service Commissioners 1996: 6) and in 1996 half the vacancies at the top two grades of the civil service were advertised, with about half the positions going to civil servants (Butler 1997: 5). Closer examination reveals that the incomers, although senior in rank, settled disproportionately at the managerial fringes of the village than at its traditional policy-making core (consistent with the bureau-shaping theory referred to earlier). Over half of the external appointments at Grades 1–3 were in management jobs, like NHS executive positions and headships of executive agencies,[6] with less than 10 per cent in departmental headships or deputy headships, which remained largely the preserve of the traditional mandarinate. Indeed, what emerged after the creation of executive agencies from 1989 was something like a two-track senior civil service, with senior departmental officials (largely career civil servants on traditional indefinite contracts) on one track, and on the other agency chief executives (and other fixed-term appointments like the Directors-General of the various 'Of-type' regulators that emerged to oversee the privatized utilities, beginning with OFTEL in 1984), many of whom came from different backgrounds inside and outside the civil service and were appointed on limited-term contracts (cf. Hood 1995). Even after the establishment of the Senior Civil Service in 1996 this division was still identifiable (cf. Hood 1998*b*), and new written contracts for senior civil servants introduced with a flourish in that year merely formalized the two-track structure for conditions of tenure.

Lateral entry to the senior civil service was far from unprecedented, but the combination of outside appointments to executive agencies, regulatory offices, and 'policy' departments was unusual by the standards of the recent past. This large minority of incomers changed the traditional structure of the village as 'run by a small group of people who grew up together' (Treasury official, quoted by Heclo and Wildavsky 1974: 76) and seemed likely to weaken the force of Heclo and Wildavsky's mutual 'rating game', involving a relatively fixed group of players interacting over decades.[7] Indeed, concerns about the erosion of the 'public service

---

[6] A quarter of the 129 agency chief executives in post in 1996 had come from outside the civil service (Cabinet Office 1996*b*: 11).

[7] Day and Klein (1997: 38) make a similar observation in their study of changes in the Department of Health between 1983 and 1995, where the influx of a new breed of managers alongside traditional civil servants produced 'a clash between a bicycle and a BMW culture'.

ethos' were expressed in a 1993 Cabinet Office report, *Career and Succession Planning*, by the 1993 Committee of Public Accounts' special report on *The Proper Conduct of Public Business*, and by some aspects of the conduct of the sale of arms to Iraq in the 1980s brought to light by the Scott Report of 1996 (cf. Foster and Plowden 1996). Indeed one senior PCA official to whom we talked linked the influx of outsiders to chief executive positions in Next Steps agencies to a decline in compliance with PCA findings: 'they are on fixed-term contracts and often from outside the public sector and they try to defend themselves and their Permanent Secretaries to protect their own positions' (I23).

Even if other changes were not simultaneously occurring (detailed later), a substantial influx of outsiders into senior executive positions put pressure on Whitehall's traditional regulatory arrangements comprising unwritten rules, arcane linguistic codes, and a career-long mutual rating system. The trend to codification of those rules, however, was not peculiar to the New Public Management era of the 1980s and 1990s. Mackenzie and Grove (1957: ch. 10) charted a trend to write down more of the operating rules of central government from the late nineteenth century to the mid-1950s. Nevertheless, developments such as the 1991 Citizen's Charter, the 1993 Civil Service Management Code, the publication of the code of Ministerial conduct, *Questions of Procedure for Ministers*, in 1992, the 1994 Code of Practice on Access to Government Information (revised 1997), and particularly a new written Civil Service Code introduced in 1996 marked a new phase in codification. The last Code was a landmark in formalizing and explicating civil-service rules of conduct in a public document corresponding to *Questions of Procedure for Ministers* (Symons 1996: 15).[8] It was paralleled by separate formal codes for board members and staff of executive non-departmental public bodies (NDPBs) introduced in the following year; and before it won government in 1997 the Labour Party declared its intention to formalize the Civil Service Code further by putting it on a statutory basis. As noted in the epigraph to this chapter, one of the senior civil

---

[8] The Code incorporated a number of earlier guidance documents, including the Armstrong Memorandum of 1985, to require civil servants to act with 'integrity, honesty, impartiality and objectivity' (CS Commissioners 1996: 23) and prohibits them from carrying out acts specified as illegal, improper, and unethical, those breaching constitutional convention and involving maladministration.

servants to whom we spoke compared this development to the changes in the City of London (with the advent of new players not socialized to the traditional unwritten rules of conduct) that led to more explicit regulation of financial markets, seeing the need to make rules explicit and institutionalize them as related to the entry of 'brash business types' into the higher ranks of the bureaucracy (I20, I21). Even though the drive to 'write things down' seems to be part of a long-term trend shaped by factors other than the entry of 'uncouth businessmen' alone, it can be seen as a regulatory response to increased lateral entry to senior public-service positions.

The codification of what had previously been unwritten or semi-written regulatory lore may partially explain why perceptions of the burden of regulation appeared to differ between traditional career civil servants (who in several cases said they were not aware of any substantial increase in regulation affecting them) and agency chief executives from outside the career service, many of whom seemed more conscious of the volume of rules and regulations and the various 'hobgoblins' that could descend on them out of the mist 'bearing regulations' (as noted in the epigraph to Chapter 2).[9] To the former group those rules and regulations were simply a written-down form of what they had learned 'at mother's knee', while to the latter, encountered for the first time, they may have seemed a more formidable corpus. What was perceived as a crushing burden of regulation by one group may have been viewed by the other as simply an *aide-mémoire* summarizing a familiar and natural body of rules.

### (b) *From old village to new town? A population explosion of organizational units*

A second element that potentially undermined Whitehall's traditional regulatory systems, especially for staffing and spending, was the addition of what could be considered a 'new town' (in the form of about 140 separately managed executive agencies) to the traditional village of twenty to thirty major departments. Again, even if other changes had not been occurring at the same time, a more than

---

[9] Hogwood *et al.* (1998: 18–19) report similar findings in a study of Executive Agencies and NDPBs.

doubling of the organizational units in the system would have put pressure on the traditional *ex ante* central approval regimes that governed Whitehall staffing and spending. The regulatory response to the 'new-town' developments had to take the form either of substituting general guidelines with *ex post* checking for the old prior approval system, or of delegating staffing and spending controls for agencies to departments, or a mixture of both.

What happened was a mixture of both. One of the biggest items of regulatory growth within central government was the development of oversight units in the 'parent departments' of Next Steps executive agencies, as what were once notionally direct line-of-command relationships were replaced by more regulatory arrangements. Indeed, the formal structure that emerged paralleled that applied for forty years in the oversight of nationalized industries, with a nominally arm's-length relationship between agency and Ministerial department, and an agreed set of targets within which managers are theoretically 'free to manage'. Given the experience of the nationalized industry regime, it is scarcely surprising that for at least some agencies, notably the Prison Service Agency (discussed in Chapter 6), informal processes similar to those experienced by the nationalized industries seem to have gone on—unacknowledged backdoor influence and string-pulling by Ministers (Lewis 1997; Barker 1998). At the official level the regulatory relationship between departments and agencies (just as with the 'Of-type' regulators) seems to have been heavily suffused with mutuality, since a key strategy for departments in keeping track of agency behaviour was to swap staff around between agency and department—a technique not normally part of the repertoire of an 'arm's-length' regulator. Moreover, the combination of policy and regulatory responsibilities in the oversight units of parent departments tended to mean regulation was overshadowed by political considerations in the same way as applies in the regulation of member state governments by the EU (discussed in Chapter 8).

The other major regulatory development consistent with the addition of a 'new town' to the 'village' was the shift of staffing and spending control systems into new styles. In both cases long-term trends away from traditional regulatory approaches were accelerated during the New Public Management era. In Treasury oversight of expenditure, as far back as the early 1950s a process of 'withdrawing the legions from the Provinces' (in Bridges' (1963: 10) evocative phrase) was in evidence—that is, the replacement of the traditional quasi-random process of unpredictable questions by budget controllers associated with detailed authorization regimes by general guidelines accompanied by more limited authorization controls for 'big ticket' items. Development of the same basic regulatory philosophy has come in several stages since then, but the regime for oversight of expenditure that emerged with the Treasury's 1994 Fundamental Expenditure Review marked a new phase in substituting a general target approach (represented by running cost targets for departments) with a hands-off regulatory style in place of the traditional oversight system. Treasury officials to whom we talked were divided in their assessment of the workability of the hands-off philosophy of regulation. Several at the 'sharp end' of overseeing departmental spending were sceptical that effective expenditure control could be achieved without specific 'windows' for the overseers to look through into the details of the departmental 'production function', while those with a more general view of the organization's mission enthused about the opportunities the new system offered for Treasury staff to take a strategic view uncluttered with distracting detail (cf. Parry *et al.* 1997). Whatever may be the correct view, the advent of another 140-plus organizational units to the client population for surveillance of spending would have severely taxed the resources of the 120-odd core expenditure controllers in the Treasury (Thain and Wright 1995: 97) if nothing else had changed, and here too the new-town development fits with the general pattern of regulatory change.

Staffing regulation involved another substantial shift from *ex ante* approval to general standard-setting accompanied by *ex post* audit and evaluation, but in this case the status of one of the key regulators changed into one of higher relational distance (RD) from regulatees. Traditional regulation of staffing in the civil service consisted of two main elements: a large central unit concerned with setting and approving details of pay and grading (plus other central personnel matters such as discipline), and the Civil Service Commissioners, created in 1855 as a regulator of the merit principle in recruitment, but operating by the mid-twentieth century as the direct organizer of recruitment into the civil service at every level. In the mid-1970s the Commissioners were responsible for running 400 competitions and recruiting 15,805 people a year, describing themselves as a 'professional selection agency' (CS

Commissioners 1976: 228) and 'an integral part of the Civil Service Department' (ibid. 8). In the late 1950s Mackenzie and Grove (1957: 38) argued that in spite of the special constitutional position of the Civil Service Commission, 'it is perhaps most realistic now to treat it as if it were a special organ of the Treasury for a special purpose', a characterization echoed by Drewry and Butcher (1984: 101) in a textbook on the civil service published over twenty-five years later.

The Commissioners began to retreat from the integral role of directly managing civil-service recruitment to that of arm's-length regulator of merit recruitment by departments for clerical civil-service staff in 1964, and the transformation from organizer to regulator was taken much further in the 1990s. Recruitment of all but the topmost positions was delegated to departments, accompanied by the development of a more extensive and formalized version of the monitoring regime formerly applied to departmental appointments of clerical staff. At the same time the prior approval powers[10] of the Commissioners were retained only for recruitment to Senior Civil Service[11] positions. The management of recruitment for executive and fast-stream positions was separated from the regulatory activities of the Civil Service Commission in 1991.[12] That change left the Commissioners with a relatively pure regulatory role, of laying down and interpreting yet another formal code expounding principles of merit selection and fair and open competition[13] and auditing compliance with the code by departments and

[10] The Commissioners' powers to approve candidates date back to the 1855 Order in Council establishing the Commission and the 1859 Superannuation Act requiring civil servants to have a certificate from the Commissioners to receive a pension. By 1981 the award of certificates had become largely a 'rubber-stamping' process and was abandoned for all posts below Executive Officer; in 1991 it was abolished altogether, but the Commissioners' written approval was still required for recruitment to positions in the Senior Civil Service.

[11] The SCS set up in 1996 contained 3,050 staff on nine pay bands including thirty-eight Permanent Secretaries (Chapman 1997: 1).

[12] In 1991 the Civil Service Commission was renamed the Office of the Civil Service Commissioners and the executive recruitment activities of the former Commission were assigned to a Next Steps executive agency, Recruitment and Assessment Services, which competed to supply recruitment services to government bodies and (amid much controversy about the presumed effects on merit recruitment) was privatized in 1996, becoming part of the Capita Group. Recruitment for 'fast-stream' positions was then run by a consortium of departments, which also used Recruitment and Assessment Services as a contractor for managing the process.

[13] A Recruitment Code drawn up in 1995 to spell out and tighten up the rules in response to a perceived 'free for all' which had developed among departments after

agencies.[14] That role was formalized by a new 1995 Order in Council under which the Commissioners' main responsibility was conceived as standard-setting and checking on 'quality control' (see Clark *et al.* 1994). At the same time (as noted later), the Commissioners' RD from their clients increased.

The other traditional element of staffing regulation was oversight of civil-service pay and grading. As noted in Chapter 2, substantial formal deregulation took place in this domain, in the sense that what was once an army of more than 1,500 central-agency oversight staff was cut down by two-thirds, with responsibility for pay and grading of all but the highest ranks delegated to departments and agencies between 1991 and 1995. This development, one of the few clear-cut instances of deregulation that we found within government, can be seen as a partial return to the pre-1919 style of civil-service regulation, before the Treasury solidified its grip on pay and grading across all departments, with pay and grading regulated only indirectly through 'bottom-line' cash controls. The current central-agency interest in civil-service pay was described to us as 'an employer federation interest, not a direct employer interest' (I20), with central *ex ante* controls on pay having been largely superseded by the Treasury's post-1994 running-cost controls and the various value-for-money regulators that have sprung up in the new Whitehall (discussed below).

### (c) *Regulating patronage in the new public service*

Moving from a largely closed-career civil service, in which politicians' ability to select the topmost bureaucrats was limited to a

the withdrawal of the Commissioners from management of executive recruitment in 1991 accompanied by minimal guidance to departments (I21; CS Commissioners 1996: 3).

[14] The audit process aimed to cover every department and agency on a three-year cycle and was contracted out to private personnel specialists, with PE International conducting fifty-four audits in forty-two departments and agencies in 1996–7 (Chapman 1997: 3). The Commissioners' 1996–7 report noted 167 breaches of the Recruitment Code, all relatively minor (ibid.). When breaches were discovered, the Commissioners' response varied according to the perceived seriousness of the offence. Arrows in their quiver included (in roughly ascending order of throw-weight) talking to the Permanent Secretary of the offending department, conducting a further in-depth audit (if compliance was seen to be breaking down, for instance because of the advent of managers from outside the civil service who did not see the point of the rules), indicating dissatisfaction in their published annual report, or commenting publicly on the breach, for instance in giving evidence to a Select Committee (I20, I21).

choice among an existing set largely preselected for ability, to a system in which over 150 senior appointments were added to politicians' patronage in the sense that they were available to be filled by lateral entry, also had implications for the traditional system of regulating merit appointment. The old Civil Service Commission, headed by a senior serving civil servant and constituting what amounted to a branch of a central department, was at best a fragile counterweight against Ministerial pressures for politically motivated appointments as the scope for patronage expanded. For instance, the public protest made by the First Civil Service Commissioner over the appointment of Derek Lewis as Chief Executive of the Prison Service Agency in 1993 was an indication of the sort of strain the Next Steps agencies put on the CSC regime. In addition, the creation of a substantial number of senior civil-service positions on fixed-term or limited-term contracts put pressure on traditional informal mechanisms—what Foster (1996, 1998) describes as the 'conversations' between Ministers and civil servants that substituted for more formal processes in other countries for protecting civil servants from Ministerial browbeating.

Against that development it is perhaps understandable that the Civil Service Commission was reshaped as a more formal and independent regulator in the mid-1990s and that the scope of CSC's operations was expanded into something approaching a general regulator of the civil service (I21). The independence of the CSC as a regulator (and its RD relative to the civil service) was increased by the appointment in 1995 of an outsider with a business background as First Civil Service Commissioner rather than a career civil servant (though the staff of the CSC remained civil servants as before). The rationale of that move was described to us by one very senior official as reflecting the fact that 'civil servants come from a culture of trying to please Ministers, outsiders do not' (I21). In addition to the appointment of an independent head, the CSC's regulatory scope was expanded in two ways. First, the Commissioners were constituted as the final arbiters of complaints received under the 1995 Civil Service Code by civil servants alleging they had been asked to act in breach of the Code. This change replaced an older, less formal system in which the Head of the Civil Service had been the point of contact for civil servants wishing to complain about improper demands being made of them by Ministers.[15] Second, the

[15] This development stopped well short of the Inspector General regulatory model suggested to the Treasury and Civil Service Committee in 1985 by Sir Douglas Wass

scope of the Commissioners was expanded from involvement in civil service recruitment to participation for the first time by the First Civil Service Commissioner in the senior appointments committee SASC chaired by the Head of the Civil Service which considered recommendations on promotion to the highest posts in the civil service.

A third extension of merit regulation over public-service appointments was the creation for the first time in 1995 of a CSC-type overseer of quango appointments: the Commissioner for Public Appointments (CPA). As with the CSC, the CPA (which oversaw the application of the merit principle to approximately 1,000 bodies outside the civil service) was headed by an independent outsider[16] appointed by Order in Council, laid down and interpreted a codified body of rules for recruitment, and monitored departmental compliance through a cycle of audits contracted out to a major consultancy firm, with each appointing department visited once every three years (Commissioner for Public Appointments 1997). Like the CSC, the Commissioner generally encountered a compliance culture and avoided a naming and shaming approach: as a senior CPA official put it, 'the yellow cards tend to be given in private to Permanent Secretaries, the red ones are for public use and include being named in the annual report but are very much a last resort' (I29). The CPA and new-style CSC represented a move towards more formal and independent regulation (albeit from a low base) which in part can be seen as a response to an increased potential for patronage both within and outside the civil service.

## 3. REGULATORY 'CREEP'?

The argument above is that many of the changes that took place in the regulation of Whitehall's village over the 1980s and 1990s

to oversee the interaction between civil servants and Ministers (Bogdanor 1987: 38). The first line of approach remained that of using internal complaints procedures within departments or agencies, but it was clearly a partial move towards the creation of an independent 'whistle-blowers' ombudsman', and in the first year of the operation of the system the Commissioners received six times as many approaches as had been made to the Head of the Civil Service in five years under the older system (Chapman 1997: 5).

[16] Also a retired businessman (Sir Len Peach), but in this case a former head of another regulator inside government, the Police Complaints Authority, amounting to a rare instance of an individual developing a 'career' of regulation in government.

could be seen, in retrospect at least, as a response to the twin pressures of more senior appointments from outside the career civil service and the addition of more separately managed organizational units, both of which were closely linked to New Public Management developments. But there were other changes in the regulatory landscape that appear less closely related to those changes: the take-off of anti-corruption regulation fuelled by concerns about sleaze, the reconfiguration of central government audit away from its traditional focus on executive-level regularity, and the development of new modes of cross-Whitehall regulation on top of the three or four traditional forms described at the outset. Many, though not all, of these instances of advancing regulation were associated with the regulators that are linked with, or report to, Parliament, such as the National Audit Office.

### (a) The rise of the 'sleaze-busters'

One of the generic regulatory trends within UK central governments in the 1990s was the rise of the 'sleaze-busters', watching over the 'proper conduct of public business' by Ministers and civil servants. Some of these developments may have been triggered by the advent of more outsiders into senior positions in Whitehall undermining the traditional high-compliance culture based on mutuality and unwritten rules absorbed over a lifetime career. But the impulse to step up sleaze-busting regulation inside government appears to have stemmed from other causes too, since the urge to codify the rules of behaviour and set up commissioners of the great and the good in monitoring and policing roles extended to Parliament and local government and was directed as much against the conduct of politicians as to civil servants. What emerged was a pale shadow of the ever-expanding anti-corruption 'industry' in parts of the USA (notably New York), with its constantly widening definitions of what counts as corruption, conflict of interest, and impropriety imposing increasingly stringent procedural and bureaucratic limitations on government (cf. Anechiarico and Jacobs 1996). But it seemed to be animated by a similar egalitarian mood of distrust of high public office-holders and a preoccupation with sleaze[17] not seen since the early 1970s.

[17] Many of the sleaze-busting regulatory developments derived from the Nolan Committee on Standards in Public Life, appointed in 1994 in response to public and

Accentuated sleaze-busting regulation took several forms, and linked to other regulatory developments discussed elsewhere, such as successive moves to 'open government' and the transformation of the Civil Service Commissioners into a higher-RD style of regulation. One of those forms was the extension of Civil Service Commission-style policing of merit appointments from the civil service to quangos, by the creation of the Commissioner for Public Appointments (discussed earlier). A second was a partial move away from a wholly internalized regulatory system for overseeing the conduct of MPs, by the appointment of a non-elected official, a former Comptroller and Auditor-General, as Parliamentary Commissioner for Standards in 1995. The Commissioner had little independent power, but the advent of an outsider into this sensitive domain was a notable step away from the principle that MPs collectively regulate their own conduct. A third was the addition of more anti-sleaze provisions into existing regulatory regimes, for example over declarations of conflicts of interest and auditing procedures or the mid-1990s transformation of the Cabinet Office/ OPS Machinery of Government unit into the Machinery of Government *and Standards* Group (our emphasis) with a substantial role in standard-setting for probity and regularity. Many of these developments had more impact on public bodies outside the core of central government, like 'fringe bodies', universities, and quangos, than on Whitehall's traditional village, and whether these changes represented a secular trend towards a US-style anti-corruption regulatory industry or merely a one-off response to a temporary media and public mood of the early 1990s remains to be seen. Indeed, the traditional regulatory machinery for ensuring probity and regularity in central-government financial administration seems to have changed little in response to 1990s' concerns with sleaze, perhaps because the problems were seen to lie in quango appointments and behaviour rather than the financial working of departments, or perhaps because the probity regulation system was already more formal than many of the other traditional mechanisms for regulating the Whitehall village.

media perceptions of a sleaze explosion in government. Such perceptions were not new: corruption scandals in the early 1970s led to the establishment of a Royal Commission on Standards of Conduct in Public Life and an (effectively voluntary) register of interests for MPs. The Nolan Committee (1995: 15) found that much of the anxiety was misplaced but nevertheless made recommendations for stepping up anti-sleaze regulation over government.

## (b) *Public audit with added vitamins*

A second dimension of regulatory 'creep' was the advent of a new style of public audit in central government, with the transformation of the Exchequer and Audit Department into the National Audit Office (NAO) in 1983.[18] That transformation took the public auditor out of direct Treasury control of 'pay and rations' into the hands of a Parliamentary Public Accounts Commission (a change associated with a substantial increase in the staffing and spending of the audit office, as shown in Chapter 2) and gave the audit a statutory mandate to add value-for-money audit to its traditional mandate to conduct 'tick and turnover' regularity audits.

That development paralleled the move of public auditors into the value-for-money business in other countries (notably the General Accounting Office in the USA) and with enhanced value-for-money audit in local government associated with the rise of the Audit Commission (discussed in the next chapter). That move produced a different relationship between the audit office and departments, since value-for-money assessments are a form of policy analysis never far removed from assessment of 'policy' itself, which in the theology of public audit the NAO is formally debarred from considering. In the process, the NAO's activities came to impinge more directly on policy work undertaken in person by senior civil servants. One senior interviewee suggested there was a long-term shift in the NAO's activity from a system in which 'little people' in the audit office challenged other 'little people' in government departments for their executive lapses, with Permanent Secretaries in their role as Accounting Officers becoming involved only as spokespersons for their departments when the issues ricocheted up to the Public Accounts Committee (IP1). The emerging system, he claimed, was one in which public auditors increasingly criticized senior public officials for policy decisions for which they were directly responsible, as in the Pergau dam affair of 1992 (a dam in Malaysia financed by the UK government as a development aid project, but apparently in exchange for purchases of British arms by

---

[18] The 1983 Act made the Comptroller and Auditor-General and his staff officers of the House of Commons rather than civil servants, removed Treasury control from recruitment, grading, and salaries of NAO staff, established a Parliamentary Public Accounts Commission to consider the NAO's spending estimates, and empowered NAO to examine the efficiency and effectiveness of central government departments and fifty other bodies, but precluded it from looking at matters of policy.

the Malaysian government),[19] raising the stakes and the political temperature.

Even so, the transformation of public audit appeared to have less dramatic effects on the traditional core of Whitehall than the parallel process occurring in local government through the activities of the Audit Commission. Unlike the Audit Commission NAO did not publish league tables of saints and sinners in Whitehall, but concentrated on case-by-case reports. Unlike the Audit Commission NAO was obliged by convention to clear its reports with departments before publishing them, which made it difficult for the organization to engage in studies of issues involving several departments. Unlike the Audit Commission NAO had to temper its criticisms to the sensitivities of a backbench committee (the Public Accounts Committee) which was effective in putting pressure on the bureaucracy only when it works on a bipartisan basis. Unlike the Audit Commission's District Auditors NAO auditors did not operate in a context where Ministers and civil servants could be surcharged for unlawful expenditure. Moreover, many of NAO's most savage criticisms of public-service misconduct in recent years were directed at the activities of non-departmental public bodies, notably in a damning attack on the management of the Welsh Development Agency in 1993 and the catalogue of failings identified in the Public Accounts Committee's 1994 special report *The Proper Conduct of Public Business*.

In the 1950s and 1960s the standard criticisms of central government public audit were that the system, reflecting its Victorian origins as part of Gladstone's overhaul of public expenditure control, worked well to ensure probity and regularity but was weak at assessing value for money and had major gaps, notably for university and NHS spending (cf. Mackenzie and Grove 1957: 330 and Normanton 1966: ch. 9). Such criticisms are now obsolete, given the enhanced and extended audit process that the contemporary NAO pursues. The NAO remained more inhibited in the stance it could adopt towards central government departments than was the Audit Commission towards local and health authorities. But the

---

[19] Aid payments for the dam were promised by Mrs Thatcher in 1989 while negotiating for a separate £1.3bn. arms deal and approved by the Foreign Secretary in 1991 despite ODA objections (to the effect that the dam was poor value for money). The affair was investigated by NAO in 1992, leading Malaysia to suspend government contracts with the UK.

expansion of audit capacity, as a reaction to potential embarrassments created by putting public organizations on a longer leash than before, was a process that came to reach directly into the work of Whitehall's traditional policy-advice mandarinate as well as the new managers on the fringe of the village.

### (c) *New or extended cross-Whitehall regulators*

A third element of regulatory 'creep' was the development of new forms of cross-Whitehall regulation to augment the traditional trio or quartet described at the outset of this chapter, and the extension of existing cross-Whitehall regulation. As shown earlier the traditional Treasury staffing and spending regulation changed in nature, with a radical shift away from prior approval to general guidelines and aggregate targets. Some of that regulation became more codified in the process, as with the various guidelines incorporated in the 1993 Civil Service Management code and the increased formality of the Treasury's procurement regulation regime, developing as part of EU regulation over member governments (discussed in Chapter 8).

The Parliamentary Commissioner for Administration (PCA), though its resource base expanded (as part of the ombudsman explosion noted in Chapter 2), did not stake out new regulatory territory in the same way as the public audit office, and its activities remained overwhelmingly oriented towards grievance-handling through an MP 'filter' on a case-by-case basis. In contrast to the public audit office, its RD relative to the villagers at the topmost level waxed and waned, with most Parliamentary Commissioners (including the first) coming from the ranks of senior Whitehall mandarins following the tradition established for the Comptroller and Auditor-General (on which the PCA's office was loosely modelled) and others coming from the legal world outside Whitehall. Within the PCA's office (again in contrast to the NAO), staff continued to be civil servants on secondment, meaning lower RD at the staff level than for NAO, and that may be linked to the use of informal methods of conducting business at the lower levels of the sanctions hierarchy.[20] Some changes in regulatory style developed,

---

[20] The approach taken by the PCA's office to obtain compliance from departments depends according to its judgement of the nature of the case. One senior PCA official elegantly labelled these cases as different types of port wine, that is 'tawny'

such as the PCA's move (against the rival claims of the Data Protection Registrar) into the role of arbiter of cases over the open-government rules introduced under a White Paper of 1994 and increased emphasis, according to PCA staff we talked to, on 'promoting good administration' by 'informal methods' (I23), because (it was claimed) ' "encouraging change" is . . . best achieved by persuasion'. The PCA made some moves to enunciate positive principles of good administration, for instance in cooperating with the Cabinet Office to produce *The Ombudsman in Your Files* (1995*a*) a guide for departments on how to avoid maladministration. But the scope for any dramatic move by the PCA towards the role of general regulator of good civil-service administration seems limited, because the PCA risked a legitimacy deficit if it moved far from its quasi-judicial role focusing on casework.

In contrast to limited changes in the regulatory role of the PCA, the new cross-Whitehall regulators included the burgeoning set of quality and efficiency regulators noted in Chapter 2—including those that developed within OPS/Cabinet Office to promote efficiency, agencification, minimal regulatory burdens on business, and maximal customer-responsiveness by government and 'standards'. Though the boundaries and titles of these regulators changed over time (particularly with the shift from Conservative to Labour incumbency in 1997), the phenomenon showed no sign of receding and indeed freedom of information legislation pending at the time of writing was due to add another regulator to the set.

The nature and dynamic of this cross-Whitehall regulation are problematic. Some of these developments may have stemmed from discontents with, or the limitations of, pre-existing regulators. For instance, the Citizen's Charter Unit and its activities from 1991 may reflect the limited development by the PCA of a regulatory role in laying down general principles for good administration. The Unit went beyond drawing up and disseminating general 'principles of public service' (standards, information and openness, choice and

---

cases that could be handled at director level, 'ruby' cases needing to be referred to the Deputy level, and 'vintage' cases requiring involvement by the PCA in person (I23). The PCA also employed an escalating hierarchy of responses to non-compliance, from informal resolution at the lower end to high-level reports brought before the PCA's Select Committee at the other end (cf. Harlow and Rawlings 1997: 439–40), and 'shots across the bow' of Permanent Secretaries in the middle range (I23).

consultation, courtesy and helpfulness, putting things right and value for money (PM's Office 1994)) to develop schemes of 'enforced self-regulation' through requiring public-sector bodies to draw up codes and monitor their compliance with them. The Deregulation Unit, originally established in 1985 and subject to two later revamps, including a change of title to 'Better Regulation Unit' in 1997, was part of a reaction against the failure of other regulators to include considerations of compliance costs to business in their assessment of departmental performance. OPS's monitoring of Next Steps agencies, reporting on their performance indicators and targets, amounted to a task NAO might have performed had it operated along the lines of the Audit Commission.

However, the way these new cross-Whitehall regulators operated seems to be a far cry from some of the regulators of local services described later in this book. Though they tended to work on the basis of developing codes and guidelines, their regulatory role was limited and their RD from departments low. They tended to be staffed by high-flying mid-career generalist administrators in classic Whitehall village mould, competing for a place in the sun at the centre of government and close to policy. The standard style of such regulators was to include a compliance officer located in each of the departments, loosely modelled on the systems traditionally used for financial and personnel administration.[21] The role of such compliance officers is likely to be ambiguous, as to whether they function as agents of the regulator or of the regulatee, and the regulators at the centre typically lacked any 'hard' sanctions. Far from the ability to recommend closure of institutions or impose financial penalties, they had no formal sanctions at their disposal. Consequently they were heavily dependent on persuasion and on the image of being linked with a successful initiative;[22] their role tended to focus on negotiation and often stressed rewards (as in the 'Chartermarks' sponsored by OPS) rather than penalties to obtain compliance. In the analytic terms of Chapter 2, these actors were at the low end of the regulatory continuum.

[21] That is, the Accounting Officers (whose duties were first defined in 1872), Principal Finance Officers, and Principal Establishments Officers (dating from 1919) that are the compliance officers for each department for financial and personnel administration (Mackenzie and Grove 1957: 36).

[22] One said, 'we worry about losing a high-profile case because it would damage our credibility around Whitehall, so we have dropped cases that look likely to fail' (16).

## 4. CONCLUSION

In reshaping other 'troublesome' parts of the public service, White-hall's villagers did not experience regulation as draconian as that they visited on schools (where regulators were given the 'nuclear weapon' of recommending closure of units deemed 'failing') or local authorities (where compulsory competitive tendering regulation put public-servants' jobs on the line). That pattern is consistent with our discussion of relational distance (RD) in the last chapter, since the RD of most Whitehall regulators tended to be low relative to their regulatees, and the sanctions available to those regulators were limited. Indeed, in some ways regulation seems to have been part of a strategy of 'dynamic conservatism' by the villagers, in an effort to preserve traditional characteristics, for instance in retaining merit appointment and taming uncouth businessmen.

Nevertheless, Whitehall was not immune from the regulatory mood sweeping through the British public service in the New Public Management era. More of the once unwritten lore of the village was codified, and more regulators separate from general civil-service management emerged, though the perceived impact of those developments seems to have been greater for those at the fringe of the traditional village—such as politicians, with new regulatory restraints on their appointment powers and the managers down the line (in whose ranks more outsiders have appeared, potentially weakening the traditional mutuality culture)—than for its traditional core. An important source of new regulation was the creation of Next Steps executive agencies in 1988 which created managerially separate organizations operating within a regulatory framework out of units that were previously part of a single department. Such a process put heavy strain on the traditional central-agency mechanisms for regulating staffing and spending. But even for the centre, some movement was discernible, for instance in the way that value-for-money public audit came to reach into the policy work of senior civil servants rather than the executive failings of the middle level. Moreover, the development of EU regulation over member governments' activity (discussed in Chapter 8) added a new regulatory dimension to life in the Whitehall village. Not all regulatory growth was successfully 'bureau-shaped' away from the centre.

# 5

# Mirror Image or Double Whammy?
# Regulation and Local Government

Local government is more regulated than is central government. There is no surcharge for ministers and civil servants.

Statement from seminar of regulators,<br>LSE, 7 March 1997

The audit is indeed the bridle by which the various
local administrators can, with the greatest readiness and
certainty, be guided to what is right, and restrained from what
is wrong; and its importance therefore can hardly be
overestimated.

N. Chester, quoting a nineteenth-century<br>Poor Law Commissioner

## 1. TWO REGULATORY TRADITIONS

Since the nineteenth century the central–local government
relationship has been essentially regulatory, in that the oversight
mode of control discussed in Chapter 3 has been important (with
the associated information-gathering tools of inspection, audit,
and authorization, and to a less degree certification and adjudication). But the degree of oversight has varied over time and
between different services and functions, and so has the mixture of
oversight and mutuality in the central–local government relationship. Oversight has grown in fits and starts and occasionally
decreased, but the long-term trend is a striking growth in both its
scope and intensity. In the recent past oversight has been mixed
with competition as a behaviour-modification tool in new regulatory hybrids.

Like the European Commission today (discussed in Chapter 8),
UK national government in the nineteenth century delivered few

public services to the people directly, but regulated other bodies responsible for provision. It focused chiefly on 'high' politics, the national issues of defence, foreign policy, imperial affairs, law and order, and collecting taxes to support these preoccupations. It mainly left 'low' politics, the carrying out of internal domestic tasks, to local institutions (Bulpitt 1983).

Legislation conferring powers on local authorities was largely enabling. It determined institutional structures, powers, and obligations but did not normally specify standards in the sense of the level of service to be provided, or the mode of delivery. Local authorities were accountable to Parliament or central government only to a limited extent, where statutes empowered central government to undertake a 'light' regulatory role. That approach was embodied in the 1835 Municipal Corporations Act, establishing a line of accountability that ran to local electors who voted for councils which discharged the authority granted them by Parliament. They were self-governing local authorities, responsible for local services, under a low degree of central oversight.

The legislative framework within which such bodies operated derived from 'public' statutes establishing their broad structure and functions and private legislation initiated by the local councils themselves (Prest 1990). To finance their activities they did not depend on grants from national taxpayers. They levied a local property tax (the rate) which was justified by the doctrine that local property should pay for local services from which it benefited. In their handling of public money municipal corporations were audited not by any national authority but by three borough auditors, two elected annually by the local voters and one chosen annually from among members of the council and known as the mayor's auditor (Golding 1962).[1]

While parliamentary, Ministerial, and administrative oversight over municipal government was light, law courts exerted greater formal control by applying the *ultra vires* doctrine. The increasing importance of statutes as the basis of local-authority powers gave the doctrine potency, though in practice the courts applied it flexibly (Loughlin 1996: 45). In rural areas county Justices of the Peace in Quarter Sessions exercised a close watch over how JPs in

---

[1] This local audit process, mandated by statute, is an example of 'enforced self-regulation' (Ayres and Braithwaite 1992) of a kind common in EU regulation of national governments today, as discussed in Ch. 8.

Petty Sessions and the parishes carried out their administrative tasks.

However, even in the nineteenth century there was another regulatory approach different in style from the loose oversight over boroughs by central government. That was the tight-rein approach to local-government regulation reflecting the Benthamite strict-inspection approach discussed in Chapter 1, championed by Edwin Chadwick and embodied in the 1834 Poor Law Amendment Act, the 1848 Public Health Act, and the Education Act of 1870. It was also behind the establishment in 1836 of the General Register Office to superintend the local collection of statistics of births, marriages, and deaths, and of the national district audit service created in 1868 to keep a central check on certain local accounts. Seeing local authorities as corrupt, inefficient, and parochial, those advocating tight-rein regulation stressed national supervision, inspection, professional and uniform standards, and regular reporting: all the features of the oversight mode discussed in Chapter 3.

The coexistence of the Chadwickian oversight approach to local-government regulation with the looser style of oversight embodied in the 1835 Municipal Corporations Act is shown in two consecutive sentences from the report of the Royal Sanitary Commission of 1871 (16): 'The principle of local self-government has been generally recognized as of the essence of our national vigour. Local administration, under central superintendence, is the distinguishing feature of our government.' Ever since the nineteenth century the two regulatory traditions expressed in these two sentences have been in tension. The value of local self-government was continuously declaimed, but domestic issues periodically became 'high' politics, and national government responded with laws requiring local bodies to tackle what were seen as pressing national needs, with varying degrees of national supervision, monitoring, inspection, standard-setting, and sanctions. Ambivalence remained about whether local government was responsible for national services locally administered, under intense oversight, or for local services under a loose form of regulation from the centre.[2]

---

[2] For the study of centre–local relations in the nineteenth century see Bellamy (1988); Best (1971); Finer (1952); Greenleaf (1983; 1987); Mandler (1990); Parry (1993); Smellie (1946).

Over the twentieth century central government increasingly intervened in 'low' politics, placing new statutory responsibilities on local authorities and extending their activities from services to local property to welfare-state provision. The legislation often empowered national government to regulate local authorities in detail for these new tasks. To finance the new services more of local government's resources came from central grants financed by national taxpayers, and the national audit service (District Audit) gradually supplanted locally elected or appointed auditors for checking the legality of local authorities' expenditure.

By the 1960s John Griffith's (1966) landmark study of British central–local government relations argued that patterns varied according to the nature of the different services and the different institutional cultures within departments as well as among them. Griffith constructed a threefold typology, involving a continuum from a *laissez-faire* relationship at one extreme (where local government was left to operate with little central control or standards) to a *promotional* relationship at the other extreme, where central government identified national needs and exhorted local authorities to achieve what it saw as the highest possible standards. Between these positions was a *regulatory* relationship, in which central government laid down national minimum standards, aiming to ensure that local authorities at least met the floor standards but leaving them free to do more if they wished. One of the analytic problems of Griffith's scheme is that what he termed the 'regulatory' relationship, falling in the middle of his continuum, was potentially the most draconian of the three, since in that case central government adopted a formal, detailed, prescriptive, and punitive approach to national minimum standards in contrast to the persuasion deployed in the 'promotional' style.

These relationships were not static. Services moved among Griffith's types depending on their national political salience. The general twentieth-century trend was a movement away from the *laissez-faire* style (against a background of a 'direct-service culture',[3] a substantial proportion of local-authority finance deriving from general taxation, growth of local authorities in employment and public spending, and the use of general public

---

[3] As Vincent-Jones (1998: 7) points out, the comparatively large size of UK local authorities made direct-service provision possible to a greater extent than applied to other European states, so that the 'direct-service provision problem' addressed by CCT regulation typically existed to a smaller extent elsewhere.

expenditure as a tool of macroeconomic management) but, even so, central government imposed few explicit national standards over services for most of the century. When the Layfield Committee on Local Government Finance surveyed central–local government relationships in the mid-1970s, standards about process were common but not national standards about the amount and level of services local authorities should deliver (Layfield 1976).

Although local government in England and Wales was reorganized into fewer and fewer units (400 instead of 1,100) under the 1972 Local Government Act, in the name of greater efficiency and strengthening local authorities' independence against central government (Vincent-Jones 1998: 7), national government, in fact, strengthened its regulatory grip over local authorities in the 1980s and 1990s. Though still not prepared to take over the running of local services directly, it was dissatisfied with both the way local services were provided and their substance. Apart from legislative changes removing further responsibilities from local authorities (transferred to the private sector, boards, and central departments), central government altered the audit arrangements for local authorities and tightened its regulatory controls. The revised audit system introduced under the 1982 Local Government Act had the effect of increasing RD between auditors and local authorities by removing local authorities' ability to choose their auditors (cf. Day and Klein 1990: 14) and introducing a substantial proportion of auditors from the private sector with different training and background, yet still equipped with independent legal powers over surcharge and disqualification from office.

In the tightening of regulatory controls by central government over local government, the most notable feature was a new regime for compulsory competitive tendering (CCT—allowing local authorities to provide specified services directly only if the work had been won by their organization in a competitive tendering process), which introduced a new mixture of oversight and competition and had a potential 'reign of terror' element in that it required public servants periodically to compete for their own jobs against rival bidders.[4] After 1988 local taxation provided about only one-fifth of local government's income, and local government spending

---

[4] Though, as Vincent-Jones (1998: 8) points out: 'In fact, CCT failed to transfer provision away from direct labour to the private market and to encourage significantly diversity of provision, since the majority of service contracts were awarded in-house following competitive tendering.'

and taxing powers were limited by the introduction in 1984 of a regulatory regime that capped local authority budgets.

Over this period the relationship between central and local government could no longer be characterized as a generally light oversight regime. Finding reduced scope for a prominent role in high politics, central government had found a new role in low politics. Ruling colonies in the Empire was replaced by regulation of Britain's internal colonies—its counties, towns, and cities (Jones and Stewart 1985; Jones 1993; 1997). Central government was now regulating not only *how* local authorities should carry out their functions (process controls) but also in many cases the level and nature of the services they should provide (output controls). Apart from a few services (like leisure) in which it had little interest, central government pursued a strategy of increasing regulation, mixing heightened oversight with new elements of competition.

## 2. OVERLAPPING AND COST-UNCONSCIOUS REGULATION

Chapter 2 sketched a pattern of multiple and overlapping regulators for the UK public sector as a whole, with striking overall growth over the 1976–95 period. As was shown in that chapter, local government was facing a growing army of central regulators, with regulators of local government increasing more than for central government in staff and spending. It also faced a segmented structure of oversight, reflecting the different departments into which central government is divided and which have regulatory power over local authorities (notably the departments responsible for education, transport, health, agriculture, environment, social security, police, and civil defence). There was little coordination between the activities of the various departmental overseers of local government, or of the various inspectorates, auditors, and ombudsmen, as noted in Chapter 2 (echoing Day and Klein's (1990: 60) observation that different scrutineers of services for the elderly tended to work in isolation, ignoring the potential for 'economy of effort' and jointly producing 'inspectorial overload'). Indeed, there were marked differences in styles and approaches among the various regulators, and periodic tensions and conflicts: for example, between the generalist orientation of the Audit Commission and the more professionally oriented approach of the specialized inspectorates (IEE9).[5] A London borough Chief Executive saw not only inconsistencies in approach between the Audit Commission and OFSTED, but also inconsistencies among different auditors, with no strong coordination by the Audit Commission over their activities (IEE11).

Central departments responsible for functional services and the associated inspectorates have tended to embody the Chadwickian regulatory tradition, and the same goes for the Treasury, which from the early 1980s saw local-government spending as a major component of overall public expenditure that needed to be controlled as part of the public-expenditure planning total just as if it were central-government spending. Only the department responsible for the general well-being of local government (the Department of the Environment in the 1976–95 period) contained the light-rein regulatory tradition, but it was increasingly overridden by the Chadwickian approach within central government.

That regulatory structure changed in three main ways over the period considered here. One was the creation in 1994 of central-government offices for the regions, putting together four departments with responsibilities for urban regeneration (Environment, Transport, Employment, Trade and Industry) under a single Regional Director in each region and bringing regulation closer to local government. A second was the creation of two major general local-government regulators in the form of central non-departmental bodies, namely the Commission for Local Administration (1974) to investigate citizens' complaints of maladministration by local authorities and the Audit Commission established in 1982 (Hollingsworth *et al.* 1998). Although appointed by central government, the Audit Commission is an independent national body intended to act as a counterweight to the professional inspectorates and district auditors themselves (both of which were seen by central government at that time as having too low an RD from the professional communities they oversaw). The

---

[5] An Audit Commission official said the relationship between the Commission and the inspectorates varied, ranging from joint teams (with the Social Services Inspectorate), through sharing staff (OFSTED and the Police Inspectorate) to the Fire Services Inspectorate which was 'a little removed'. The last appeared 'uncomfortable in having a big beast roaming around the jungle' but was mainly supportive of the Commission's reports (I41).

Commission was intended to exercise its counterweight role by appointing auditors (many from the private sector) over local authorities, with powers to recommend surcharge and disqualification from office, and by ensuring local authorities achieved value for money, often expressed as the three 'Es' of economy, efficiency, and effectiveness (Day and Klein 1987: 50).

A third development, only in its early stages at the time of writing is the best-value regime announced in 1997 and intended to replace CCT, under which local authorities would have more freedom to decide how services were provided as long as they conformed to a set of monitoring and evaluation practices, to be approved by the Audit Commission, including 'benchmarking' of practice against other local authorities. It remains to be seen whether or how best value develops, but from a regulatory perspective the initiative could be seen as a reaction against the discredited command and control approach of CCT by instituting what is ostensibly a more 'reflexive' regime (Vincent-Jones 1998: 10–11) that would be closer to the mirror-image pattern of regulatory change discussed in Chapter 1.

Chapter 2 observed that the various regulators in government tended to apply a 'Nelson's eye' to the notion of compliance costs, while those at the receiving end of regulation tended to be more aware of the costs of the obligations imposed on them by their regulators. This pattern was displayed in the regulation of local government. Central overseers—like DOE, OFSTED, SSI, the Commission for Local Administration—were dimly aware of the compliance-cost issue, but put little effort into calculating such costs (IP2; I3) and if pushed to think about them tended to guess they were about the same as the direct administrative costs of regulation (I35). By contrast, local-government regulatees complained generally of the costs imposed on them by having to meet 'unfunded mandates' imposed by central regulators (IP2): a former chief executive of a London borough declared that neither the ombudsman nor other regulators ever costed their interventions, even though they 'cost a bomb' (IP5). But such regulatees rarely seemed able to put more than the vaguest figures on such costs: a chief executive of a London borough told us 'at a rough guess 5 per cent of total local authority costs could be judged to be associated with covering the needs of external regulatory bodies'—but it was only a 'rough guess' (IEE11). Failure to cost compliance in a precise and sophisticated way by the regulatees, and failure by the local-authority associations to come up with any convincing overall figures, would seem only to encourage the 'Nelson's-eye' approach to compliance costs by the central regulators. And indeed the 'Nelson's-eye' approach appeared to be adopted by local authorities themselves when they were the regulators, as with inspection of social services provision (IEE5), where the move to outsourcing in the 1980s had sharply increased the regulatory role of local authorities (Day and Klein 1990: 4).

Against the background of regulatory growth, the complex of overseers and the changing overall style of regulation, the rest of this chapter explores four interrelated themes in the regulation of English local government mainly on the basis of interviews with regulators and regulatees—relational distance, formality, sanctions, and the link between regulatory changes and central administrative control.

## 3. VARIATIONS IN RELATIONAL DISTANCE

Relational distance (RD) was introduced and discussed in Chapter 3 as a way of understanding the social distance between regulator and regulatee. But for the central regulators of local government, there was no reliable pattern of high RD corresponding with rigorous regulation, and low RD with more flexible and sensitive regulation. It may be that Whitehall cultures cut across what a simple RD explanation would predict. The central departments, the Treasury and components of the Department of the Environment, Transport, and the Regions (DETR), exhibited high RD, and even expressed a disdain for the low quality of local councillors and officials (IP2; Jones and Travers, 1996). That approach went with draconian regulation in some cases (notably rate-capping and CCT), but in other domains those departments practised light-rein regulation. The social-service inspectorate had low RD relative to its regulatees, yet its oversight was a mixture of a rigorous inspectorial approach and elements of bargaining and negotiation (Day and Klein 1990: 27) (the case of OFSTED will be discussed in Chapter 7). On the other hand, the police and fire inspectorates exhibited low RD and a much less rigorous regulatory style, favouring persuasion rather than sanctions.

Nevertheless, RD helps to bring out three important variations among the different regulators of local government. First is the difference between the inspectorates and the Audit Commission. The former tended to be professionals, inspecting each other, whereas the latter involved higher RD, as discussed earlier (an Audit Commission official described its perspective as 'a lay view, an external view' (I42). Second, there is a distinction between the top staff and those at the 'coal-face' engaged in inspection, as with the Local Commission for Administration. The former usually exhibited a higher RD than the latter who tended to have experience of local government. Third is the difference between public-sector and private-sector regulators, as with auditors drawn from the public service and those from private-sector accounting firms. But the consequences of this distinction in practice are hard to assess. An official at the Audit Commission noted that some local-government bodies expressed a preference for public-sector auditors. But he felt it was unlikely that local authorities would be at a disadvantage with a private-sector firm, 'given the usual long working relationships that, in practice, become established over time' (I41), implying that the theoretically higher RD achieved by using private-sector auditors in the post-1982 regime was weakened by contract frequency.

Moreover, the effects of RD may be modified by the career paths of local-government regulators. While many may have come from the ranks of those they regulate, both at the top and the coal-face, they tended not to return, either because they were so senior and retired on giving up their oversight role, or because they moved on elsewhere, as with many in the audit world into the private sector. So the regulatory experience itself may be a process encouraging higher RD, even separation.

Interviews revealed varied ideas and doctrines about practices affecting RD. A member of the Audit Commission told us he 'did not lose any sleep' over possible conflicts of interest with Commissioners who had previously been local-authority administrators, and saw the value of their previous local-government experience as 'less because they know where the bodies are buried and more because they understand how the systems in local government work' (I41).

To avoid cosiness, a former chief executive of a London borough argued, 'it is good that auditors are changed from time to time'

(IP5). Such rotation, urged an Audit Commission official, was not solely to protect against excessive familiarity between auditor and auditee, but also to give staff 'more varied experiences and challenges' and 'to exercise a degree of competition between the audit firms', even though rotation might create an element of disruption for local government (I41). A chief executive of a London borough felt it helped communication to have the auditors as regulators-in-residence, physically located in the authority's own premises (IEE8).

A chief fire officer stated that although fire inspectors often had practical experience within the service, there existed 'no cosy relationship'. They were 'retired fire officers with no axe to grind and appointed by royal warrant. It is difficult to see how you could make them more independent' (IEE9). A divisional fire officer observed that inspectors with local-government backgrounds 'have been very critical' (IT4). An Acting Director of social services noted that SSI operated a system of secondment from local authorities, which 'helps to promote the exchange of ideas', but, as with fire inspectors, they would not inspect their own authorities (IEE5 and I34).

A very senior inspector of social services recruited lay people to inspection units through advertisement. They had to be trained and supported by the more traditional inspectors with local-authority backgrounds (I13). Thus to the core of 'low-RD' professional inspectors was added a diverse group of 'high-RD' lay people. Likewise, a divisional fire officer saw benefit in lay inspectors, as 'introducing the perspective of the commercial world into evaluations of efficiency' (IT4). But a chief fire officer was sceptical of the value of lay inspectors, since such inspectors might be 'hood-winked' or might duplicate the role of auditors or elected councillors (IEE9). A leading inspector of fire services said lay inspectors had been introduced for 'political reasons': 'they had to appear "not subject to service capture", in the words of the prime minister.' His view was 'they had been useful in getting more of a public and business perception of fire-safety legislation, but they were never going to have any long-term impact' (I34).

RD was an issue for regulation inside local authorities as well as for central–local relationships. For instance, a London borough chief executive observed that the authority's regulatory unit for social services (which inspected both private and local authority facilities) was located within the chief executive's department rather than within social services, 'to promote independence and efficiency, and to reassure councillors and outside bodies that objective standards are being applied in providing the service' (IEE11). And as local authorities move towards increased outsourcing of service provision RD becomes a central issue of institutional design for regulation of local services.

## 4. REGULATORY FORMALITY AND JURIDIFICATION

Over the period 1976–96 there were many signs of central government oversight of local authorities becoming increasingly formal in both senses discussed in Chapter 3, namely reliance on explicated rules and reliance on punitive sanctions. There was more routinization and proceduralization with recourse to written rules and hierarchy in place of understandings and conventions. In the past central-government regulators had normally kept punitive powers (like sending in commissioners or taking over some function from a failing local authority) as a default mechanism of last resort, but now punitive elements came more to the fore. When central government found it could not get its way with local authorities by the methods of mutuality (informal conversations, appeals, persuasion, and advisory circulars), it resorted to heightened forms of oversight, such as the CCT regime, explicit performance indicators, and even proposals for centrally appointed teams to take over not just particular schools or local-authority departments but whole local authorities.

Hence, whereas once the relationship with local government could be presented as a partnership in which both central and local government were engaged cooperatively in a common enterprise (the mutuality mode), sometimes of improving services and raising standards, and at other times of restraining expenditure, in the 1980s both sides appeared locked in confrontation and parts of the regulatory relationship moved from a compliance equilibrium (a mutuality style in which flexible compliance by regulatees goes with flexible enforcement by regulators) to a 'deterrence equilibrium' (a hyper-oversight style in which minimal compliance by regulatees goes with aggressive enforcement by regulators) (Scholz 1991: 118). Mutuality in the form of informal collaboration and partnership receded as local-authority regulatees responded negatively and aggressively to central government's oversight initiatives. In turn the latter resorted to more formal and punitive means to compel compliance, with more comprehensive and intensive legislation, including sweeping new powers for Ministers to determine local-authority behaviour, usually through legislative instruments (Loughlin 1996).

Going with this increasing confrontation was an element of increased juridification, in the sense of more litigation to settle disputes about the meaning of laws and regulations, and increased recourse to legal rules and lawyers for determination of rights and responsibilities previously left to politicians and officials (Laughlin and Broadbent 1993; Loughlin 1996). Juridification in the 1970s and 1980s was not a return to the nineteenth-century style of rural JPs engaged in administrative supervision. Rather, the courts became more involved in adjudicating disputes between central and local government for two main reasons. First, rules and standards written into statutes and statutory instruments became more explicit and detailed about the nature of services and how they were to be provided, increasing the potential for dispute over interpretations of the rules (Loughlin 1996: 368). Second, since reconciliation was impossible through informal and political channels in the mutuality mode, both sides increasingly resorted to the courts to resolve their differences.[6] Local authorities challenged the legality of more central-government actions, especially over grant allocations, and in response central government devised ever more comprehensive and detailed laws and regulations, including clauses in legislation that gave ministers discretionary powers to vary statutes. Increased input from judges in turn changed the way local and central government did business, leading them increasingly to take legal advice to make their decisions acceptable to the courts, which made the relationship between central and local government, and

---

[6] During the 1990s there seemed to be an ebbing of legal challenges, perhaps because both central-government departments and local authorities came increasingly to rely on taking legal opinions before they made their decisions: but that trend seems to signify the continuing importance of juridification rather than its erosion.

decision-making processes within local authorities, more formal and juridified.[7]

The shift from a mutuality-based compliance equilibrium to an oversight-based deterrence equilibrium in central–local regulation came about largely because the electoral cycle brought to power in local authorities parties opposed to the Conservative Party which formed the national government. The Conservative Government had different policy priorities from those of elected councils dominated by their political opponents, and proclaimed a crusading ideological mission to curb and redirect local spending and taxing, 'roll back the state' at local level and enhance the role of market discipline. But in spite of a general rhetoric of 'deregulation' and the introduction of competition in new forms, sharply intensified formal oversight, embodied in legislation, was necessary for the centre to attain its goals in local government.

That increased formality showed in the ever-expanding role of the Audit Commission as a waste-watcher as well as a probity regulator, and in a growing number of reports by the various inspectorates, often about individual authorities, schools, old-people's homes, and child-care institutions. Government-appointed public inquiries were increasingly used to investigate failings in particular authorities, mainly in social services. New legal provisions required local authorities to make papers available to the public and to publish more information about their activities. Local authorities felt themselves exposed to ever more form-filling demanded by central government. Primary and secondary legislation constrained their discretion, sometimes in great detail, as with the regimes for CCT, expenditure control and the obligation to publish a variety of centrally determined performance indicators.

A DOE Deputy Secretary told us regulation had become 'increasingly formal over the past twenty years, because there was a tendency for local authorities to try and get away with things unless

---

[7] A Deputy Secretary at the DoE claimed there was more judicial review which meant 'you had to be more careful when drafting papers' (IP2). A senior member of the Commission for Local Administration said 'everyone is conscious of the possibility of being reviewed these days' (I5). A very senior inspector of social services found there was a growth in judicial review, as local authorities tested the law (I3). From the local-authority perspective, an acting Director of Social Services in a London borough declared court cases had 'impacted on the system' and observed 'there was a worry about diverting front-line resources to managing legal systems as a result of recent Acts' (IEE5).

they are prohibited' (IP2). But not all our interviewees shared such perceptions of increased formality for all aspects of the central–local regulatory relationship. For instance, for professional inspectorates, one former chief executive of a London borough detected a move towards less formality, making them more helpful for local authorities than in the past (IP5). Many of our interviewees testified to a continuing pattern of informal relationships between central and local officials lying behind the increasingly prescriptive statutes and statutory instruments, for example through informal face-to-face meetings and attendance at conferences to 'gain information and exert informal pressure' (IP2; IEE5, IEE10). And a leading inspector of fire services emphasized that inspectors spent time with senior members of brigades, elected members and council officials. The aim was 'to try to get them to do things the Inspectorate wants. . . . It is very close combat—you do not have the privilege of using heavy artillery from a distance' (I34).

Moreover, relationships between central regulators and local authorities were far from universally antagonistic. Professionals locally sometimes sucked in central overseers as allies to promote certain service standards against other professionals in their local authority and their councillors (reflecting Day and Klein's (1990: 38–40) models of cooperative and collusive relationships between inspectors, members, and officers). For example, a chief fire officer told us he could use the inspectorate's reports to push policies previously resisted by local councillors and trade unionists (IEE9). And some regulators may function much more like 'rat-catchers', available to perform a service for local-authority managers rather than an alien force bringing central pressures on local authorities to make charges they found unpalatable. Day and Klein (1990: 51) describe a case of an SSI inspection initiated by a local authority as a means of allaying public concern after problems came to light in a residential home, and likewise auditors in their 'regularity' role may assist local authorities to detect embezzlement by employees.

Hence in regulation of local government, despite generally increased formality and a growing element of juridification, mutuality in the form of informal interactions and reciprocal dependence by no means disappeared. On paper, oversight regimes could seem formal and cold, but the way they were applied could involve mutually supportive relationships. Indeed, a London borough chief executive noted that informal dealings between local officials and central regulators were open to abuse. 'The establishment functions on the basis of personal contacts in which informal processes account for much of the decision-making.' Corruption can ensue, in the sense of 'the bending of situations' by personal contacts, 'the "all jolly good chaps" ethos endemic to the way business is done in this country with handshakes and drinks' (I8).

## 5. LADDER OF SANCTIONS

In combination formal law and informal practice usually created a ladder of sanctions to deal with recalcitrant local authorities. Like regulators in many other domains (as noted in Chapter 3), central-government overseers of local authorities tended to think of a 'ladder of sanctions', including many not set out in statute or formal documents but present in conventional behaviour. Overseers tended not to bring out their big guns at the outset, except to deal with some obviously determined offender. The style was seen as 'British common sense', involving informal dealings between administrators preferring to do deals and settle matters with as little fuss as possible, rather than legalistic, formal, and impositional. If that style broke down, there was a step up the ladder, involving more senior officials or even political masters, and then finally, if that failed, to deployment of the rigours of formal law as a last resort. A serving chief executive of a London borough saw a test of local authority management as its expertise in 'stopping situations getting out of control' (I8).

Formal law usually laid down a ladder of sanctions but left discretion over their use to the regulatory bodies. Hence bodies like the Audit Commission and OFSTED had an escalating array of actions, moving in each case from informal oral suggestions to more formal written communications delivered by more senior officials, followed by formal warnings and eventually to published criticisms which could be followed by further sanctions. A former Controller of the Audit Commission saw its role, under his leadership, as a kind of management consultancy to local authorities.[8] 'I was not after anyone. My role was to offer a service to the local

---

[8] Recalling Day and Klein's (1990: 13) characterization of the Commission as 'a policeman constantly tempted to turn consultant'.

authority clients.' For him, a clear ladder of sanctions started with informal early discussions, 'speaking softly and hauling some authorities back from the brink', then escalated to warnings, until finally the stages of public reports and surcharge actions, coming from local auditors, were reached (IP8). Another Audit Commission official felt the organization's current view was that 'incentives work much more than sanctions' and that it was best to begin with a 'light touch' rather than 'an adversarial approach' (I41).

Perceptions of the nature of non-compliance tended to shape the way sanctions were used. For example, a DOE Deputy Secretary, although admitting the department had few weapons to deploy directly against local authorities, argued its response varied according to whether there had been 'a simple mistake or deliberate transgression' (IP2), for example over CCT. Even so, the DOE seemed to look on with world-weary scepticism over other alleged local-authority failings, simply moaning that little could be done, as with Lambeth, Hackney, and Liverpool. In the Social Services Inspectorate, a very senior inspector said 'inspection works better as a collaborative task', but noted the importance of the Minister's power to issue a direction to local authorities if SSI reports were not taken seriously. Even though the power had never been used, its potential threat was persuasive, focusing the minds of senior people in local authorities (I3).

The inspectors of police and fire appeared reluctant to impose their views. Despite criticism by the inspectorates, certain local authorities were allowed to continue for years in their old ways, since the services had to be supplied. A senior figure in the Fire Services Inspectorate said 'we use persuasion rather than formal sanctions . . . we spend more time talking out difficulties . . . ultimately it would not be possible to impose solutions' (I34). The Commission for Local Administration preferred 'prevention to cure'. The Commissioners talked to the local-authority associations and the Local Government Management Board, and sought to ensure the Commission's views did not come as a surprise to a local authority which took a different view from that of the Commission on whether maladministration had occurred (I5).

The weapon of publicity was used to varying degrees by regulators to bring pressure to bear on recalcitrant local authorities. Some deliberately courted the media, using them almost as their operational arm, like the Audit Commission (IP8). A former official at the Commission declared 'the production of evidence in the public domain of financial incompetence increases the pressure for improvements. . . . Only if you appear in the front page in the local newspaper will members take it seriously' (I35). The Commission for Local Administration used the media with more discretion, but a senior ombudsman observed 'the oxygen of publicity is the biggest sanction' (I5). A former chief executive of a London borough observed that although there was 'a disposition to keep disagreements private', the DOE did 'go public' at times with press notices alerting local MPs and the local media about something it disapproved of (IP5). Other regulators, like the social services, police, and fire inspectorates, kept a distance from the media, relying on their parent departments for publicity and on publication of their own annual reports. A leading inspector of fire services felt the media 'would get in our way as they only try to sell airtime. . . . A high-profile launch of a report could prove counter-productive and we do not have the necessary resources to deal with the media. . . . Media exposures tend to make people defensive and reduce the possibility of gaining a truthful response' (I34). Indeed, one serving chief executive of a London borough described a 'public-interest report' from auditors, which would result in media interest and a full council meeting, as 'the equivalent of being put in the public stocks' (I8).

Hence our interviews suggested regulators were sophisticated in their awareness of what would be most persuasive for their clients. They saw it as common sense to seek to persuade rather than deploy heavy weapons at the outset, but they did not start with light artillery if they judged they were meeting with a high degree of recalcitrance from the outset. Nor did they bring out the heavy artillery if they judged little could be achieved for political or other reasons. So escalation up the regulatory ladder was not an automatic or mechanical process, and—to echo an observation made for many other of the regulators considered in this book—the array of sanctions often appeared as more a quiver of arrows than a ladder.

## 6. REGULATION AS A MIRROR IMAGE OF DECLINING CENTRAL CONTROL?

Chapter 1 suggested the growth of regulation in government might be considered a mirror-image or corollary of changes taking place in operational management. But the idea of mirror image does not fit the development of the relationship between central and local government between 1976 and 1996. Growing arm's-length regulation over local government was not associated with any relaxation of central control, as either cause or consequence. There was both more arm's-length regulation and less freedom at the operational level, a pattern which is not accurately described as a mirror image.

Back in the 1970s, however, it looked as if regulation of local government might follow a mirror-image pattern. The 1976 Layfield Committee recommended that local government should have considerable discretion in decisions about service levels, local expenditure, and taxation, drawing most of its income from local taxes. On the Committee concern was expressed that to balance this substantial operational autonomy there should be a national audit body to reassure the public and national government that local authorities were spending public money in a legal and proper manner. This anxiety led to the recommendation for what later became the Audit Commission. Thus in response to a proposed decentralization of responsibility to local government there was a corresponding proposal to establish a regulatory body to monitor and supervise local authorities—in line with the mirror-image theme.

In the event, however, the central–local government relationship did not develop in the direction the Layfield Report had hoped in the 1980s and 1990s. Instead of more operational autonomy for local authorities there was less. Central government exercised ever-tighter direct controls over the functions that remained with local authorities, while at the same time stepping up arm's-length regulation. Even the Audit Commission, although seeking to win the confidence of local government in its early years, was widely seen by the mid-1990s as a means for imposing the wishes of central government on local government. Other new regulatory bodies were set up to inject national standards for particular services into local authorities, like the SSI and the various regulators of education to be discussed in Chapter 7. Existing inspectorates, like those for the police and fire services, became more active. As the mid-nineteenth-century Chadwickian approach had focused regulation on specific functions, so each central department now used its inspectorate to regulate the way local authorities carried out what it regarded as services for which it was held responsible, contributing further to the uncoordinated and *ad hoc* nature of regulation over local government.

Central government responded to criticism of this two-pronged attack by arguing it was in fact decentralizing, not to local government but to other organizations like school governing bodies and individual users of local services. It claimed it needed to control and direct local authorities not just to promote national policy objectives, but also to break the dominance of local monopoly suppliers of services, as in its championing of compulsory competitive tendering. Hence the importance of regulatory changes combining oversight with competition through markets or quasi-markets. Compulsion was needed because producer-dominated local authorities were reluctant to privatize or decentralize services to other institutions. Thus an element of the mirror-image perspective can be detected in central government's justification for its centralizing measures. It was seen as a case of increasing regulation, albeit temporary, to bring about a longer-term decentralization of local-authority activities.

Indeed, a senior DOE civil servant asserted that the Department's New Public Management style consisted of reducing controls over process, and before action took place, and instituting more *post hoc* regulation using performance indicators to focus on value for money (IP2). Such a strategy can be fitted into a mirror-image perspective, but it was not the perception of local-authority regulatees who felt the changes amounted to more central control and correspondingly less discretion for them. From that viewpoint it seemed the increased oversight was simply to achieve the goals of central departments against the wishes of local authorities which had their own mandates to do things differently. There was thus *both* more direct central control *and* more arm's-length regulation, not more regulation because of increasing operational autonomy.

But a mirror-image process could more clearly be seen inside local authorities. They were required by central government to distinguish the tasks of setting policy and commissioning provision from service-delivery. As they did so, they enhanced the cores of their internal structures to play a more defined role as policy-setters and regulators of the institutions that delivered services, both within and outside the authority. This development was apparent in a number of local-authority services, paralleling the adoption of a purchaser–provider split in most local functions, from homes for children and old people, to direct-labour building and maintenance activities. Direct-service organizations inside local government became units of decentralized management separate from those parts of the authority that devised policy, drew up the contracts for service-provision, and monitored and regulated operational performance. Local authorities' central core organization became increasingly focused on an arm's-length regulatory approach, both towards their own organizations and towards private or voluntary organizations. Moreover, inside the corporate centres of local authorities, central government increased the internal regulatory role of officials, insisting on an officer to ensure processes were conducted with propriety and enhancing the role of the financial officer to warn of illegality and improper expenditure. But the regulatory role of local authorities grew not only because of central-government requirements but also from their own initiatives, such as the devising of performance standards to regulate those providing services to local citizens, anticipating the national-level Citizens' Charter of 1991.

Where local provision was contracted out to the private sector, as in social services, a number of our interviewees, including a senior inspector of social services and an Acting Director of Social Services in a London borough, stated that private-sector facilities received a more rigorous inspection than public ones (I3; IEE5). Although this perception of more rigorous inspection of contracted-out facilities was not shared by those we interviewed in the prisons sector (discussed in the next chapter), such development fits with both the RD and the mirror-image perspective, in that oversight has tightened as activity has become more decentralized. Moreover, a problem with contracted-out services, as identified by a London borough chief executive, was that there was 'a huge confusion about where complaints should go, whether to the client or the contractor' (I8), and the chief executive of another London borough felt that even though services were contracted out, 'the image the public has of a service is slow to change', and 'they still tend to expect the council to be responsible' (I11). Such a view also supports a mirror-image perspective, to the extent that local councillors (particularly from the non-Conservative parties which came to dominate local government in the 1980s and 1990s) might be expected to want to regulate more closely private contractors, in which they had little trust and to which they had been unwillingly obliged to contract out functions, than public-sector organizations.

Hence the mirror-image perspective introduced in Chapter 1 seems to have a mixed application to the regulation of local government. It seems more appropriate for the changing relationship between the organizational core of local government and those providing local front-line services (sometimes with local-authority inspectors and central inspectors hunting as a pack), than for relationships between central and local government more generally. What at one level appears as a mirror image looks more like a double whammy at another level.

## 7. CONCLUSIONS

This chapter suggests that regulation of local authorities by central government has moved to a more marked form of the oversight style discussed in Chapter 3, although it seems to have been mitigated in practice by some degree of mutuality. Juridification increased, too, with effects on the working practices of both central and local government. The fragmented and *ad hoc* structure of oversight, reflecting piecemeal institutional development, was complex and difficult for citizens to understand. Yet we found little enthusiasm among regulators for centralizing inspection and regulation of local authorities into a single all-purpose body. An Audit Commission official thought 'it would be unhealthy . . . too big and too powerful. . . . And there would be the danger of putting too many eggs in one basket.' He preferred a 'hybrid regime', with more coordination of the timing of inspection and audits but a continued differentiation of roles, with the Audit Commission 'working on the basis of a central model and the various inspectorates continuing with their own work responding to the distinctive needs of different areas of public service' (I41).

The various overseers of local government are accountable in different ways for what they do. Apart from inspectors who are civil servants inside departments or local-government staff working inside local authorities who are responsible to directly elected bodies, regulators tend to be detached from such direct lines of democratic accountability. It is often unclear who are their public or their clients, to whom they are supposed to be accountable, and we found little evidence of mutual accountability on the part of such regulators to one another. Most regulators are chosen by central departments after consultation with affected interests. Their accountability tends to be focused on the reports they produce and publish. They are as accountable as the public requires them to be—which is not much. Indeed such bodies have usually been set up with some independence from political authorities as a means of handling what institutional analysts term the 'commitment' problem (that is, ensuring the survival of an institution or policy beyond the political coalition that brought it into existence (Horn 1995)). Those who complain about lack of accountability, in the tradition of American criticisms of a 'headless fourth branch of government' (in the famous phrase of the 1937 President's Committee on Administrative Management (1937: 32)), misunderstand the reason such bodies were set up in the first place—to be independent of direct-line hierarchies.

Of the two nineteenth-century regulatory traditions for local government noted at the outset, the Chadwickian seems currently to be dominant. Local government has been subjected to a plethora of overseers exercising ever-tighter controls, despite the fashion for decentralizing managerial, executive, operational, and implementing responsibilities to devolved organizations. At the centre many see regulation as designed to encourage self-regulation and self-management, yet from the regulatees' perspective the various regulators often seem an external intrusive pressure seeking to enforce uniformity. However, just as the Chadwickian approach experienced setbacks during the nineteenth century, so the recent intensification of central oversight over local government may in the future find itself replaced in a reaction favouring more mutuality.

# 6

# All Bark, No Bite? The Regulation of Prisons in England and Wales

> My experience of inspecting, and no one does that more
> than the Armed Services, is . . . that it was pointless to have
> the opportunity that I knew inspection presented with
> an inside feel for the organization and not having the
> opportunity to deploy that in a way that it could be properly
> used.
>
> Sir David Ramsbotham, HM Chief Inspector
> of Prisons, 1995

This chapter examines regulation of prison standards by arm's-length oversight bodies with highly developed 'detector' instruments but much less developed 'effector' instruments—in formal terms at least. In principle such a structure should be expected to produce outcomes similar to those predicted by Wilson and Rachal (1977), as discussed in Chapter 1—that is, limited ability on the part of public-sector regulators to influence the public bureaucracies they oversee, because of a lack of prosecutorial powers or comparable sanctions. In large part that is what can be observed, but there appear to be some exceptions.

Prison regulation is important not only because of the sheer scale of this policy domain (with over 60,000 prisoners and an annual budget of over £1.5bn. in the mid-1990s) but also because, like others in the care of the state in 'total institutions', prisoners are vulnerable to mistreatment, particularly by lower-level custodial staff who may ignore the rules they are supposed to follow (Livingstone and Owen 1993: 290). Hence the case for oversight regimes to act as a counterweight to potential abuse of the special powers of the state in such domains.

## 1. THE DENSITY OF REGULATORY STRUCTURE

Prisons in England and Wales were subject to one of the densest patterns of regulatory oversight of any public-sector activity in the UK (see Figure 6.1). Each public prison was liable to inspection at any time by its individual local Board of Visitors, a quasi-independent central inspectorate (HM Chief Inspector of Prisons), and (for food hygiene) by local-authority Environmental Health Officers, as well as by the various divisions of a central government executive agency, the Prison Service (for example, for security and catering). In addition to internal prison procedures, prisoners'

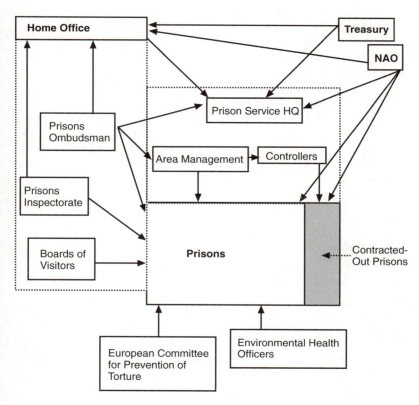

Fig. 6.1. Prisons regulation in England and Wales

grievances could be aired through Boards of Visitors, a Prisons Ombudsman, and the general Parliamentary Ombudsman (through MPs), each of which might use grievances to highlight prison failures. Prisons whose operation was contracted out to private firms not only faced all those regulators but were also subject to oversight by their own local Prison Service Controller with a permanent presence within the prison—one of a comparatively rare breed of 'regulators-in-residence'.[1] Additionally the prisons system more generally was subject to financial oversight by the Treasury and NAO, supranational regulation through the inspection and reporting functions of the European Committee for the Prevention of Torture (the 'torture people' in the shorthand terminology of one of our interviewees (I40)),[2] as well as private oversight by pressure groups outside government (notably the Howard League for Penal Reform and Prison Reform Trust) which helped to shape the activity of bureaucratic regulators.

A potential strength of such a complex and overlapping regulatory system is redundancy—if any one overseer is captured or ineffective others are available as back-up or counterweight. But duplication also exposed prisons to inconsistent and competing requirements. Where efforts were made to coordinate the activities of different overseers, it tended to be for sharing of expertise[3] or for one regulator to back up another's activity,[4] not to reduce burdens on regulatees. Like most other public-sector overseers, the various prison regulators had little idea of what compliance costs their activities created.

[1] Other cases of regulators-in-residence were Auditors in local authorities, Meat Hygiene Service inspectors at abattoirs, and Customs and Excise officials at bonded warehouses.

[2] This committee, the only supranational body with oversight powers for UK prisons, had three main functions: 'to organize a programme of visits, to conduct such visits, and to draw up reports in the light of such visits' (Evans and Morgan 1992: 591).

[3] e.g. HMCIP drew on NAO for assessing financial aspects of contracted-out prisons (HM Chief Inspector of Prisons 1996), OFSTED for evaluation of educational facilities (I22), and the SSI for inspection of young offenders' institutions and women's prisons. Such linkages had the further effect of bringing prisons informally within the remit of other regulators.

[4] e.g. HMCIP tried—not always successfully (I22)—to link with Boards of Prison Visitors, include checks on access to the Prison Ombudsman and Boards of Visitors in its inspections, and claimed the European Committee for the Prevention of Torture was heavily dependent on it (I1).

We found evidence of linkages and cooperation within the prison regulators' world, but also rivalry, competition, and conflicting standards, for example in opposition by the Chief Inspector of Prisons to the creation of a separate Prisons Ombudsman in 1994. Indeed, competition was at the heart of the 'director' element of the prison oversight system, with inherent contradictions between humanity and security, and the oversight regimes embodying those values.[5] For instance, after two major prison breakouts (at Whitemoor and Parkhurst) in 1994–5, the Prison Service was required to place renewed emphasis on security, a change in behaviour which may have pleased security scrutineers, but drew adverse comment from HMCIP, finding rehabilitation functions were adversely affected (HM Chief Inspector of Prisons 1995: 1).

Although it may have unintended benefits in preventing capture and enhancing control through 'opposed maximizers', it is hard to see the regulatory overlap and redundancy as a product of conscious institutional design. Rather, successive changes in the prisons regime over the past two centuries (summarized in Figure 6.2) frequently added new parts to the oversight system but seldom took anything away.[6] Institutional change typically consisted of adapting existing structures or adding new layers. Three main forces seem to have shaped the process.

First, until nationalization in 1878, prisons were run locally, either privately or by magistrates, and the legacy of this era remained, notably in the form of local lay bodies (Boards of Visitors for each prison) continuing to inspect and oversee what had become a central-government service. Boards of Visitors, which included local magistrates, were appointed by the Home Secretary and traced their lineage back to the oversight role of Justices of the Peace.[7] National inspection was itself a legacy of local provision,

---

[5] A clear example of an oversight process involving 'selective inhibition of opposed maximizers' or 'collibration', in Dunsire's (1978; 1990) terminology.

[6] The main twentieth-century exception was the removal of disciplinary functions from Boards of Visitors in 1992: Prison (Amendment) Rules, 1992. SI 1992, no. 514.

[7] Both as inspectors appointed by Courts of Quarter Sessions to visit county Houses of Correction (17 Geo. II, c. 5 (1744)) and as local prison administrators. The nationalization statute required the Court of Session to appoint Visiting Justices for each gaol, empowering them to visit every part of the prison and see every prisoner (Prison Act 1877, s. 14).

**Oversight**

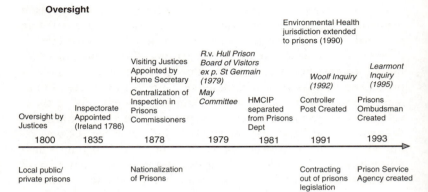

FIG. 6.2. Prisons administration and oversight: path dependency—
England and Wales

since it dated from 1835.[8] When the prisons were nationalized the
inspectorate was retained, but became virtually invisible within
the internal-management functions of the Prisons Commissioners
(Morgan 1985: 107; McConville 1995: 655–6, 668). This change
greatly reduced the transparency of prison administration since
inspectors' reports were not published. Even reports on particular
scandals were largely internal and confidential (Webb and Webb
1963 (orig. publ. 1922): 235–40).

Second, the prison oversight system was shaped by successive
responses to *ad hoc* inquiries, spurred by particular incidents or
crises to which Home Secretaries felt obliged to respond (cf. Lewis
1997: 15). Each of the three major institutional reforms of the last
twenty years followed that pattern. The creation of a reinvigorated
prisons inspectorate to function as the Prison Service's 'official

[8] Five independent inspectors of prisons were appointed on a statutory basis in
1835 (5 & 6 William IV, c. 38). This move was part of a more general 'policy boom'
in independent inspectorates in that era (see MacDonagh 1977; Rhodes 1981: 1–2),
but there were Irish precedents for prison inspection (26 Geo. III, c. 27 (I) (1786));
50, Geo. III, c. 103 (1810)). Although the Inspectorate established in England and
Wales in 1835 was not given enforcement powers, its early reports, critical of local
prisons, undermined support for local administration, both shoring up the Inspectorate's power and building support for greater central control of prison standards
(McConville 1981: 170–3, 254–5; Ignatieff 1989 (orig. publ. 1978): 188–9).

critic' (Lewis 1997: 28), followed the 1979 May Committee Report (May 1979: para. 5.61; Morgan 1985).[9] The creation of a non-statutory Prisons Ombudsman in 1994 was a response to an inquiry into serious riots at Manchester Strangeways Prison, recommending the appointment of an independent lay adjudicator for prisoners' complaints (Lord Woolf and Tumim 1991).[10] The establishment of the Prison Service as an executive agency and the contracting-out and market-testing of some prisons also followed recommendations from the Woolf report, supported by a government review of the organization of the Prisons Department (Lygo 1991).

Third, even though specific changes were introduced in response to inquiry reports, institutional developments in prison oversight also reflected broader public-sector reform themes, including reform of inspection arrangements, increased emphasis on lay adjudication and grievance-handling (Prisons Ombudsman 1996: paras. 1.1, 1.2), devolution of operational responsibilities to executive agencies regulated by departments, market-testing and contracting out of functions once provided on a permanent monopoly basis by public bureaucracies. Formally, the creation of the Prison Service Agency in 1993 was a case of mirror-image developments as characterized in Chapter 1, with loosening central direction accompanied by new forms of arm's-length oversight. But the mirror-image proved hard to realize, and indeed there seems to have been elements of a double whammy development akin to that described for local government in the last chapter. Relations between the Home Office as regulator and the Prison Service Agency as regulatee were problematic from the start. Division of financial responsibility between the two units was unclear (cf. Public Accounts Committee 17th Report, HC 234 1995–6); the Home Secretary appeared to want to intervene in operational matters which were formally the agency's responsibility (cf. King and McDermott 1995: 54; Lewis 1997: 117–18), but did not want to accept responsibility when things went wrong and indeed sacked the Director-General of the

[9] HM Chief Inspector of Prisons was appointed and removable by the Home Secretary, with no enforcement powers, but with duties to publish reports save where security was at issue (Prisons Act 1952, s. 5A, as amended by Criminal Justice Act 1982).

[10] Replacing a proposal for the establishment of a statutory Prison Disciplinary Tribunal. A Prisons Complaints Commission for Scotland was also set up in 1994 on a non-statutory basis (Scottish Prisons Complaints Commission 1995: 3–4).

Prison Service in 1995 in circumstances that continue to attract controversy (Lewis 1997; Barker 1998).

The development of contracted-out prisons, beginning in 1992,[11] was accompanied by new oversight arrangements laid on top of the existing controls which applied equally to public and contracted-out prisons. All the regulatory machinery used for public prisons—notably HMCIP, the PO, and Boards of Visitors—applied to contracted-out prisons too (Harding 1994: 68; Ryan 1994: 248). And the contracted-out prisons effectively operated within the pre-existing Prison Service framework but with a reallocation of certain management and oversight responsibilities, and a relationship with the Prison Service which was, at least formally, governed by contract rather than simple command (cf. Harding 1997: 40). Prison Governors were replaced by 'Directors', who had the same powers and responsibilities as Governors, except that they were not allowed to handle the allocation of 'punishments', like conducting adjudications or segregating prisoners.[12] The Prison Service operated as a regulator rather than a manager of contracted-out prisons, managing contracts, overseeing compliance, and checking the suitability of those employed as custody officers.[13]

## 2. DETECTION AND STANDARD-SETTING

### (a) *Information-gathering*

The Home Secretary was formally responsible for 'regulation and management' of prisons, issuing Prison Rules for that purpose

---

[11] Criminal Justice Act 1991, ss. 84–8; Criminal Justice Act (Contracted-Out Prisons) Order 1992 (SI 1656); Criminal Justice and Public Order Act 1994. The first contracted-out prison was the Wolds (1992), followed by Blakenhurst (1993), Doncaster (1994), and Buckley Hall (1995), with more private prisons being built at the time of writing (Prison Service 1995: 30; see also Harding 1997: 7).

[12] The legislation attempted to preserve for public officials tasks involving the allocation of punishment, with Directors responsible only for administering punishment (Harding 1994: 65, 68–71; 1997: 27 ff.). Directors expressed resentment about having fewer powers than public-sector governors (ibid. 40, 45), largely because they could not use disciplinary functions to manage prisoners (James *et al.* 1997: 93).

[13] It was intended to apply some aspects of the contracted-out prisons regime to other prisons which were to be market-tested, notably for the setting of key performance indicators (KPIs), but up to the time of writing that had not happened. Only one prison (Strangeways) was market-tested and since Treasury rules on market-

under prisons legislation.[14] But these responsibilities were devolved in two directions: management to the Prison Service and prison Governors (Directors in contracted-out prisons), and regulation to several bodies including the PO and HM Chief Inspector of Prisons and, for private prisons, Controllers.

The Home Office was itself a regulator of the Prison Service, and strengthened its detector capacity for that purpose after the Prison Service became an executive agency in 1993. After two politically embarrassing prison escapes in 1994 and 1995, and (according to Barker 1998: 13) problems experienced by senior Home Office officials in being 'out of the loop' of direct dealing that developed between top Prison Service staff and prison ministers, a Monitoring Unit was set up in the Home Office in 1995, with its head reporting directly to the Permanent Secretary (I40). Using classic oversight information-gathering instruments, the Unit monitored the Prison Service's planning, target-setting, and performance against targets; and required the Prison Service to submit quarterly returns on its performance.[15]

While the main external regulators of prisons lacked strong effector powers, in the sense of formal sanctions against non-compliance, they did have such powers for detection. The right to carry out on-site inspections of prisons was routinely used. Visitors and inspectors were both entitled to visit prisons at any time and gain access to all areas. Visitors often had their own keys, which could be important in more than a symbolic sense (cf. Rock 1996: 308), and prison Controllers within the contracted-out regimes also had their own keys.

The detector role comprised set-piece inspections in the classic oversight mould discussed in Chapter 3, but also included elements of randomness. The May Committee (May 1979: paras. 5.61–5.62) recommended the new prison inspectorate should focus on thematic inspections and reports rather than routine inspections, but the statutory duties of the Chief Inspector were not specific, beyond an obligation to inspect prisons and report to the Home

testing appear not to have been honoured after the in-house team won the bid, it remained subject to management by the Prison Service (HM Chief Inspector of Prisons 1996; Harding 1997: 146–7).

[14] Prisons Act 1952, ss. 47, 52. Prison Rules 1964, SI 1964, no. 388, as amended.

[15] The unit was merged with other parts of the Home Office to form an Efficiency and Consultancy Unit in 1997.

Secretary.[16] Over time HMCIP varied the emphasis placed on thematic inspection as against the regular five-year inspections inherited from the previous inspection regime (Morgan 1985: 112); in practice, most prisons underwent full inspections only every six to seven years.

Quinquennial inspections, involving a five-day visit announced long in advance, were supplemented by three-day follow-up visits, normally unannounced. In this way contrived randomness was mixed with oversight in the detection regime. Indeed, some HMCIP staff thought more use should be made of short unannounced visits and long visits should also be unannounced, since (predictably) teams working on five-year inspections tended to be 'snowed' with voluminous paperwork prepared for their visit (I1), and unannounced follow-up visits provided incentives to Governors/Directors to act on recommendations made after full inspections (I22).

For the Prisons Ombudsman (PO), whose stated objective was 'to provide an independent grievance system for prisoners which is fair and even-handed and which contributes towards a just and effective prison system',[17] any randomness in detection was produced by the complaints it happened to receive (in practice most came from long-term prisoners rather than remand or short-term prisoners (Prisons Ombudsman 1997: 12)). At the outset it was anticipated that the PO would mainly work reactively in information-gathering, responding to complaints submitted, but the PO also had the power to visit prisons and used it to interview staff and prisoners (Prisons Ombudsman 1995: 12). Its terms of reference allowed it 'unfettered access' to all Prison Service documents relevant to an investigation, but unfettered access was defined to exclude advice or reports to Ministers (PO Amended Terms of Reference, May 1996, para. 11), and in effect the Prison Service could decide whether documents requested were relevant to a particular investigation, and therefore to be disclosed. The PO reported difficulty in obtaining information from the Prison Service, not just because of delay but also because the Prison Service

---

[16] Prison Act 1952 s. 5A, as amended by s. 57 Criminal Justice Act 1982.

[17] The PO initially aimed to produce reports on most eligible complaints within eight weeks of receipt and on all complaints within twelve weeks, but these targets were not achieved because of delays in obtaining information and were later extended (Prisons Ombudsman 1997: 20–1, 25).

removed papers from files, claiming the material was either irrelevant or security-sensitive (Prisons Ombudsman 1997: 19–20). The PO's lack of statutory status and authority may partly have accounted for such difficulties.

Contracted-out prisons were more closely monitored than public prisons. They were subject to more specific standards and exposed to a wider range of audits, carried out by both Controllers and the Prison Service. For instance, all minor assaults in contracted-out prisons had to be recorded and reported to the Prison Service through the Controller, but there was no equivalent requirement for public prisons. Both the Controller and Director of the contracted-out prison in our sample believed the prison was 'overregulated', creating compliance costs higher than they needed to be (I28; IEE3).

Controllers of contracted-out prisons, who combined the prison Governor functions not held by Directors with oversight of the management of their prisons against the contract specification (Creighton and King 1996: 16–17), were generally senior Governor-grade Prison Service staff who might expect to return to Governor appointments after the end of their term as Controller (I28). As noted earlier, these 'hybrid' overseers were unusual in functioning as regulators-in-residence, working on the premises of the regulated prison. Mixing monitoring with direct responsibility over discipline proved difficult in the early days of the first contracted-out prison, the Wolds (James *et al.* 1997: 92), and Controllers aimed to develop their own independent information systems to check on that provided by the company running the prison (to which controllers had routine access, except for confidential financial information (HM Chief Inspector of Prisons 1996)).

### (b) *Standard-setting*

As noted earlier, the basic provisions for prison conditions were set down by the Home Secretary in the Prison Rules.[18] Orders provided

---

[18] After a shift in judicial thinking, the Prison Rules became justiciable as a matter of public law, but their breach did not give rise to any private-law remedy, which meant in practice damages for breach of the Rules were rarely available, and prisoners' ability to secure compliance with regulatory standards though litigation (alongside the work of the regulators) was limited. See Livingstone and Owen (1993: 18–20).

guidance on interpretation of the Prison Rules, and advice and information to Governors (formerly 'Circular Instructions') were regularly issued to Governors. The Prison Rules embodied some standards on the treatment of prisoners (Vagg 1994: 211–13) and after HMCIP's first annual report, the Prison Service produced a set of standards in 1984 for prison buildings. The Woolf Report recommended further development of standards, and supranational norms, like the European Prison Rules, created further pressures for such development. However, from the outset HMCIP did not see its role as just auditing the compliance of prisons with existing standards but also raising those standards (I1).

Moreover, linked to the contracting-out of prisons was a move to more precise specification of standards for each individual prison (James *et al.* 1997: 62). This practice spilled over to some degree into public prisons, attracting praise from some commentators (Harding 1994: 65). Prison contracts, issued by the Prison Service and monitored by the Controller of each contracted-out prison,[19] contained detailed specifications about discipline, complaints, and treatment of prisoners generally (Birkinshaw 1994: 17, n. 48). Performance measures were predominantly output-based, marking a move away from traditional public-sector concern with inputs (Harding 1994: 71), and in one contract there were 232 variables by which performance might be evaluated (I3).[20] Contracts specified 'key performance indicators' (KPIs), but Controllers could monitor items other than the KPIs. For example, where a prison met the KPI over *provision* of educational facilities, the Controller might move to examine the *take-up*, even if take-up of such facilities was not referred to in the contract (I28).

As noted above, this 'contract culture' of greater formalization and specification of standards spread to public prisons which became subject to operating standards, towards which all prisons and young offender institutions were supposed to work (Prison Service 1995: 30). Indeed, a senior Prison Service official mooted the idea that contractual standards and regulators similar to Controllers should apply to public and private prisons alike (I7; cf. Learmont

[19] Criminal Justice Act 1991 s. 85.
[20] There is some evidence to suggest contracted-out prisons generally provided prison conditions at the reasonably high level of their contractual specification, and that by 'cross-fertilization' the model public-sector regime was based on the specifications for contracted-out prisons (Harding 1997: 139–44).

1995: 106). But the 'contracts and Controllers' regime for contracted-out prisons operated within a context in which operating companies were strongly motivated to hold their existing contracts, bid for further contracts, and strengthen the case for further contracting-out generally. Without such incentives for a compliance culture the regulatory regime could be expected to have different effects.

Contracting-out changed HMCIP's work, drawing it into more concern with value for money and enabling it for the first time to use a form of 'yardstick competition' (that is, circumstances where there is no direct competition between different service providers but the existence of more than one supplier gives the regulator comparative information about costs and quality (Armstrong *et al.* 1994: 75)). HMCIP was quick to highlight innovations in the management of contracted-out prisons which improved prison conditions and could be adopted in public prisons, hoping to spread good practice more effectively (I1; Harding 1994: 82).

## 3. EFFECTOR SANCTIONS: HIERARCHIES, QUIVERS, AND REWARDS

Of the main prison overseers only Controllers of contracted-out prisons had formal powers to punish for non-compliance, but the other regulators developed their own methods for inducing behavioural modification. Like the local-government overseers discussed in the last chapter, those regulators sometimes used a ladder of escalating sanctions if the desired modification was not forthcoming, but often saw their repertoire of possible actions as less like a ladder than a quiver of arrows, graduated in weight and varying in form, from which the response judged most appropriate for the task in hand was chosen. Where regulators lack heavy artillery, as in the case of the prison overseers, it may be attractive for them to place the emphasis on rewarding good performers, rather than sanctioning the bad. Examples of that approach included publicizing best practice, as was done by HMCIP and the Citizen's Charter Unit, rewarding prisons with 'Charter Marks'. But HMCIP also had other arrows in its quiver, notably critical reports which could damage Prison Service careers, and its willingness to use that weapon suggested that relations between HMCIP and the Prison Service were not wholly cosy. HMCIP seemed to be respected by the Prison Service, partly because of the experience and expertise of HMCIP staff (I4) and partly because Governors believed HMCIP would not flinch from revealing problems.

However, there were nuances to this arm's-length relationship. Governors could see HMCIP as their ally on some issues, since HMCIP enhanced Governors' bids for more funding to improve conditions and make prisons easier to run. So Governors and senior Prison Service staff had incentives to share information about problems that could be attributed to resource limits and often seemed supportive of HMCIP's work (I3, I4, I7). Indeed, the Director-General of the Prison Service and the Chief Inspector met about once a month and had similar objectives on many issues (I7).

Factors likely to shape regulatory responses to non-compliance include the regulator's beliefs about the causes of such behaviour and the relational distance (RD) between regulator and regulatee. In public prisons non-compliance with regulatory norms was commonly seen as resulting from under-resourcing or incompetence. But contracted-out prisons were seen by regulators as better resourced and managed, and consequently regulatory compliance or non-compliance was more likely to be seen as stemming from 'amoral calculation' (Kagan and Scholz 1984) on their part.

### (a) HMCIP

HMCIP's approach to maintaining and improving prison standards was a mixture of education and 'shaming', dependent on its perceptions of why non-compliance occurred. Strong emphasis was laid on 'educating' Governors and prison staff, drawing their attention to problems at the earliest opportunity (I1), discussing draft reports with Governors before sending them to the Home Office, and discussions between the Chief Inspector and Governors of how to improve prison regimes immediately after an inspection team had identified problems (I22). What HMCIP saw as a general improvement in prison management in the 1990s also changed its role: instead of concentrating on identifying clear gaps in prison programmes (for instance in provisions for sex offenders), as in the past, it was now more likely to be faced with the task of evaluating how good such programmes were (I1).

Although HMCIP had no formal power to impose its recommendations, it consciously used varying levels of response in attempting to achieve compliance (see Figure 6.3)[21]. The lowest-level response consisted of informal remarks made to Governors or Directors during or after inspections. A higher-level one was to identify problems and make recommendations in inspection reports submitted to the Home Office, for publication. That meant sharing the details with the Prison Service, the Home Office, and the wider readership of HMCIP reports. But though the publication of critical inspection reports was HMCIP's main sanction for non-compliance, it was not wholly independent in deploying that weapon since reports were published by the Home Office after consideration by the Home Office and the Prison Service, and HMCIP often complained about long delays in publishing inspection reports. Such delay was officially attributed to administrative failures rather than obstruction (HM Chief Inspector of Prisons 1995: xi–xii), but a former Director-General of the Prison Service said of the publication of HMCIP reports that the Service 'had always played a delaying game, agreeing to publication only six, nine or even twelve months after the report had been completed—by which time the service could excuse deficiencies and deflect criticisms on the grounds that the report was hopelessly out of date and the problems now rectified' (Lewis 1997: 28). HMCIP itself declared that the practice of putting out a Prison Service press statement, combining both information on steps taken since the inspection and rebuttal, created more delay, and made 'something of a mockery of the report' (HM Chief Inspector of Prisons 1996).

A further step up the ladder of sanctions was to make comments directly to the Director-General or Home Secretary. This approach was not a routine response to failure to follow HMCIP recommendations and was used only when HMCIP attached great importance to the issue, or thought the matter was of great urgency, as with the serious security problems it identified in its 1994 inspection of Parkhurst Prison (I1).[22]

---

[21] This figure comes from the work of Ayres and Braithwaite (1992), who argue an effective and responsive regulatory system is likely to work mostly at the base of a pyramid of sanctions but to have the capacity to invoke higher-level responses if compliance is not achieved.

[22] Two months later there was a serious escape from Parkhurst which led to the immediate removal of the governor and the ultimate removal of the Director-General after the 1995 Learmont Inquiry report.

FIG. 6.3. HM Chief Inspector of Prisons: a credible hierarchy
of sanctions?

A new form of sanction was introduced in 1995 when the Chief
Inspector withdrew an inspection team from Holloway Prison on
the grounds that conditions were so poor that inspection could
serve no useful purpose.

Holloway was dead in the water. It was not decent, it was filthy. Relationships between the staff and inmates were non-existent. Meal times were
wrong. The reception was wrong, prisoners were left in the cold while
being processed. People were locked up from their meal at 3.30 p.m. to
7 a.m. the next morning. (I22)

Refusal to inspect was a technique the Chief Inspector (Sir David
Ramsbotham) had developed in his army career, and was aimed to
cause embarrassment and inconvenience to Prison Service staff and
Ministers. In that case, the immediate effect was to draw the Home
Secretary into the operational issues of Holloway—an intervention
justified on the grounds that under the Prison Service Agency
Framework Document the Home Secretary was responsible for

acting on matters of 'grave public and parliamentary concern' (I40). The next result was the removal of the prison Governor (as recommended by the Chief Inspector) and the diversion of resources into Holloway from other parts of the Prison Service (I7). Refusal to inspect is a tactic that seems unlikely to be used often, partly because it creates hostility in the central Prison Service administration and Home Office, and partly because of the risk of degrading other sanctions.[23] Nevertheless, Ramsbotham on occasion used the rhetoric of a regulator with real powers, for example, speaking of 'closing down' a wing of HMP Bristol on the grounds that the cells were too small (I22), even though he possessed no such power.

Use of the media was another potential weapon in the hands of the Inspectorate, given the level of media interest in prison conditions and the consequently high media profile of HMCIP, but that weapon was not used routinely and its usage seemed to vary over time and from one Chief Inspector to another. Judge Tumim seemed more willing to talk to the press in critical terms about prison conditions in the latter part of his tenure as Chief Inspector, because he felt he was no longer asked for his advice by the Home Secretary (I1). His successor, Sir David Ramsbotham, criticized newspapers 'hellbent on sensationalizing comparatively minor incidents, appearing to mount an unremitting attack on the Prison Service as a whole' (HM Chief Inspector of Prisons 1996). But HMCIP used press notices and media interviews with the Chief Inspector to increase the newsworthiness of its published reports, and on occasion deliberately used the media to shame a reluctant Home Office into action, notably over the provision of integral sanitation in all prisons.

## (b) *Controllers of contracted-out prisons*

With contracted-out prisons, legal sanctions for breach of contract were available to the Controller, and on Wilson and Rachal's (1977) argument, discussed in Chapter 2, that could be expected make behaviour modification easier. As in other regulatory contexts, such power may secure compliance (Hviid 1995), even if it is

---

[23] At the time of writing, the tactic had been used only once since the Holloway incident (in 1997, when an inspection team was withdrawn from Glen Parva Young Offenders Institution, *Sunday Times*, 13 Apr. 1997).

seldom deployed. But as noted earlier, a more powerful spur for cooperation seemed to be the power of the Prison Service not to contract out further prisons, or not to award contracts to particular firms, meaning prison-operating companies had little incentive to test the limits of what they were strictly required to do by contracts. One prison Director described a largely informal relationship in which contracts were at the margins rather than the centre and Directors generally did what was asked of them whether or not they were contractually obliged to do so (I3).

Nevertheless, Controllers and Directors were aware of the formal hierarchy of sanctions available for breach of contract. Ultimately a contracted-out prison could be reclaimed by the Prison Service, but this 'nuclear option' was seldom if ever likely to be used, and most of the time lower-level sanctions were more important (Harding 1997: 105). Before formal contractual sanctions were invoked the Controller was likely to see the Director informally and follow up with a letter (perhaps copied to senior management in the prison-operating company (I28; cf. Harding 1997: 106) if the Controller was especially concerned). When it came to formal contractual sanctions, the first stage was a default notice, followed by a financial penalty if the matter was not remedied within twenty days, but because of the incentive structure described above the financial penalty stage was rarely reached.[24] One Controller saw financial penalties as 'a sledgehammer to crack a nut for most incidents' (I28). In his prison seven default notices had been issued in two years, but none had ever reached the stage of financial penalty, perhaps because the prison maintained a half-time post of Compliance Officer.

HMCIP has reported cases where it was surprised financial penalties were not imposed, and this pattern is attributed by Harding (1997: 107) to 'regulatory softness'. But it could be that different ways of securing compliance were found more effective, or that a financial penalty seemed to the Controller to be an excessive response, and no lower-level sanctions were available.[25] It remains to

---

[24] The first reported case arose when the company running HMP Blakenham lost control during a disturbance and was subjected to a £41,000 penalty, withheld from the next payment to the company (Harding 1997: 106; James *et al.* 1997: 158). Details of later penalties and improvement notices served on contracted-out prisons can be found in HC Deb. 302, cols. 54–5, 1 Dec. 1997.

[25] At the time of writing, a new system of penalty points had replaced the original structure of sanctions in the contractual arrangements for HMP Bridgend.

be seen whether the system will follow the pattern of contracting in the NHS, with greater formalization of incentives in contracts used as the basis for an aggressive approach to enforcement in which purchasers routinely pursue penalties (Hughes *et al.* 1997: 270–3), or whether it will follow the pattern of local-authority contracting-out, in which aggressive enforcement of contractual conditions has been seen to be ineffective and gradually replaced by a return to more cooperative relations (Vincent-Jones and Harries 1996).

## (c) *The prisons ombudsman*

The PO's main effector power was to adjudicate on complaints deemed to be 'eligible grievances' and make recommendations to the Prison Service Director-General, though the PO's annual (and six-monthly) reports were also used to draw attention to systematic failings highlighted by complaints (Prisons Ombudsman 1997: 31–2). Examples of such failings included persistent misapplication of categorization rules, routine failures to follow adjudication procedures, and disclaimers issued by the Prison Service over the holding of prisoners' property (Prisons Ombudsman 1995: paras. 8.7–8.10). Moreover, the PO could make recommendations even when complaints were not upheld, and often did so. The overwhelming majority of PO's recommendations were accepted by the Prison Service,[26] though the acceptance rate was slightly lower than for the Parliamentary Ombudsman (close to 100 per cent) and some other public sector ombudsmen.

The PO's office found some different approaches to compliance in contracted-out prisons compared with public prisons. For instance, in the first two years of operation there were no complaints at all to the PO from the contracted-out prisons, perhaps because most of their prisoners were on remand and therefore unlikely to develop long-term grievances. Moreover, private prisons had more freedom to resolve minor complaints through monetary compensation, for example about loss of property (I3), meaning the PO was less likely to be drawn into such issues. So when complaints from contracted-out prisons did arrive on the PO's desk he was likely to treat such complaints more seriously because of a perception that

[26] In 1996, 88% were accepted, with only 8% rejected outright, and 4% partially rejected (Prisons Ombudsman 1997: 31).

contracted-out prisons had greater capacity to resolve complaints flexibly.

## 4. EXPLAINING CONTRASTING REGULATORY CULTURES: RELATIONAL DISTANCE, INDEPENDENCE, AND REGULATORY LEVEL

Regulators' decisions about how to view those they regulate, and how to treat their infractions were in part shaped by relational distance (RD), as discussed in Chapter 3. Some prison regulators had high RD, being appointed for their independence rather than for their particular expertise of prisons. Others were 'poachers turned gamekeepers', regulating people they knew of old. The RD hypothesis discussed in Chapter 3 suggests such regulators would have the advantage of knowing the system well, but would also be likely to display some form of regulatory capture, with formal standards tempered by sympathy for regulatees in what could 'realistically' be asked of them (Makkai and Braithwaite 1995). Other factors seen as likely to increase the risk of capture include high frequency of contact between regulator and regulatee and the size of the regulated industry (see Chapter 3).

Though Harding (1997: 37) sees regulation of contracted-out prisons as likely to be characterized by 'capture', several features of prison regulation had the effect of reducing the risk of capture. First, as noted earlier the sheer number of regulatory actors made overall system capture difficult. The regime consisted of a complex 'regulatory space', comprising multiple actors reacting to one another in changing ways, not the simple bilateral relationship assumed by classical capture theory (Hancher and Moran 1989). For example, the contracted-out prison director who tamed his Controller, would still have to contend with the Area Manager, the Board of Visitors, and HMCIP. Second, the regulatory system as a whole displayed mixed characteristics on 'risk factors' for capture. Most points on the spectrum were represented in RD and frequency of contact.

Within the set of prison regulators, two had high contact frequency with their prison. Local Boards of Visitors were appointed for independence rather than experience, but Controllers of contracted-out prisons were the opposite: typically they were experi-

enced prison governors, overseeing Directors with similar backgrounds and experience. The other two regulators (HM Chief
Inspector of Prisons and the PO) had low contact frequency with
individual prisons, and examination of the staffing arrangements
for their offices showed they were hybrids, with high RD for the
head of the office, while the senior staff had considerable prisons
experience and expertise.

Since the creation of the office in its current form in 1982, HM
Chief Inspector of Prisons has been a lay appointment. At the time
of writing the office was held by a former army general (Sir David
Ramsbotham, appointed in 1995), and his predecessor (Stephen
Tumim 1987–95) had been a County Court Judge. Physically,
HMCIP's office was located within the main Home Office building
in Queen Anne's Gate, reflecting the dual role intended for HMCIP
as overseer of prisons and adviser to the Home Secretary. Tumim
claimed that in spite of lack of specific prison-service expertise, 'if
a principal task of an inspector is to ask very basic questions and to
press for answers, then the advantage may lie with a lay inspector'
(Tumim 1992: 5), because such an individual might be less inclined
to accept arguments that things have always been done in a particular way. Moreover, high RD at the top of HMCIP was balanced by
the Chief Inspector's dependence on a senior staff drawn largely
from the Prison Service, typically at governor grade (HM Chief
Inspector of Prisons 1995: 74; Rock 1996: ch. 10), and in practice
the senior staff did much of the inspecting.

The personality of the Chief Inspector was important in shaping
the regulatory regime. Judge Stephen Tumim's appointment in
1987 led to a restoration of regular five-yearly inspections, and
HMCIP became more of a crusader for improvement of prison
conditions (HM Chief Inspector of Prisons 1995: xv), a change in
approach that would have been difficult for someone steeped in
Prison Service ways. Tumim kept HMCIP outside the management
agendas of the Home Office and the Prison Service, partly through
careful selection of thematic topics for report, which implicitly set
new and higher standards for prisons. Tumim made much of successes like regularizing meal times ('lunch not before 12 and tea not
before 4' (I1)) and achieving accelerated commitment from government to provide integral sanitation in cells, ending the practice of
'slopping out' (Tumim 1992: 9; HM Chief Inspector of Prisons
1995: xv), though Vagg (1994: 48–9) claims HMCIP had little

overall impact on the improvement of prisons conditions since its establishment in 1982.

The first PO, Sir Peter Woodhead, was a former Admiral, and the PO's office was formally part of the Home Office, though operationally independent from the Prison Service and physically based at some distance from both the Home Office and the Prison Service to 'emphasize the Ombudsman's independence' (Prisons Ombudsman 1995: para. 2.3). Despite the expectation that Woodhead would prove less of an embarrassment to the then Home Secretary than Tumim had been as HMCIP, 'Woodhead turned out to be his own man, popping up on the media to express trenchant views about the service and even publishing his own preliminary report without clearing it with Ministers' (Lewis 1997: 123). But the extent of the PO's independence was limited because the office had no statutory basis and, unlike the Parliamentary Ombudsman, had no parliamentary committee to operate as an effector in pressing for compliance with recommendations (Richardson 1993: 321). In spite of the generally high level of compliance with PO recommendations, noted above, some interviewees told us there was a general perception in both the Home Office and the Prison Service that the PO need not be taken too seriously (I4).

For contracted-out prisons, the cooperation noted earlier between Directors and their Controllers may partly be attributed to low RD between Controllers and Directors. In most cases they had a common background as prison Governors and consequently the lowest RD of any prison regulator, which was further increased by close physical proximity on account of the Controller's role as regulator-in-residence. In a report on the Wolds Prison HMCIP found some uncertainty about the roles of the Director and Controller and noted the Controller was effectively a lower-grade Governor than the Director and considerably less experienced (Harding 1994: 74; cf. also Shichor 1991: 120).

Given the close relationship and frequency of contact associated with supervision of contracted-out prisons (and contracted-out services generally), it is clear why capture is considered a high risk (Harding 1997: 48). But, as argued earlier, the role of other regulatory actors within the regulatory space may qualify this conclusion. In particular, independent inspection by HMCIP provided oversight more rigorous than in other countries with contracted out prisons (ibid. 1994: 80). And while in some Australian jurisdictions the equivalents to UK Controllers as monitors of contracted-out prisons were located outside the prisons, the reduced risk of excessive cosiness in regulator–regulatee relations may be counterbalanced by concerns about whether the monitoring job can be done effectively by an arm's-length regulator (ibid. 73–4).

## 5. CONCLUSION

Three main themes emerge from this account of prison oversight. First, regulatory arrangements for prisons were remarkably dense, with overlap among institutions producing both duplication of functions and competitive pressures. The institutional structure of regulation was baroque, with new regulatory arrangements laid on top of older ones, with little apparent concern for cost or overall design. It is scarcely surprising that some saw the arrangements for overseeing contracted-out prisons—the latest example of the 'layering' process—as over-regulation.

In terms of the analysis of regulatory methods in Chapter 3, the standard-setting process approximated to the competition mode, while the detector process (the most developed part of the regulatory system) was a mixture of oversight and competition and the effector element was little developed in the way of formal powers in the hands of overseers. But the detector role was problematic for some regulators, notably the PO, which faced some obstruction from the Prison Service and an unwillingness in the Home Office to allow examination of complaints affecting its policies. Absence of any statutory basis made the PO's mandate subject to change at the discretion of the Home Secretary, undermining the credibility and independence of the office.

But although Wilson and Rachal's (1977) claim that public-sector regulators will find it hard to modify the behaviour of their charges in the absence of formal sanctioning powers is broadly consistent with much of what we observed in prison oversight, prisons regulators nevertheless developed a range of effector responses to failure to comply with standards, using arrows that at least sometimes seemed to find their target. For instance, HMCIP used its statutory independence to provide a robust and critical view of prison conditions, though it could achieve improvements only by persuading and shaming government. Controllers wielded a big stick, but it is not clear whether this fact, the more general incentive structure faced by the contractors who operate prisons, or the low RD between Controllers and Directors explains the general compliance culture of contracted-out prisons. Moreover, it may be that improvements in prison administration which are widely, though not universally, attributed to contracted-out prisons[27] were more a product of the break with the old regime, and from operating largely in new buildings and with good initial levels of resourcing, than a product of a well-designed regulatory regime.

Third, we found a mix of regulatory cultures, partly influenced by varying RD between prisons regulators and those they oversaw. However, as has been shown, the relational distance hypothesis is complicated by the existence of hybrid patterns of RD in two regulator organizations (HMCIP and PO) in which RD was high at the topmost level but lower for many other key staff. This model of mixed RD is a way of combining independence and expertise not in a single person, but in a single office.

If the central rationale for arm's-length regulation of prisons is to act as a counterweight to the 'information asymmetry' produced by the closed and hidden character of prisons, the emphasis on the detector role of overseers makes sense. But the lack of powerful effectors to deploy against breach of standards created the risk of lack of credibility on the part of prisons regulators, even in their core information-gathering role. Indeed, prison oversight seems to exemplify some of the best and worst features of public-sector regulation. On the one hand, there are signs of excessive regulation by competing agencies because of a 'Nelson's-eye' approach to evaluation of cost, linked to difficulties in effecting behaviour-modification without formal sanctions. On the other hand, in circumstances where highly charged political issues make it difficult to arm independent regulators with heavy artillery, there may be real advantages of multi-regulation and mixed institutions for such features as RD and frequency of contact, in reducing the risks of stagnation or capture in the regulatory regime.

---

[27] For the methodological difficulties in comparing public and contracted-out prisons over value, standards, and conditions see James *et al.* (1997: ch. 2).

# 7

# From Secret Garden to Reign of Terror? The Regulation of State Schools in England

> The principle of zero tolerance [of poor performance in schools] will be adhered to unflinchingly.
>
> Dept. for Education and Employment, 1997

> Dans ce pays-ci il est bon de tuer de temps en temps un amiral pour encourager les autres.
>
> Voltaire, *Candide*, 1759

This chapter explores a regulatory dynamic rather different from the effector-free regime for prisons regulation discussed in the last chapter. In this case there is also a complex institutional jungle of regulators and a heavy emphasis on detector activity, but the information-gathering style has been a mixture of oversight and competition elements, and (in contrast with the expectations of Wilson and Rachal (1977)) the regulators acquired heavy artillery for their effector role of behaviour-modification—perhaps because their target was at local- rather than central-government level. But it is one thing to equip regulators with 'nuclear weapons', another for those weapons to be effectively deployed in the close combat of educational politics.

As with prisons, the State regulated education before it became a direct provider of the service. The establishment of a central inspectorate in 1839 to report on schools to the government (Blackie 1970), shortly after the creation of the first prisons inspectorate, was a key part of the Chadwickian approach to the regulation of local services, as discussed in Chapter 5, but at that time most schooling was provided by the Church, not the State. With the advent of direct State responsibility for the provision of schools, beginning about a century ago and now amounting to approximately 90 per cent of total primary and secondary education, the regulation of schools took on a different character, as a case of regulation inside government.

The regulatory regime changed several times over a century. After the creation of the national inspectorate in 1839, a 'Revised Code' of 1862 linked school inspection with state funding (meaning inspectors could determine which schools received funding and which did not) and with a system for paying schoolteachers by results based in many cases on examination performance (Selby-Bigge 1927: 261) which lasted until 1898, when it was abandoned because of perceptions that it skewed teacher behaviour into concentrating on more able pupils at the expense of the less able. After the collapse of the 'performance-pay' approach to school inspection, the link between funding and school inspection was broken and a non-punitive successor regime aimed at examinations of schools 'in the round', with full-scale inspections of secondary schools roughly every five years being attempted from 1902.[1]

Yet successive changes in school inspection and regulation did not produce a stable and universally acclaimed service. Indeed, few parts of the British public sector saw as much regulatory change in the 1990s as schools in England and Wales. Those changes were fuelled by a perception, becoming widely accepted by the major political parties, that the British economy was underperforming because of inadequate basic schooling provided by public authorities. Regulatory change in the 1990s was linked to broader policy developments since the mid-1970s justified in terms of lifting economic performance through school improvements.[2]

During the 1980s and early 1990s, education regulation was reformed in several ways in an attempt to raise standards. Out of the generic types of control discussed in Chapters 1 and 3, the emphasis was laid on increased competition and increased oversight, and less mutuality in the sense of professional control over

---

[1] That target had become a ten-year cycle by the 1920s and by the 1950s the idea of any specific cycle of inspections had been abandoned altogether (DES/WO 1982: 12).

[2] In 1976 the Labour Prime Minister James Callaghan initiated what he called a 'Great Debate' about the standards and quality of public education in Britain (Feintuck 1994), arguing that British schools were not educating pupils to a standard adequate to sustain a modern industrial economy. This theme was taken up with relish by the subsequent Conservative Government and sustained by the Blair Labour Government.

schools by teachers and local-authority administrators. A National Curriculum was introduced for the first time, stipulating what should be taught and how. Parents were given new freedoms to choose their children's school. Examination league tables were published, listing the performance of every school in the country. And education reforms were influenced by a more general doctrine that 'purchase' and 'production' of public services should be more clearly divided. For instance, the century-long role of local authorities as direct managers of schools was modified by laying more direct responsibilities for staffing and budgeting on school governors and creating a competitive regulatory regime in which schools might opt out of local-authority oversight into an alternative central-government regime.[3] It was even suggested that the policy changes in the later 1980s reversed the previous division of responsibilities between public authorities and head teachers, with the former becoming responsible for decisions about curriculum and assessment and the latter becoming managers of staff and resources (Wilby 1989). Richard Laughlin and Jane Broadbent (1997) argue that the sum of the changes extended central-government control over the teaching profession in the name of a market-type rhetoric of competition and contracts which was used to undermine professional autonomy and mutual accountability in teaching.[4]

In the process, the institutional arrangements for school inspection were radically overhauled with the replacement of the former HM Inspectorate of Schools by a new non-Ministerial department, the Office of Standards in Education (OFSTED). The government's declared aim was to put schools 'under the watchful eye of the new and powerful Chief Inspector of Schools' (Department for Education 1992), and Wilcox and Gray (1996: 2) suggested the OFSTED regime was one of the most ambitious scheme of schools inspection in the world. Some elements of the mirror-image pattern discussed earlier can be detected, since local authorities found their role changed from direct day-to-day managers of schools to that of

---

[3] The Blair Labour Government announced its intention to return opted-out schools to local-authority control, thus removing the element of regulatory competition over schools (but not apparently further education colleges, which had been removed from control of local authorities altogether).

[4] They draw on a framework of 'markets', 'hierarchies', and 'clans' developed from Ouchi (1979) to argue that the reforms of the 1980s and 1990s were designed to undermine the clan-type qualities of mutuality and increase the hierarchical element of oversight.

arm's-length overseers in the years after 1989, and at the same time oversight from OFSTED, the Audit Commission (as discussed in Chapter 5), NAO, and other bodies increased. Performance indicators were collected and published (either by the Department for Education and Employment or by the Audit Commission) with the intention of encouraging improved performance. The Blair Labour government created a Standards and Effectiveness Unit within DfEE in 1997 and also announced its intention to take powers to close 'failing' schools, on the recommendation of OFSTED.

School inspection illustrates several themes discussed in Chapters 2 and 3. First, it is an oversight regime that developed rapidly over the 1990s. Second, resources invested in national inspection sharply increased. Some of this increase resulted from a deliberate switch from local-authority advice to central inspection, but the overall effect was to add to the national resources invested in the regulation of schools. Third, a conscious effort was made with the creation of OFSTED to increase relational distance (RD) and reduce 'professional capture' of the regulators by using lay inspectors and contracted-out inspection.

Fourth, the post-1992 OFSTED inspection system used more explicit 'written-down' oversight procedures than in the past, in an attempt to standardize regulatory style and make assessment more consistent and objective. Standard-setting approximated to the ideal-typical oversight style identified in Chapter 3, while information-gathering and behaviour modification was a compound of the oversight and competition styles. Fifth, school quality (or 'standards') gained greater public prominence. Each of these five issues is discussed in turn in this chapter, after a brief overview of the many organizations involved in regulation of schools in England.

## 1. THE REGULATORY JUNGLE

As with prisons, schools (and other educational institutions) in England were subject to multiple, sometimes overlapping, overseers, embodying different values, coordinating their various actions to only a limited extent[5], and varying in the extent to which

---

[5] There were occasional examples of joint working, like periodic collaboration between OFSTED and the Audit Commission and between the Audit Commission and the NAO.

they were seen to be politicized.[6] Many of these bodies had been fairly recently created and the whole institutional structure was subject to frequent reform. At the centre of the regulatory regime was OFSTED, headed by a high-profile Chief Inspector of Schools charged 'to improve standards of achievement and quality of education through regular independent inspection, public reporting and informed advice' (DfEE 1997: 150, para. 17.8). The Chief Inspector had a general duty to inform the Secretary of State about educational quality, standards achieved, adequacy of financial resources available to schools, and the cultural, moral, and spiritual development of pupils at schools. More specifically, the Chief Inspector was responsible for organizing inspections of primary and secondary schools on a six-year cycle, through competitive tendering for such inspections linked with a system of accrediting Registered Inspectors for schools.

But OFSTED was not the only pebble on the regulatory beach. Local education authorities (LEAs) also remained important. Though they had been left with less direct control over schools, they still operated as first-line regulators of over 23,000 schools in England, for example through internal audit,[7] and were in turn the main objects of the central-government regulators. Other key regulators included the Funding Agency for Schools (FAS), a central-government quango operating the rival regulatory-cum-funding regime which schools could opt for instead of local-government regulation,[8] and the DfEE as the central-government department responsible for education in England. In general DfEE and its predecessors preferred to regulate through independent or satellite

[6] At the time of writing, a broadly similar array of regulators—though with differences of detail and nomenclature—operated in Wales, Scotland, and Northern Ireland, making the UK total number of school regulators up to three or four times greater than those discussed here. But the arrangements may well change in the future, particularly with the advent of a Scottish Parliament responsible for school inspection from 2000 (Scottish Office 1997).

[7] 'LEAs still remain responsible for monitoring the progress of institutions' (Audit Commission 1989) and could, in extreme circumstances, resume control over a school. And they retained other regulatory responsibilities, like internal audit, which created familiar tensions at middle-management level (one head teacher we spoke to accused LEA auditors of 'counting calculators' rather than checking contracts for value for money (IEE3)).

[8] FAS had responsibilities analogous to those of LEAs for grant-maintained schools which had opted out of LEA regulation and funding. In the late 1980s it was responsible for approximately 1,000 state schools in England (about 5% of the total), providing funding and monitoring financial and managerial performance.

bodies rather than directly, though it had formal powers to regulate directly[9] and had policy and monitoring groups concerned with standards and effectiveness. Among the alphabet-soup of arm's-length regulators surrounding DfEE were SCAA (the Schools Curriculum and Assessment Authority, created to regulate the National Curriculum and oversee school examinations); NCVQ (the National Council for Vocational Qualifications, responsible for developing and promoting vocational qualifications),[10] TTA (the Teacher Training Agency, responsible for funding and quality control of teacher training), and EAB (the Education Assets Board, responsible for determining the property, rights, and liabilities to be transferred from LEAs to a school when it became grant-maintained).

Beyond these education-specific overseers were more generalist regulators with responsibilities for schools, like the local government ombudsman and the Audit Commission, discussed in Chapter 5, which was concerned not only with audit in the narrow sense but also with assessing the economy, efficiency, and effectiveness of schools as part of its wider oversight role over local government. But the movement of schools out of LEA control into the alternative central-government FAS funder-regulator regime meant the central-government auditor, the NAO, became responsible for auditing opted-out schools (as well as expenditure by further education colleges, universities, and the DfEE) and seemed to be viewed, together with FAS, as a 'light regulator' by such schools in comparison to the LEA regime. Though schools did not present the pattern discussed for prisons in the last chapter, with new regulators being added without anything ever being taken away, head teachers and LEAs faced a complex and multiple array of regulators. Indeed, several of the head teachers we interviewed were only dimly aware of the full panoply of regulators watching over them.

## 2. REGULATORY DYNAMICS

Multi-organizational complexity and frequent reform churning up of the institutional landscape of regulation are unique neither to the

---

[9] Conferred under the 1944 Education Act (s. 68), to give directions to local authority or school governors if they were acting or preparing to act 'unreasonably'. Such powers were very rarely used.

[10] At the time of writing it was proposed to merge SCAA and NCVQ into a single Qualifications and Curriculum Authority.

world of education (the prison system, discussed in the last chapter, has similar features) nor to the late twentieth century. In the mid-nineteenth century, schools regulation also involved multiple and often conflicting organizations, including HMIs, the Local Government Board, and the Poor Law authorities (Gosden 1966). And the basic institutional separation between regulation and policy-setting at the centre, and service-delivery by local institutions remained, in spite of radical reforms to school management. 'Direct rule' from Whitehall has rarely even been considered, and policy variation has amounted to changes in regulatory style.

If there was anything distinctive about the regulation of schools in the 1980s and 1990s, it seemed to lie in the intensifying speed of change and the extent to which the regulatory agenda returned to the Benthamite or Chadwickian style discussed earlier, with arm's-length central inspection of competence accompanied by draconian powers and an extreme form of Bentham's 'tabular-comparison' principle (Hume 1981: 161) for public management, in the form of publication of data on schools' performance based on centrally prescribed standards.

A move to more intensive central inspection of performance linked to powerful sanctions for those deemed to be 'failing' included moves to put inadequate performers under different management (described in Section 5 below), the development of more frequent inspection deliberately embodying greater relational distance (described in Section 4), and the extension of central inspection beyond individual schools to LEA educational management. Thus the DfEE's Standards and Effectiveness Unit, created in 1997, took a keen interest in the performance of LEAs as monitors of school performance, DfEE requested OFSTED to look closely at the performance of particular LEAs,[11] and at the time of writing proposed to extend OFSTED's responsibility for school inspection into a duty to inspect all LEAs, jointly with the Audit Commission,[12] accompanied by powers for government to impose new management on a failing LEA paralleling the regime for individual schools.

The move towards an intensified form of the Benthamite

[11] Notably Calderdale in 1996–7 and Hackney in 1997.
[12] See DfEE 1997, ch. 3: 24–36. The Audit Commission already undertook similar inspections of social services departments jointly with the Social Service Inspectorate (Audit Commission 1997).

'tabular-comparison' approach to school regulation was reflected in central government's stipulation of a standard National Curriculum under the 1988 Education Reform Act, linked with national-service standards prescribed in the 1991 Parent's Charter and Education (Schools) Act 1992 and with requirements on LEAs to publish performance indicators about schools' examination results.[13] In addition to the publication of league tables of schools' examination results, publication of the Audit Commission's performance indicators, value-for-money studies, and management letters was also designed to encourage parents, governors, and the wider public to put pressure on schools to improve and to provide a justification for regulatory interventions against failing schools by the DfEE.

More generally, the regulatory regime of the 1990s differed in style from that operating in the middle years of the century, in that the perception by politicians of a 'secret garden' (Wilcox and Gray 1996: 32) of education experts shielding schools from public accountability and scrutiny was replaced by a more open and adversarial kind of oversight. The consensual or compliance-oriented oversight style of an earlier generation was replaced by more confrontational deterrence-oriented regulation, with the central regulators armed with heavier weapons and a battery of published information designed to stimulate improvement through fear and shame as well as the more concealed competition of the past. Moreover, as Broadbent and Laughlin (1998) point out, shaming through OFSTED inspections differed from other regimes such as prison inspection in that it was individualized, directed to individual teachers and not just head teachers.

## 3. INCREASING INVESTMENT IN CENTRAL INSPECTION

As noted earlier, the creation of OFSTED in 1992 was a major landmark not only in schools regulation but in inspection more generally. OFSTED was expected to be tough on low standards;

[13] At the time of writing, this 'audit trail' was being extended by requiring each LEA to produce educational development plans with measurable—and therefore auditable—performance targets (DfEE, 1997, ch. 3: 28–9) to be scrutinized by OFSTED and the Audit Commission.

standards were to be measured with an emphasis on examination performance, and inspections were be largely contracted out, in contrast to the previous regime in which inspectors were normally full-time civil servants. The decision to contract out the inspection function was part of a concerted effort by the Thatcher and Major governments to distance the oversight of school standards from what national politicians saw as a trendy, left-leaning, professional establishment (Wilcox and Gray 1996: 32).

The regime which OFSTED replaced combined a very limited inspection of schools by full-time central inspectors (involving only about 150 schools a year), physically based in the central department responsible for education in a way that allowed close communication between inspectors and policy civil servants (Loughlin 1992: 77–84). The central inspectorate's activities were supplemented by advice and inspection by LEAs and limited school self-evaluation (Wilcox and Gray 1996: 25). The then Education Secretary (Kenneth Clarke) claimed it would have taken about 200 years for the central inspectorate to examine all schools (Harris 1993: 174). In 1985 a Department of Education and Science circular encouraged LEAs to inspect schools regularly, but LEA staff seem to have preferred to play an advisory rather than an inspectorial role[14] even though the perceived need for inspection and evaluation of schools increased, as direct LEA oversight and management of schools declined with financial delegation to schools in the 1988 Education Reform Act. In 1988 the then Secretary of State, Kenneth Baker, proposed there should be 'inspection in all its forms' (meaning LEA, national, and school-based examinations of education) and in the following year the Audit Commission (1989) also argued for more inspection by a mix of institutions.

On the face of it, the new OFSTED system of inspection, introduced in 1992, involved a step change in spending on school inspection from the centre, with a 300 per cent increase in real terms in the budget devoted to national inspection between 1980–1 and 1995–6. But the increase in the overall resources (taking national and local together) devoted to schools inspection was rather less dramatic. If the expenditure devoted to LEA advice and

---

[14] Stillman (in 1989) found LEA advisers spent less than 10% of their time on inspection (Wilcox and Gray 1996: 28).

inspection (and subsequently switched away from those activities) is added to the pre-OFSTED HMI figures, the creation of OFSTED involved only a small increase in total inspection resources. It is the increased spending on the *national* system of inspection which is spectacular, with £120 million being transferred to OFSTED from LEA budgets—a feature which created local-government hostility to the system at the start (I31). The result was a system designed to produce a full inspection of each school every four years, or 25 per cent of schools every year, about forty times more than the previous regime.[15]

## 4. RELATIONAL DISTANCE— LENDING DISENCHANTMENT TO THE VIEW?

Relational distance (RD), as discussed in Chapter 3, was central to the late twentieth-century debate over school inspection, but the issue had also been debated in the nineteenth century. Bishop (1971) cites parliamentary commissioners appointed to examine school inspection of schools in the 1860s arguing 'schoolmasters . . . were unfit for the office of inspectors who should be equipped, by previous training and social position, to communicate and associate upon terms of equality with the managers of schools and the clergy of different denominations.' But the lack of practical classroom knowledge on the part of inspectors which this doctrine of 'superior status' produced led to friction between teachers and inspectors[16] and later it became common for inspectors and inspected to be part of the same world of education professionals (Day and Klein 1987: 174).

RD re-emerged as an issue in schools inspection from the 1970s with concern by politicians that inspectors had been captured by the educational establishment and were too close to those they inspected, forming (together with teachers and LEA advisers) the secret garden referred to earlier, which excluded most parents and the general public (IEE10). A 1992 White Paper expressed the view

[15] This system contrasts with the approach taken by the Scottish Education Inspectorate, which inspected only 4% of schools each year to build up a national picture of standards and performance (supplemented by visits to all secondary schools every two years) and did not publish reports (I31).

[16] Head teachers and education professionals we interviewed expressed concerns which seemed closely to mirror those of teachers in the 1860s (I26, I31).

that inspection, advice, and teaching had been blurred in such a way as to damage educational quality and declared: 'too often there was no clear distinction between inspection and advice, so that sometimes inspectors told schools what to do and then checked up to see if they were doing it—rather than their proper task of evaluating whether or not it worked . . . hence from next year all schools will be subject to regular and rigorous inspection' (Dept. for Education 1992).[17]

The OFSTED style of inspection was intended to increase RD in the system by introducing a clearer distinction between inspection and advice, with OFSTED concentrating on the former (Wilcox and Gray 1996: 10). In 1992 the then Secretary of State (John Patten) envisaged a new breed of inspectors as 'big cats prowling on the educational landscape' (Learmouth 1996: 55). In that spirit, the Education (Schools) Act 1992 required inspections to be conducted by a registered inspector with the assistance of an inspection team consisting of 'fit and proper' persons, who (in the spirit of the Chinese Imperial Censorate)[18] might not have any connections with the school and needed to have received training approved by the Chief Inspector. Ministers rejected the view that registered inspectors should be drawn exclusively from former teachers, although they acknowledged that most registered inspectors would, in fact, be so (Harris 1993: 179). In practice OFSTED inspection teams involved many former LEA inspectors, with about half run by LEAs and the other half by other organizations (Matthews and Smith 1995).[19]

A further attempt to increase RD in school inspection was the introduction of lay inspectors in the 1992 Education (Schools) Act,[20] intended to bring the viewpoint of individuals outside the

---

[17] According to Learmouth (1996: 55), 'HMI were seen as too remote and theoretical, often peddling the latest trendy ideas to, presumably, gullible teachers' and 'LEA inspectors often described themselves to their schools as "critical friends", thus bringing upon themselves calumny for having too cosy a relationship with schools.'

[18] Hood (1998a: 80).

[19] But those LEA inspectors found themselves working in a quite different framework, since they came under pressure to win bids for inspection contracts to earn their keep and found the pace of inspection work had become harder, in what used to be a comfortable job (IEE1).

[20] Schedule 2, Part 1, sect. 3 of the Act required the registered inspector to ensure at least one member of each inspection team was a 'layperson' in the sense of having no personal experience in school management or educational provision and 'whose primary function on the team is not that of providing financial or business expertise.'

professional educational world directly into the practice of school inspection (in practice seeming to herald a greater focus on general efficiency (Hustler and Stone 1996)). In addition to lay inspectors and current or former LEA inspectors, OFSTED inspectors were largely drawn from a new breed of recently retired people who had become 'portfolio workers' (either for LEAs or private firms undertaking school inspection) and often lived far away from the schools they inspected. Hence inspection teams did not have the professional cohesiveness of full-time bureaucrats working alongside one another on a permanent basis, and were often together only for the one week of an inspection.

Indeed, as noted in Chapter 3, the post-1992 OFSTED regime of school inspection allows us to explore further the link between RD and regulatory formality in the sense of the disposition to impose sanctions on regulatees. Accordingly, we explored all OFSTED inspections of secondary schools in England from 1993 to mid-1997 (3,599 inspections in all) as a further test of the experience and contact-frequency hypotheses discussed in Chapter 3. Three types of inspection team were included in the analysis—private firms, local-authority teams inspecting schools outside their LEA area, and local authority teams inspecting their own LEA. In this case, we could compare the behaviour of the teams playing on home ground with those playing away, could follow Grabosky and Braithwaite in defining regulatory formality as punitiveness, and could measure it in terms of the propensity of an inspection team to declare a school to be in need of special measures (conventionally regarded as 'failing inspection', a fate experienced by sixty-seven English secondary schools over 1993–7).

This analysis revealed strong support for both the experience and contact-frequency hypotheses. LEA inspection teams were less likely to declare a school to be in need of special measures when dealing with schools in their own area than private inspection teams operating in any area or LEA teams inspecting schools in another area. Contrary to what some interviewees confidently told us about LEA inspection teams being tougher on their own schools than other teams (IEE6), the aggregate figures, summarized in Table 7.1, show a different picture. The overall proportion of secondary schools failed in this survey was 1.9 per cent. But the proportion failed by inspection teams from their own LEAs was

TABLE 7.1. *Secondary schools inspected and 'failed' by different types of OFSTED inspection teams, 1993–1997 (%)*

| Inspections | Own LEA teams (1) | Other LEA teams (2) | All LEA teams ((1) + (2)) (3) | Private teams (4) | Private or other LEA teams ((2) + (4)) (5) | All teams (6) |
|---|---|---|---|---|---|---|
| Inspections conducted | 30.2 | 22.3 | 52.5 | 47.5 | 69.8 | 100 |
| Inspected schools declared failing | 1.3 | 1.8 | 1.5 | 2.4 | 2.2 | 1.9 |

only two-thirds of the percentage of schools failed by teams from private firms or other LEAs.[21] Moreover, we found the failure rate for all LEA inspection teams (taking 'home' and 'away' teams together) was just under two-thirds of the rate for private inspection teams. This analysis suggests that regulatory formality in the sense of punitiveness was likely to be at its highest when RD took the form of a private inspection team dealing with a local-authority school.

These findings only indicate an association between RD and regulatory sanctioning, and do not say anything about the form and direction of the causal link. It may well be that OFSTED tended to commission 'away' teams to conduct inspections of schools it saw as problematic. Indeed, one of our interviewees from an inner-London local authority (IEE10) suggested the authority would have been barred from inspecting its own schools as a contractor for OFSTED because it would not have been expected to be independent when acting as a judge in its own cause and commented that the authority

needed some strong medicine to improve. A major benefit of the OFSTED inspection has forced people who in the past had disliked identifying schools 'failing' to face up to the need for measuring performance and dealing with the difficult tasks such as the removal of incompetent staff.

[21] If we ignore the private firms and focus only on the difference between LEA inspection teams operating at home and away, the result is weaker but still positive, as can be seen from Table 7.1.

So it may well be that the commissioning of an out-of-area inspection team to look at a particular school seen as problematic may in part have been a self-fulfilling prophecy.[22]

Apart from the structural changes intended to increase RD, the style of the post-1992 Chief Inspector of Schools (the head of OFSTED) differed from those of pre-OFSTED Chief Inspectors. The first head of OFSTED was a career academic, Professor Stewart Sutherland, who managed the establishment of OFSTED and adopted a consensual style towards schools. But Sutherland's successor (appointed in 1995 and reappointed by the Blair Government in 1998) was Chris Woodhead, who had been a teacher, then a teacher trainer, and latterly an educational administrator in local government. Given Woodhead's background (of low RD relative to his regulatee charges), it might have been expected that he would have adopted a low-key consensual approach. But in fact Woodhead was outspoken in criticizing poor standards in teaching and educational administration, finding himself condemned by some as putting a political 'spin' on inspection reports (IEE1, IEE6), while others heartily approved his move away from a previous style in which HMI inspections were seen as too soft or too close to the teaching profession (IEE2).

While the structural changes were dramatic, the effect on the day-to-day practice of inspection was harder to assess. A leading study of school inspection concluded that although there had been radical changes in the institutional landscape of inspection in the 1990s, 'the core methodology . . . remains stubbornly familiar' (Wilcox and Gray 1996: 140)—suggesting that what inspectors did on the ground had changed less than working relationships and the spin put on inspection reports. But many claimed the system had moved sharply towards the pressure (or deterrence) rather than the support (or compliance) end of the regulatory continuum (Learmouth 1996: 58–9). Laughlin and Broadbent (1996; 1997: 288) have found varying responses by schools and head teachers to OFSTED inspections (including use of OFSTED inspections by head teachers as a free 'health check' and a means to exert pressure on staff seen as problematic) and they note there have been at-

---

[22] It is possible too that private teams (even if composed of former teachers with a close knowledge of the local area) might have a stronger motivation to be tough than LEA teams, so that institutional motivations might have an effect independent of RD, but our data do not allow us to test for this possibility.

tempts by teachers to protect their traditional professional autonomy by various devices producing formal compliance with inspections without changing teachers' classroom behaviour. But they argue that the evolutionary effect of assessment systems of the OFSTED type is that those who resist are filtered out and less likely to rise to key positions such as headships, reducing the level of resistance over time.

## 5. REGULATORY SANCTIONING AND REWARDS: 'NUKING' THE RECALCITRANT

As noted earlier, the effector elements linked to school regulation and inspection have varied over time, from the nineteenth-century payment-by-results regime linked to inspection to the more advisory style of the mid-twentieth century. What is notable about 1990s changes in school inspection is the development of greater codification of what had once been implicit 'lore' of school inspection together with the adoption of the contracting-out regime,[23] and a return to an ostensible 'reign of terror' approach linked to the addition of 'nuclear weapons' to the regulators' armoury.

As with prisons, discussed in the previous chapter, several behaviour-modification responses were available to OFSTED and other regulators (like the Audit Commission) if they found failures in the schools or LEAs they oversaw. These measures ranged from gentle pressure exerted by the local publication of a mildly critical OFSTED report or by worse-than-average examination figures through to recommendation for a school to close.[24] Many teachers and governors seem to have perceived this array of threats and sanctions as graduated steps towards an unpleasant set of consequences.

Like HMCIP in prisons, OFSTED's central weapon was information and publication, but it was linked to a competitive league-table approach to performance that was much less emphasized in the prison regime. Publishing OFSTED inspection reports (together with examination results and other performance indicators) was

---

[23] Notably in *A Framework for the Inspection of Schools*, published by OFSTED to expand upon the general duties of inspections laid down in the Education (Schools) Act 1992, sect. 9.
[24] See DfEE (1998: 26–7) for a robust official account of the ladder of sanctions.

intended both to improve schools' performance through anticipated reactions by schools before they faced inspection (OFSTED
1995a: 5) and also to influence schools indirectly by better informing parents to make choices about schools. Local newspapers also
commonly published details of inspection reports, creating additional pressures on schools to improve their performance.

Moreover, the OFSTED regime differed from the HMCIP one in
the effector weapons available to regulators if publication of information alone failed to change behaviour. If they judged a school to
be 'at risk' or 'failing', registered inspectors (after notifying the
Chief Inspector and stating in their reports whether or not the Chief
Inspector agreed) could propose special measures to improve the
school. Such proposals had to be reported to the Minister of Education, to whom the LEA and the school concerned were required
to report what steps they intended to take to make the required
improvements. The school had to produce an action plan within
forty days, and would be reinspected a year later to check the
plan was being carried out. LEAs were also empowered under the
Education Act 1993 to suspend delegated financial and management control and, in some circumstances, to appoint additional
governors.

If these measures failed to effect the desired improvements,
'nuclear weapons' were available in the form of central powers
to close schools or impose changes in management. Under the
1992–7 Conservative Government, the Minister of Education had
(and in one case exercised) the power to impose an 'Education
Association'—a board of experts appointed by the Minister—to
take over the running of a school.[25] Moreover, if the imposition
of such an association failed to improve a school (or if the
Association proposed it) the Minister could decide to close a school
altogether.

However, it is one thing to possess nuclear weapons, another to
use them. Up to the time of writing central government had taken
the initiative to close only one school and had approved the closure

[25] If he or she considers that 'the school's action plan or the local authority's
proposals for action are inadequate, [or] where he is not convinced of their ability
to implement their plans effectively or where action goes ahead as set out in the plan,
but monitoring shows it is inadequate or it not being implemented effectively.' The
building up of mid-range sanctions is consistent with the proposals of Ayres and
Braithwaite (1992) for 'responsive regulation'.

of another school claimed to be failing by OFSTED reports. Hackney Downs school in London was closed by the Secretary of State in 1995 after the Education Association appointed by the (then Conservative) government advised closure, having failed to produce substantial improvement. In another case, the Ridings School in Calderdale, which had similarly been heavily criticized by OFSTED inspectors in 1996, new management was installed by the LEA after a brief closure of the school, but in this case the management was deemed to have improved the school sufficiently to avoid closure. A third case, St Richard of Chichester School, was closed by the LEA (London Borough of Camden) in 1997 in the light of a highly critical OFSTED report which chimed with the LEA's own view that the school was 'failing'.

It may be that such a modest deployment of heavy weaponry is all that is sufficient *pour encourager les autres*, but it contrasts notably with the stern zero-tolerance school-closure rhetoric of the OFSTED regime under the Major and Blair Governments. And an armoury consisting only of nuclear weapons without effective lighter armaments for graduated responses can easily lead to 'cliff-edge' chicken games that the nuclear power finds hard to turn to its advantage. Perhaps fearing major political embarrassment in handling substandard schools in Labour-controlled LEAs, the Blair Labour Government in 1997 aimed to add lower-level effectors to the regulatory repertoire in the form of an institutionalized system of early warnings to schools which fell short of failing but had serious weaknesses in management or performance, to be followed by a graduated set of sanctions available to the LEA and Secretary of State.[26]

However, in principle powerful effector sanctions linked with an increasingly formal oversight regime brings a distinctive quality to schools regulation, linked to a political imperative to create a push for higher standards. Similar trends were detectable for other locally delivered services (such as social services, subject in the 1980s and 1990s to greater regulatory oversight by the SSI and the Audit Commission) and in the 'uniformed' services of police and fire, there has long been relatively tight central control over local provision, linked to central inspection. But education, traditionally

---

[26] See DfEE (1997: 29–30) and *School Standards and Framework Bill*, HC Bill 95, Session 1997–8, ch. IV, iii.

more fragmented, seems to have travelled further towards formality and high-level sanctions over the 1990s than other service domains like prisons or social services, and produced both a development of provisions for 'bankruptcy' receivership in the public sector and a style of wholesale contracted-out inspection, neither of which has been adopted in other public-sector oversight regimes.

## 6. ASSESSING THE PERFORMANCE OF PERFORMANCE ASSESSORS

The oversight regime discussed above places heavy stress on formal performance indicators for schools, particularly in the form of examination results. But how can the performance of the inspection system itself be assessed? Is school inspection, like audit as claimed by Power (1997), a domain which is itself unassessable or unauditable?

OFSTED commissioned independent research on the quality of its regime, which showed relatively high—and improving—levels of satisfaction[27] with its inspections. Keele University academics and management consultants Touche Ross concluded 'the thoroughness and care with which OFSTED has approached the [inspection] task is impressive' and 'the data reveals a high degree of professionalism among all those involved in the inspection process' (OFSTED 1995*b*: 3), though they questioned whether inspection led to the maximum possible improvement and queried the effectiveness of the follow-up to inspections (ibid. 5).

Another way of gauging OFSTED's 'value added' is to look at overall changes in school examination results. After all, OFSTED inspections, along with other new regulatory activity (like that of the Schools Curriculum and Assessment Authority, the Audit Commission, and the Teacher Training Agency), were justified that they would lead to improving school performance. And since the government itself used examination results as the key performance indicator, it seems only consistent to judge OFSTED by the same criterion. If OFSTED's regulatory regime improved educational quality, then—other things being equal—there should be a per-

---

[27] Generally, between two-thirds and three-quarters of those involved with inspections viewed them as broadly satisfactory.

TABLE 7.2. *GCE A/AS level examinations in schools in England, 1979–1980 to 1996–1997: young people achieving A/AS levels (%)*

| No. | 1979/80 | 1984/5 | 1989/90 | 1990/1 | 1991/2 | 1992/3 | 1993/4 | 1994/5 | 1995/6 | 1996/7 |
|---|---|---|---|---|---|---|---|---|---|---|
| One or more | 15.5 | 16.5 | 20.4 | 21.8 | 24.4 | 21.3 | 21.8 | 22.6 | 22.7 | 22.3 |
| Two or more | 12.5 | 13.5 | 17.2 | 18.5 | 20.7 | 18.3 | 19.0 | 19.9 | 20.2 | 20.0 |
| Three or more | 8.6 | 9.6 | 12.5 | 13.6 | 15.1 | 13.7 | 14.6 | 15.7 | 16.3 | 16.2 |

*Note*: Sixth-form colleges transferred from the schools sector to further education in 1992–3, thus leading to a once-and-for-all drop in schools' performance.

*Source*: DfEE database of School and College Performance Tables.

ceptible improvement in the examination performance of schools. Indeed, in his 1996–7 annual report, the Chief Inspector of OFSTED asserted: 'The progress I described in my last report continued through 1996–7 . . . GCSE and A level results have also continued to improve' (OFSTED 1998*a*: 12). Accordingly, Table 7.2 above indicates GCE A/AS[28] level examination results for schools in England from 1979–80 to 1996–7.

Table 7.2 suggests there is no examination-based evidence for a radical improvement in schools' performance after 1992–3. For instance, the number of pupils achieving at least one A level in the four years after OFSTED's creation in 1992–3 rose by 1.4 percentage points. By contrast, in the previous two years, the corresponding increase had been 4 percentage points. There were similar, though less pronounced, reductions in the rate of improvement for two and three A levels, and similar trends can be seen for GCSEs. Moreover, a study published in 1998 sought to compare the performance of schools that had been inspected by OFSTED with a control group that had not been inspected. The research, which was heavily criticized by Chief Inspector Woodhead, suggested the 800

[28] In England A level examinations are the main university-entry examinations taken by students in their thirteenth year of schooling. GCSE examinations, typically taken two years earlier, come at the end of the compulsory schooling period.

schools first inspected by OFSTED had GCSE results which had performed in much the same way as a similar-sized group that had not been inspected (*Financial Times*, 6 May 1998).

Perhaps it will take more than four years for the benefits of OFSTED's inspections to work through to individual schools' examination performance. It may be too that other factors shaped the outcomes summarized in Table 7.2, like changing examination standards. But there is no evidence that there was any change in the severity of examination standards between 1992–3 and 1996–7 (indeed, many critics, including OFSTED (1998: 13) itself, suggested standards grew laxer rather than more rigorous) and the government made no allowances for such factors in requiring the publication of school examination performance. All that can be said at this point is that OFSTED's own performance as a 'value-adder' to school education remains to be clearly demonstrated by the measures conventionally used to assess the performance of schools.

## 7. ACCOUNTABILITY

Accountability in education was the subject of extensive debate in the 1980s and 1990s (cf. Day and Klein 1987: 165 ff.). The reforms described earlier meant central government, local authorities, and schools themselves could all be held to account in some way for educational successes and failures. The House of Commons Education Committee (1993) observed 'it is impossible to know which authority to hold accountable for any shortcoming in educational provision or use of resources.' Similar accountability issues arose for the schools' overseers. In what ways were OFSTED, the Audit Commission, and other regulators of schools accountable for their use of public money and for the way they fulfilled their legal obligations?

Both organizations employed relatively open procedures. Most complaints about the system of oversight were directed at the standard of OFSTED inspections (and, on occasion, at local authorities' internal audit) rather than at opaque decision-making. For financial accountability, OFSTED, as a non-Ministerial government department, was formally accountable to the Secretary of

State for Education and Employment, in that its expenditure
(£151m. in 1997–8) came within the DfEE's 'vote' and the
Department's annual report states: 'As a Government department,
OFSTED is subject to normal financial disciplines including gross
running costs control and cash limits' (DfEE 1997: 150, para.
17.11). But OFSTED's head, the Chief Inspector, was also supposed to be independent of Whitehall and that independence
figured large in the rhetoric for re-engineering school inspection in
1992. So to whom was the Chief Inspector accountable in a
broader sense?

OFSTED's own annual reports did not make much effort to
elucidate this question, and its 1996–7 report did not consider
accountability at all. The best its 1993–4 report could do was to
state 'we sought to increase our responsiveness to stakeholders'
views on inspection, and to contribute to the debate on educational
standards and quality' (OFSTED 1995a: 14). The 'stakeholders'
then mentioned included teachers, governors, business and reli-
gious bodies, other government departments and non-government
bodies, registered inspectors, and parents. Two surveys of stakeholders' views had been commissioned during the year.

By contrast, the Audit Commission's 1996 annual report included the following statement:

[O]perating independently of government, the Commission is self-
financing: its income derives entirely from fees charged to local authority
and NHS bodies for audit work and it receives no government grant or
subsidy. A Non-Departmental Public Body sponsored by the Department
of the Environment with the Department of Health and the Welsh Office,
the Commission has agreed a framework document with its sponsoring
departments. (Audit Commission 1996: 4)

And whereas the Audit Commission's report included performance
indicators for its activities and commissioned an independent review of its activities by a former partner of a major accounting firm
(Audit Commission 1996: 2), OFSTED described its performance
largely in terms of its own inspectors' judgements about schools'
progress rather than performance indicators based on objective
data.

Although, as noted in the previous section, OFSTED paid some
attention to assessing the quality of its own inspections, there is no

evidence that accountability was an issue given much thought by OFSTED, and overall accountability for the regulation of schools (particularly by OFSTED) seemed very limited. Given the importance attached by successive Conservative and Labour Ministers to making the secret garden of educational professionals more accountable to the world outside, the schools inspectorate was able to set about its new tasks with very few questions asked about its own answerability.[29]

## 8. CONCLUSIONS

In contrast to prisons, discussed in the last chapter, schools regulators in England did not lack for formal effector powers to modify the behaviour of their charges. Schools regulation was an ever-changing and multi-organizational world, and a dramatic instance of the resurgence of the Chadwickian approach to central regulation of local services as discussed in Chapter 5. Successive governments proclaimed inspection to be the key to improving school standards. They sharply increased the resources invested in central oversight, mixed major elements of competition with oversight in the detector regime, aimed to increase RD between regulator and regulatee, and added to the regulators' effector capacity by introducing new 'nuclear weapons' in the armoury of sanctions against schools and LEAs found to be wanting—though those weapons were used much more sparingly than the uncompromising rhetoric would suggest.

The pressure to keep turning the regulatory screw seems unlikely to diminish in the short term. Indeed, when this chapter was being drafted the regulatory changes initiated by the Conservatives in the 1980s and 1990s were being extended and entrenched by the Blair Labour government, with the exception of the 'regulatory competition' embodied in the ability of schools to opt out of LEA regulation into the FAS regime. But whether the Chadwickian approach of 'reign-of-terror' regulation will self-destruct in the longer term, as it did in the nineteenth century, is harder to say. Clear evidence

---

[29] At least, until the summer of 1998 when OFSTED appointed a Complaints Adjudicator to handle complaints made against itself (OFSTED 1998*b*). But the Adjudicator could not hear appeals against inspection judgements, only against the handling of complaints by Registered and Team Inspectors.

of its benefits in terms of examination performance remains to be produced, and underlying procedure at the 'chalk face' of inspections seems to have changed less than the surrounding institutional arrangements and rhetorical packaging.

# 8

# Eurocratic Regulation

> Issues can be taken out of the bureaucratic and into the inter-
> governmental-interinstitutional bargaining arena far more eas-
> ily in the European Union than they can be moved out of the
> bureaucratic arena in most member states.
>
> E. Page, *People Who Run Europe*, 1997

This chapter examines EU[1] oversight of UK public-sector activity, over compliance with EU norms and financial rules. Such oversight is central to the operation of the EU, because the administration of EU programmes largely works through 'indirect rule' (Daintith 1995), relying on the member states to turn its 'wholesale' policy instruments (rules and money) into 'retail' programme implementation—transposing EU legislation into national law, enforcing law, and managing the major EU spending programmes for agriculture, social provision, and regional development (cf. Lenaerts 1993; Maher 1996; Peterson 1997).[2] Given that central feature of the EU, a tension between 'light rein' and Chadwickian approaches to oversight can hardly be avoided, and regulators have perforce to mix oversight with a heavy dose of mutuality in their director, detector, and effector activities. Competition and contrived randomness seemed to be at best minor elements of the regime.

Developments in EU oversight do not easily fit either the mirror-

---

[1] For convenience we refer to institutions of the European Union as 'EU' through-out, though strictly speaking most of the regulatory activity described in this chapter falls within the narrower European Community jurisdiction. References in the EC Treaty are to Treaty articles as they were numbered in 1997 prior to the major renumbering exercise required by the Amsterdam Treaty 1997, should the Treaty be ratified.

[2] Proposals for free-standing EU-level regulatory agencies, e.g. in telecommunications and competition policy, have been contentious, raising the spectre of bureaucracies even more remote and less accountable than the Commission (Laudati 1996).

image or double whammy patterns of central direction and arm's-length regulation discussed in earlier chapters because of the absence of any 'direct-rule' tradition. But in many cases EU oversight added an extra dimension to regulatory regimes within member states, for example in audit and procurement control. And EU oversight presented a distinct pattern of regulatory formality, relational distance, and institutional development. Three features are worth highlighting.

First, while there had been a gradual movement towards relatively autonomous public-sector regulators at EU level, notably the European Court of Auditors and the European Ombudsman, such institutions were less developed than their national-state equivalents. There was little equivalence to the trend observed within the UK to create free-standing overseers of the public sector, relatively detached from service delivery or general policy-making. In practice most EU oversight was by subunits of the European Commission which combined policy and regulatory functions, with narrow regulatory objectives tending to be displaced by broader strategic and political objectives.

Second, in contrast to much regulation inside government at the domestic level, EU oversight of the public sector stressed self-regulation by member states over compliance with EU obligations. That approach was necessitated by sharp resource limits, meaning the EU's small oversight capacity needed to focus on promoting and monitoring domestic controls while concentrating regulatory resources on those parts of member-state administration of EU programmes judged to constitute the highest risk of mismanagement and abuse.

A third and related feature of EU oversight regimes was a high degree of formality in the sense both of rule-boundedness and legal sanctions, mitigated by political brokering and 'linkage politics' at the top (Page 1997: 156). As the discussion of RD in Chapter 3 would lead us to expect, the formality of the EU oversight culture reflected a lack of common professional or social backgrounds between EU regulators and member-state governments, and was partly produced by limited trust between the two institutional levels. Greater willingness to define relations in legal duties and powers, and to litigate over disputed powers or non-compliance, in principle created a hierarchy of sanctions that could support effective self-regulation by member states. But political factors militated against that outcome and EU oversight of member-state activity in domains like public procurement and subsidies to business tended to increase 'juridification' of regulation inside government at the domestic level.

## 1. REGULATORY INSTITUTIONS

EU 'indirect rule' over member-state public authorities took two main forms. One was oversight of general compliance with Treaty and other EU obligations (Figure 8.1). Such obligations included compliance with the principle of equality of treatment (Article 119 EC), competition rules (Articles 85–94 EC) and single-market principles contained both in the Treaties and in secondary legislation

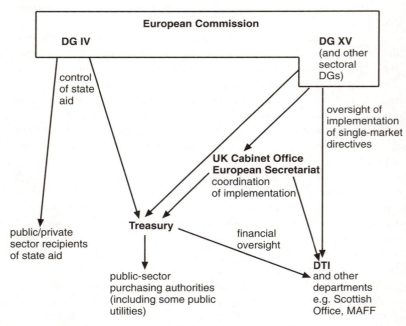

Fig. 8.1. EU oversight of UK public bodies I: implementation of treaty obligations and directives

(Articles 30–6, 100A), as well as the general principle of loyalty to the Union (Article 5 EC).

The second main form of EU oversight of member-state public authorities was financial (Figure 8.2). Though the EU was directly responsible for a large budget, including the administrative costs of its own institutions and programmes for research and development, about 80 per cent of its annual budget consisted of 'indirect' expenditure, managed within the member states. Out of total expenditure in 1995 of more than 66 billion ecu, more than 34 billion ecu was devoted to the Common Agricultural Policy and more than 19 billion to structural operations (linked with regional, social, and agricultural policies), both of which consisted mainly of indirect expenditure (European Commission 1996*b*: 82–3). This feature of EU administration produced an elaborate web of financial oversight of expenditure in the member states both by public authorities and by other actors like farmers and NGOs, on top of the apparatus of financial control and audit within each member state.

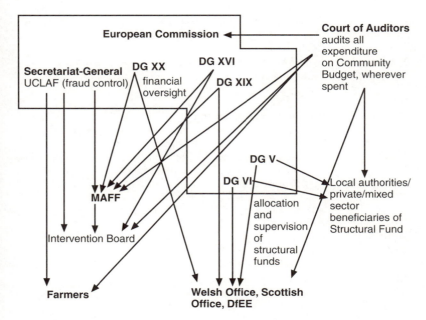

Fig. 8.2. EU oversight of UK public bodies II: financial oversight

## (a) *Hybrid EU regulation*

As noted earlier, most EU oversight of member states was conducted by subunits of the Commission, not free-standing regulators. Moreover, in most Commission Directorates-General enforcement and compliance formed only a small part of the work. The Commission had originally been established as a policy-making institution rather than as a management/oversight body,

TABLE 8.1. *European Commission Directorates-General in 1997*

| DG Number | Responsibilities |
| --- | --- |
| I | External Relations: Commercial Policy and Relations with North America, the Far East, Australia, and New Zealand |
| IA | External Relations: Europe and the New Independent States, Common Foreign and Security Policy, and External Missions |
| IB | External Relations: Southern Mediterranean, Middle and Near East, Latin America, South and South-East Asia, and North–South Cooperation |
| II | Economic and Financial Affairs |
| III | Industry |
| IV | Competition |
| V | Employment, Industrial Relations, and Social Affairs |
| VI | Agriculture |
| VII | Transport |
| VIII | Development |
| IX | Personnel and Administration |
| X | Information, Communication, Culture, Audiovisual |
| XI | Environment, Nuclear Safety, and Civil Protection |
| XII | Science, Research and Development Joint Research Centre |
| XIII | Telecommunications, Information Market, and Exploitation of Research |
| XIV | Fisheries |
| XV | Internal Market and Financial Services |
| XVI | Regional Policies and Cohesion |
| XVII | Energy |
| XIX | Budgets |
| XX | Financial Control |
| XXI | Customs and Indirect Taxation |
| XXII | Education, Training, and Youth |
| XXIII | Enterprise Policy, Distributive Trades, Tourism, and Cooperatives |
| XXIV | Consumer Policy and Consumer Health Protection |

and its capacity to function as a regulator was consequently limited (Edsberg 1994: 11; Laffan 1997). The effectiveness of its regulatory powers also varied across policy domains, with considerable scope for tension among competing overseers (Frazer 1995).

The unit with the most developed regulatory apparatus was DG IV, which had powers of rule-making, monitoring, and enforcement and could apply sanctions to both private and public actors over state aid and public monopolies (legally, DG IV's regulatory powers were exercised through the Commission as a whole: Wilks and McGowan (1996: 225–6)).[3] Indeed, the Commission's regulatory power over member-states' bureaucracies grew markedly in the 1980s as it 'shifted the emphasis in competition law away from its traditional concerns with private conduct and toward the problem of government interference with the competitive process' (Gerber 1994: 137–8).

For other EU regulatory domains, oversight was more mixed and fragmented and the mix of policy and enforcement functions was more evident, though with some trends towards greater institutional separation inside the Commission. For instance, a subunit of DG XV monitored the UK's application of the EU procurement regime, devoting about 75 per cent of its time to oversight and about a quarter to policy initiatives. In exercising such oversight, Commission officials had to deal with the same UK Treasury staff who were involved in EU negotiations over policy changes, and the desire to maintain good relations for policy-making tempered the use of formal enforcement powers (IEU3).[4]

For financial oversight, like other domains of EU regulation, the Commission was the central actor. But for agricultural and structural funds oversight was central to the activity of the DGs concerned (funder-regulators, often called 'spending departments' in EU-speak), meaning less risk of oversight being displaced by other strategic objectives. Financial oversight was also 'purer' because two DGs were devoted exclusively to budgetary oversight and financial control (DGs XIX and XX respectively). Under the terms of the Financial Regulation the Financial Controller had an

[3] The Treaty makes it clear these rules apply as much to public as to private undertakings (Art. 90(1)), and empowers the Commission to issue directives without recourse to the other institutions (Council of Ministers and Parliament) which would be needed for the more common single market (Art. 100A) directives (Art. 90(3) EC). See Scott 1996*b*.
[4] Cf. Williams (1995: 6), who makes a similar observation about oversight of member states' compliance with EU environmental law obligations by DG XI.

independence unique among Commission Directors-General, since neither the Commissioner responsible for financial control nor the Commission as a whole could issue instructions to her (Harden *et al.* 1995: 606). In addition, the establishment in 1988 of a specialized 'fraud squad', the fraud coordination unit (known by its French acronym UCLAF) within the General Secretariat of the Commission, provided for a degree of institutional and physical separation between oversight of substantive programmes and control of fraud (Ruimschotel 1994: 334).

The only fully distinct EU regulator overseeing member states' compliance with Union obligations was the Court of Auditors, based in Luxembourg.[5] The Court's members were appointed from each member state, on judicial-type fixed-term tenure. The Court focused mainly on 'regularity audits' of EU budget expenditure, together with some special studies (loosely equivalent to UK value-for-money audit), to provide assurance to the Parliament that money had been properly spent (Harden *et al.* 1995). The Court's role was heavily oriented towards detection, since it had no enforcement or sanctioning powers and was only entitled to be consulted on proposals to change the financial regulations put forward by the Commission and passed by the Council of Ministers. The Parliament's financial oversight was carried out chiefly through its Budget Committee and Budgetary Control Committee. Hence EU financial oversight displayed institutional overlap and redundancy both at the Union level and in coordination with financial overseers at member-state level.

## (b) *UK adaptation*

EU membership required the UK to modify its own national administration (Wessels and Rometsch 1996: 351). The UK's tradition of centralization is said to have aided both participation in policy-making and implementation (Dowding 1995: 141). Coordination took place through the European Secretariat, established on entry into the EU in 1973 and located in the Cabinet Office at the heart of the core executive (Bender 1991: 16; Dowding 1995: 129–30). The European Secretariat combined policy and regulatory functions, with the former often taking precedence over the latter.

---

[5] The other most notable free-standing EU regulator, the European Ombudsman, established in 1995, oversees only other EU institutions, not member states.

Regulation inside UK government adapted to EU membership in several ways. The Treasury changed its expenditure controls by adopting the EUROPES public-spending-control regime, requiring departments in receipt of Community funds to cut equivalent sums from their own domestic budgets (Dowding 1995: 139; Albert-Broulhac 1998: 223). Public-sector regulation was also modified by establishing European sections in central-government departments and European officers in local authorities (Snyder 1995: 69). In addition to its Central Unit on Procurement (seeking to spread best practice) the Treasury had a Procurement Policy Unit, which both attempted to shape EU policy and implemented EU law through statutory instruments. The Department for Education and Employment had a European Social Fund (ESF) Unit to coordinate the UK receipt of ESF funding. The Unit's Verification and Audit Section cooperated with EU regulators in DG V (Social Policy), DG XX (Financial Control), and the Court of Auditors.

The UK's implementation of the EU procurement regime shows how more flexible regulatory models can be squeezed out as member states need to use formal legal instruments to demonstrate compliance with EC norms in place of administrative measures or self-regulatory instruments that might have been used for domestic regulation (Wilks 1996: 547). At first the UK, like some other member states, implemented EU procurement rules by administrative circulars (Treasury guidelines) rather than formal legal instruments (Fernandez-Martin 1996: 97–9). But hostility to this implementation style, and concerns that it was not demonstrably effective, nor capable of entitling third parties adversely affected by breach of the rules to sue for damages, led administrative measures to be displaced by statutory implementation in the UK (ibid. 105).

## 2. REGULATORY TECHNIQUE

As noted earlier, EU overseers of member states did not have enough resources for extensive 'police patrol' regulation (McCubbins and Schwarz 1984), though they had a wide array of formal sanctions. Hence they aimed to encourage member states to develop effective domestic regulation to ensure compliance with EU obligations (which can be seen as self-regulation from an EU perspective), backing that approach up with a limited amount of independent detector activity and the application of sanctions to member states where the incentives to self-regulate were too weak.

Techniques for supporting or triggering self-regulation by member states included improving the capacities of domestic institutions—for example by publishing guidance on the application of EU rules, requiring member states to make private remedies available for breach, giving information to member-state institutions as a basis for enforcement, and promoting diffusion of oversight authority, thereby reducing the risk of collusion or capture. A second approach was to impose obligations to provide information to EU institutions, such as mandatory reporting of breaches of EU rules, and of measures taken to comply with EU Directives. A third approach was selective checking on member-state domestic oversight, for instance through inspection or on-the-spot checks.

An example of the last approach was checking of member states' financial controls. According to a Commission official, such activity

keeps the member states up to the work, and it gives us knowledge of what's happening. But it is supplementary to the effort under the regulations which the member states are required to organize. We would regard the task as being essentially one of trying to ensure that they organize themselves well. (IEU11)

Each form of financial oversight was subject to on-the-spot checks. For the structural funds initial responsibility for such checking lay with the financial controller in the responsible DG, and might involve several financial controllers where funding programmes drew on more than one of the structural funds (like the European Social Fund (ESF) and the European Regional Development Fund (ERDF)). For the ESF, DG V (the social affairs DG) audited expenditure within member states through visits generally lasting about a week and following the money from the central administration to local or regional intermediaries and thence to the funds' ultimate beneficiaries (IEU4).

For the EDRF, spot checks by DG XVI (the regional policy DG) were planned and announced well in advance. In contrast with unscheduled inspections of ESF expenditure made by DG V together with UCLAF (European Commission 1997a: 108), unannounced visits were never made. The aim was not to inspect every aspect of spending, but to encourage the creation or maintenance of effective domestic control. Commission staff selected a group of projects and then asked for all the relevant documents. 'And we also check physically what's going on to make sure the motorway is there, and so on' (IEU11).[6] In addition DG XX, which had general responsibility for financial oversight, carried out its own spot checks together with national audit institutions (IEU4) and sometimes with officials from the DG responsible for the initial financial control (European Commission 1997a: 109).

The EU's general aim was to ensure its own interests were protected with the same rigour as domestic interests. For fraud the European Community Treaty required member states to take the same measures to protect Community financial interests as they did for their own (Article 209a EC) and there was further pressure to raise the stakes by requiring the same levels of protection to be applied in all member states.[7] The EU also subsidized member states' activities to prevent and detect EU fraud, devoting 94 per cent of its anti-fraud funds to such subsidies in 1993 (European Parliament, Written Questions E-1964/94).

As noted earlier, member states were often obliged to report certain actions to the Commission. For instance, most single-market directives required each member state to report what it had done to put the new rules into effect, including the text of the implementing measures. Commission staff could then assess whether such measures complied with the terms of the Directive and take action if they did not. Likewise for the structural funds, the Coordination Regulation required member states to submit details of their financial control and management systems.[8] And all aid given by member states to undertakings had to be reported to the Commission, for DG IV to assess whether the aid was permitted under the Treaty or the Commission's various interpretive guidelines (Article 93(3) EC). But the EU's power to produce regulations

---

[6] The visit was followed by a debriefing meeting with national officials giving preliminary conclusions, a final report going to both the Financial Controller (DG XX) and the EU Court of Auditors, and a formal letter from DG XVI summarizing conclusions and suggesting improvements. There was no formal follow-up, though discovery of similar problems on a subsequent visit might lead to financial sanctions (IEU11).

[7] These measures were directed against the 'tacit assumption that fraud against the Community occurs on a bigger scale than fraud against the member states' (Ruimschotel 1994: 322).

[8] Council Regulation 2082/93 OJ 1993 L/21 Art. 23.

setting out procedures for regulating state aid (Article 94) had not been used, meaning there was no authoritative guidance on which categories of aid had to be reported.[9]

Sometimes the Commission sought to encourage member states to establish new or more effective regulatory institutions. For instance, a 1996 Commission Green Paper on procurement suggested all member states should follow the Swedish model of a formal free-standing procurement regulatory authority (European Commission 1996c: 17). Such an approach was foreign to the UK, where the Treasury's Central Unit on Procurement (CUP) did not see itself as a regulator, but rather a disseminator of best practice and appeared (from its published reports) to be more preoccupied with promotion of value for money in public purchasing than compliance with EU rules (Treasury 1996a: 1). The Treasury's Procurement Policy Division also saw its task as justifying procurement rules by reference to UK rather than EU policy (I8).[10]

In addition to stimulating self-regulation, some detector activity by EU institutions supported direct enforcement of Union obligations. With public procurement the Commission gathered its own information to enforce the rules, and had been active in monitoring since the single-market programme of the mid-1980s made procurement regulation more central to the Commission's activities (Fernandez-Martin 1996: 16). For instance, newspaper reports of contracts were cross-checked against the EU's *Official Journal*, to ensure national purchasing authorities had advertised tenders in the *Official Journal*. The other main source of information was complaints by disappointed potential contractors. DG XV investigated every such complaint, but also encouraged complainants to seek damages on their own behalf through private actions (IEU3).[11]

The mission of UCLAF (the Commission's fraud unit) was both

---

[9] Art. 94 anticipates the adoption of regulations similar in function to Regulation 17 of 1962, which set down the procedures for the Commission to monitor and enforce competition law, together with a system of penalties for non-compliance. Harlow (1996) criticizes the EU's failure to develop such regulations, though at the time of writing the EU Commission has talked of such a development.

[10] The NAO had a greater enforcement role over procurement, but even there domestic concern with value for money in public purchasing did not always chime with the EU procurement regime (I11).

[11] A ten-month study in 1990–1 revealed about 90% of procurement-related complaints handled by the Commission originated with its own monitoring programmes, and about 10% from individual grievances (Fernandez-Martin 1996: 171, n. 75).

to exercise direct oversight and to stimulate member states into checking fraud on the EU budget. The Commission's DGs or the Court of Auditors might call in UCLAF to handle suspected fraud, usually in cooperation with the DG with the relevant expertise.[12] UCLAF obtained information from member-state authorities (as part of their obligation to report irregularities and fraud) as well as from the EU Court of Auditors and other parts of the Commission. It also used paid informers, and had a freephone number throughout the Union for provision of information on fraud (European Commission 1997b: 20). In the UK, it had regular contact not only with the Treasury but also with HM Customs and Excise, the National Criminal Investigations Service, the NAO, the Department of Trade and Industry, and the Intervention Board Executive Agency, a complex of agencies forming part of a cross-national 'anti-fraud control community' (Levy 1994: 74).

However, such an information-gathering and exchanging community seemed to be the exception, not the rule. There was no evidence of a parallel for general audit work. The way the EU Court of Auditors (ECA) duplicated the work of both member-state and Commission auditors reflected a lack of trust. As a separate institution the ECA was not accountable to the Commission and its approach contrasted with that adopted in many parts of the Commission. In particular, it worked through sampling across each part of the EU budget (in contrast to the comprehensive certification of each account, as practised by the UK's NAO) and did not attempt to concentrate on high risks. By contrast, DG XX, with overall responsibility for controlling the EU budget, made extensive use of risk analysis, based on historical analysis of problems arising in particular sectors (IEU 9), and the same went for the programme of visits to member states within DG XVI (IEU11).

Mesh between the ECA and national audit institutions (NAIs) was also variable. The ECA was entitled to follow the Union budget from the Commission to its ultimate recipients, meaning that its jurisdiction was more extensive than that of the UK's NAO, which had no general power to examine the expenditure of public funds by non-State bodies (unless such power was written into particular contracts). That created an opportunity for the NAO to widen its

---

[12] UCLAF's inquiry missions, numbering about 300 a year, were generally targeted to suspected cases of fraud, though its inquiries covered expenditure of EU funds outside the Union, and tax fraud as well as expenditure fraud.

role and power within the UK by securing an agreement for NAO staff to accompany ECA officials as agents of the European Commission on visits to beneficiaries of EU funds (IEU5).[13] But the ECA staff we talked to thought national audit bodies were generally too busy to cooperate to the extent of including in their audits questions the Court would want asked (IEU7), and according to some sources, differences were so great as to render NAO audit work of little use to the ECA and vice versa (Levy 1994: 72–3). The view that cooperation between NAIs and the Court was poor is supported by evidence that Court staff tended to assume that NAIs would hide details of infractions by member-state bodies from the Court, although some NAIs seemed to be trusted more than others (IEU7).[14]

## 3. REGULATORY SANCTIONS

Unlike much regulation inside the Whitehall village (as discussed in Chapter 4), most EU oversight provided for formal sanctions against the member states. But like many of the domestic overseers described in previous chapters, EU regulators often arrayed their responses into a hierarchical order. The higher-level sanctions were used only infrequently, and through a political process rather than any automatic escalator from the lower-level ones.

### (a) *The structural funds*

In responding to infractions of structural fund rules, Commission officials were constrained by the dictates of a somewhat legalistic bureaucracy, and the influence of the European Court of Auditors,

---

[13] The ECA worked not just with the NAO but also with other audit bodies like the Scottish Accounts Commission, and with departments sponsoring Community programmes.

[14] The European Parliament's Budgetary Control Committee (BCC) was developing a role in enforcing financial discipline, but it fell well short of the support given to NAO by the UK's Public Accounts Committee. BCC's hearings were often attended by officials from DG XIX, not the officials directly responsible for the expenditure, meaning BCC's potential for disciplining individual Commission officials was more limited than that of the PAC (IEU9). BCC's work focused mainly on the Commission rather than member states, partly because of distrust of the Commission and partly because the Commission was seen as 'easier to regulate' (IEU12).

which oversaw the Commission's enforcement activity. Hence Commission officials might take a tough enforcement line on infractions that they saw as trivial (IEU11), such as spending that was 'ineligible' because it slightly exceeded the maximum percentage of EU funding to be spent on some element of a project like acquiring property. And where infractions were attributed to ignorance of the rules, there was limited discretion to 'educate' rather than enforce strictly, though, as noted earlier, there might be separate measures to improve the capacity of member-state governments and intermediaries to meet EU requirements (IEU4).

Some Commission officials administering the various structural funds showed signs of distrust of member-state authorities. One said the amount of time devoted to regulation was disproportionate

[I]n the sense that you would think that if you share objectives, and bearing in mind that there are a million ways of doing these things, it ought to be much more easy to share an agreement on the ways in which things would be done. But . . . because we are trying to pursue a particular policy and other people are trying to grab European regional policy funding for their own particular purposes, there is a constant task to be done in persuading people. (IEU1)

The risks of fraud were not uniform for all 'indirect expenditure' from the EU budget. An important feature of the structural funds was the 'additionality' principle, according to which EU funding had to be supported by 30 per cent or more of member state's own money. This principle, familiar in grant administration in many other contexts, was intended to reduce the risk of fraud by ensuring member-state governments had a strong interest in looking after their own funds, resulting in close financial oversight. By contrast, much of the agricultural spending within the Common Agricultural Policy, administered in the UK by the Intervention Board, consisted of 100 per cent grants from EU funds, and involved few actors, thus greatly increasing the risk of fraud.

The Commission had formal powers to reduce, suspend, or withdraw funds for non-compliance (Council Regulation 208/93 OJ 1993 L/21 Art. 24). But, following the 'hierarchy-of-sanctions' approach, where Commission officials doubted the eligibility of a particular project for funding, the first step was to inform the sponsoring department and engage in discussion, giving member states an opportunity to secure reallocation of EU funds to other projects, an option not available after completion of the programme.[15] Such conduct, though time-consuming for Commission staff, helped to build trust with regulatees. If an ineligible project was proceeded with, the Commission would ask the member state not to declare expenditure on that project. But formal sanctions were rarely used, and indeed the Court of Auditors criticized DG VI for not using its powers to disallow expenditure often enough (Levy 1994: 73).

Nevertheless, the power to disallow expenditure meant Commission scrutiny of expenditure was regarded by national bureaucrats with greater trepidation than NAO scrutiny. On one occasion DG XVI discovered systematic and serious eligibility errors and made a 'net correction' to a whole programme, cutting the total funds available. The Commission's legal capacity to make such corrections was contested by some member states (EUI11), since net corrections are reserved for cases of 'significant failure within the member state to meet the obligations under Article 23(1)'. An increase in the use of formal sanctions by DG V in the mid-1990s was attributed to participation by a wider range of institutional players with less knowledge of the EU requirements, following the introduction of broader partnership arrangements (IEU4).

For the ERDF most cases of withdrawal of money from the UK on grounds of ineligibility were responses to initiatives by the UK government itself, informing the Commission of an infraction and requesting action (IEU1). Thus Commission funding sanctions have often been used by the UK government to bolster its own objectives. One major exception was a dispute between the UK and the Commission over RECHAR, a Community programme of aid for restructuring coalfield areas affected by pit closures. When the UK government failed to provide extra funds to local authorities to take part in the programme, the Commission withheld over £100m. in grants on the grounds that the UK had failed to meet the additionality criterion. Only with a general election imminent in 1992 did the British government announce it would

---

[15] e.g. the issue might be scheduled for discussion at a meeting of the monitoring committee of the relevant programme which involved both member-state and Commission representatives and met at least twice a year (European Commission 1997a: 15; IEU1, IEU4), or if uncertain over eligibility, Commission officials might take the matter back to Brussels seeking 'the guidance of . . . superiors' (IEU1).

comply, allowing the Commission to release the funds (Rhodes 1997: 153–4).

A combination of political sensitivity and limited powers checked the capacity of the Court of Auditors to operate as a free-standing regulator. Rather it functioned chiefly to supply information to other overseers, notably the Commission, but also NAIs, and to provide some degree of parliamentary accountability for the Commission (Pollitt and Summa 1997: 331).[16] The Court had few formal 'effector' sanctions, and relied on the power of reporting to secure behaviour modification. Some of its reports were published, including its annual report, its *Declaration d'Assurance* to the Parliament and some of its special reports. But it also reported privately through 'sector letters' to bodies it had audited. Such letters were sent to the NAI of the member state and, though formally consisting only of advice, might strengthen the NAI's hand.[17]

### (b) *Implementation of directives*

The Commission's formal enforcement powers over the implementation of EU directives by member states were exercised within a more general political context of negotiating new initiatives as well as compliance with existing obligations. There were five stages in formal proceedings under Article 169 EC to enforce member-state obligations (infringement proceedings), and the use of this provision had dramatically increased since 1978 (Mendrinou 1996: 2). The process started with a complaint (which might come from the Commission itself).[18] A formal letter then went to the member state inviting observations on the complaint, followed by a reasoned opinion on the complaint from the Commission. The fourth stage

---

[16] Harden *et al.* (1995: 624–5) note tension between the Parliament's Budgetary Control Committee and the Court: 'In the view of the Committee, the Court should be no more than a technical adjunct to its own work rather than a free-standing body with its own role in the institutional balance of the Union.'

[17] The letters also went both to DG XIX (budgetary control) and the part of the Commission responsible for oversight of the sector concerned (Harden *et al.* 1995: 618).

[18] In 1997 the European Ombudsman concluded that the Commission had failed on several occasions to keep complainants informed of the progress of complaints (European Ombudsman 1997: 59–73). Procedural changes following this finding are likely to increase the formality of the early stages of Art. 169 infringement proceedings.

was judicial proceedings against the member-state government before the European Court of Justice, which had the power to condemn member states for infringing Treaty obligations. In 1991 the Commission succeeded in securing a fifth stage (introduced in the Maastricht Treaty), under which it could seek a fine against a member-state condemned by the Court, in subsequent proceedings (Article 171(2) EC; Snyder 1995: 57).

Within this five-stage enforcement procedure most cases were settled after the second stage and few reached the judicial stages. Of 1,209 cases initiated by the Commission against member states in 1993, over 60 per cent were resolved after receipt of a letter of formal notice, 30 per cent were settled by the issue of a reasoned opinion, only 6 per cent were referred to the Court of Justice, and less than 1 per cent reached judgment. In the latter category—eight cases in all—the Commission was successful in seven (European Commission 1996a: 113). The long-run trend seemed to be for more cases to be settled after the issue of a formal notice, thus reducing the importance of the 'hidden jurisprudence' of the Commission's reasoned opinions (Snyder 1995: 63; Mendrinou 1996: 2). Snyder (ibid. 62) suggested infringement disputes were increasingly being resolved by negotiation, either within the Committee of Permanent Representatives of the member states (COREPER) or in package deal meetings between the Commission and member-state governments, meaning specific legal obligations formed only a part of a larger negotiating picture.

Infringement proceedings involving the UK tended to be resolved at an earlier stage than applied to the EU as a whole; for instance, in 1993 75 per cent of cases were terminated after the issue of letters of formal notice. Some other member states had an even larger proportion of cases resolved at this early stage (like Denmark, with 90 per cent in 1993), but the general pattern suggests a level of compliance culture within the UK government higher than that in many other member states (cf. Mendrinou 1996: 4–6), perhaps enhanced by the hitherto centralized nature of British government which meant disputes among different levels of government were rarely able to spill over into infringement proceedings.

Over procurement, member states had to transpose Community directives into domestic law and then enforce the legislation. Infractions by public purchasing authorities included failure to transpose, incomplete transposition, and disregard for the substantive rules (Fernandez-Martin 1996: 153). The last was the commonest form of non-compliance encountered by DG XV, which took a particularly serious view of failure to advertise tender details in the *Official Journal*, since that was seen as undermining the whole procurement regime (IEU3). Other infringements by purchasing authorities included: bypassing standard procedures by excessive use of negotiated procedures, intended to be used only in exceptional circumstances like extreme time pressure; failing to publish all the particulars required in the *Official Journal* notice; confusing the criteria applicable to checking the suitability of candidates with those required for award of contracts; and breach of more general EU principles like 'non-discrimination, equality of treatment, transparency, and mutual recognition' (European Commission 1996c: 9–12).

Following standard bureaucratic behaviour patterns, the Commission directed most of its enforcement activity to infringements it could readily detect. Hence transposition failures figured large, as well as contracting failures drawn to the Commission's attention through the publicity they attracted (Fernandez-Martin 1996: 153). With infringements in contract award procedures the Commission gave most attention to contracts that had not yet been awarded, since at that stage the problem was easier to remedy and the Commission could litigate to suspend contract award procedures (Armstrong and Bulmer 1998: 139). Cases of continuing non-compliance, particularly failure to transpose Directives, were brought to 'package meetings' held between DG XV and the relevant government departments involved with single-market matters (in the UK, the Treasury for procurement and the DTI for most single-market legislation). Most issues were resolved before or at such meetings (IEU3).

Officially, the Commission's enforcement policy was 'the systematic initiation of Article 169 EC proceedings against any known alleged violation and the encouragement of private persons and individuals to address complaints to the Commission's services' (Fernandez-Martin 1996: 25). But for complaints about non-compliance by purchasing authorities these powers were not in fact used frequently (IEU3), since 'experience has demonstrated that the procedures provided for under Article 169 of the EC Treaty are not capable of ensuring rapid and effective redress'

(European Commission 1996c: 16). Accordingly the Commission had suggested it be given direct administrative enforcement powers against purchasing authorities, similar to its powers for competition law under Regulation (EEC) 17/62 (European Commission 1996c: 16).[19] In a climate where subsidiarity is heavily invoked, member states are unlikely to agree to such an enhancement of Commission enforcement powers, but the position was different where EU expenditures were involved, since direct enforcement powers could be invoked in such cases, as will be shown below.

### (c) *State aid*

For state aid to undertakings the main sanction for substantive breach of the EU rules was the requirement that aid granted illegally should be repaid by the recipient to the state. But the Commission aimed to use the advance notification requirements on member states proposing to grant aid to clarify member-state obligations before any aid was granted. For example, when the UK government privatized the Rover car company, selling it to the privatized British Aerospace, it notified details of a planned cash injection of £547m. into Rover ahead of the sale. The Commission required this sum to be cut by £331m. When an *ex post* scrutiny of the sale by the UK's NAO showed the UK government had paid more than that sum to British Aerospace over the deal, the Commission required British Aerospace to repay £44.4m. to the UK government.[20] This example shows interlocking oversight activity at EU and national-government level, with *ex ante* Commission scrutiny followed by *ex post* scrutiny by the National Audit Office, revealing failures to follow the requirements of the prior scrutiny, that in turn led the Commission to impose sanctions.[21]

---

[19] Similar suggestions have been made for financial controls, but have not been acted on (Sherlock and Harding 1991: 34).

[20] Representing the additional payments plus a partial reflection of additional tax concessions. The Commission did not require any repayment to reflect the NAO's view that Rover had been sold to British Aerospace at much less than its market value, but 'hinted that it would in future be unsympathetic to closed bids as part of a privatization' (Graham and Prosser 1991: 126–8).

[21] This decision was later annulled by the ECJ on procedural grounds—Case 294/90, *British Aerospace plc and Rover Group Holdings plc* v. *EC Commission* (1992) I—ECR 493.

## (d) *Cross-sanctioning*

The Commission could also respond to non-compliance with EU norms by 'cross-sanctioning' (Hood 1986: 79), involving mutual support by different DGs. For example, UCLAF routinely informed the relevant DG when it discovered fraud in spending programmes, finding sanctions exercised within particular spending programmes to be frequently more effective than formal measures against member states for inadequate fraud-control systems (IEU10).

Other opportunities for cross-sanctioning included the possibility of applying financial sanctions for failure to follow environmental rules, for example over environmental impact assessment, which breached funding conditions (IEU11) and failure to follow procurement rules. Financial controllers in DG XX and the DGs responsible for the structural funds included in their 'regularity' checklists items for compliance with environmental principles, procurement rules, and other EU norms (IEU9). For procurement, the rules were precise enough to make checks by other parts of the Commission straightforward. Moreover, against the requirement of the structural funds regulations that all co-financed expenditure respect relevant EU policies,[22] DG XV cooperated closely with the DGs responsible for the structural funds, and monitored expenditure from those funds to ensure procurement rules were followed as contracts were issued. If it found non-compliance, DG XV routinely informed the responsible DG (DG V or DG XVI), which could then withhold the relevant funds (IEU3; European Commission 1996c: 35–6).

In principle, cross-sanctioning of this type could be applied to other matters like compliance with equality norms, though such norms are more difficult to translate into standard tick-the-box checking methods. EU financial control was not limited to regularity in a narrow sense; rather, it sought to ensure spending complies with EU norms more broadly conceived,[23] by supplementing the standard financial-control checklist by more detailed checklists tailored to the particular risks of each sector (IEU9).

But there are sharp practical limits to the cross-sanctioning

[22] Council Regulation 2081/93 OJ L 193/5 Art. 7(1). See European Commission (1997a: 113–26).
[23] Cf. Daintith's (1979) discussion of the use of government procurement for social policy objectives.

approach to regulatory enforcement. Like any complex bureaucracy the Commission was not a monolith, even though it was a single legal entity. There could be tension between one part of the Commission wishing to secure compliance with the procurement rules, while another was mainly concerned to 'move money' (Armstrong and Bulmer 1998: 139). The Court of Auditors has criticized the failure of the regional and environmental policy DGs (DGs XVI and XI respectively) to apply cross-sanctions for non-compliance by member states with environmental rules (Richardson 1996: 282–3). Such tensions and 'underlaps' are normal features of bureaucratic behaviour, even though cross-sanctioning generally seemed a stronger feature of regulation of public authorities at EU level than it was within the UK.

## 4. CONCLUSIONS

One of the features apparently distinguishing 'Eurocratic' regulation of British (and other member-state) governments was the existence of formal effector sanctions to a greater extent than typically applies to regulation inside UK national government. If Wilson and Rachal's (1977) argument that regulators of government are normally limited in their ability to modify behaviour by the absence of formal sanctions at their disposal, Eurocratic regulation ought to be an exception. Moreover, the availability of credible, high-level responses at the apex of a hierarchy of sanctions might provide the conditions for effective self-regulation on the part of member states, following Ayres and Braithwaite's (1992) well-known 'enforced self-regulation' doctrine. But although the promotion of member-state self-regulation was stressed by overseers in the Commission, EU institutional dynamics seemed to work against any effective application of the enforced self-regulation approach. Those dynamics tended to lead both to excessive use of formal sanctions for minor infractions and failure to use those sanctions for major violations, severely damaging the potential for effective self-regulation on the Braithwaite model.

Underenforcement occurred where EU regulation was politicized, and EU oversight bodies typically combined regulatory with broader political functions, in contrast to the trend in the UK's New Public Management era to separate regulatory from more general policy functions. Only the Court of Auditors and the financial arms of the Commission (DG XIX and XX) were relatively 'pure' regulators. Such hybridization of regulation worked against the automatic 'enforcement escalator' in Braithwaite's ideal of enforced self-regulation (cf. Mendrinou 1996: 17) by reducing the credibility of firm sanctions being automatically deployed in response to flagrant and repeated breaches of obligations by member-state institutions. EU regulation involved a high-level balancing act, in which considerations of future cooperation and broader Union politics often outweighed narrower regulatory considerations.

Overenforcement—the routine application of high-level sanctions for minor infractions to an extent that seems excessive from an instrumental regulatory perspective—might be partly explained by the high level of 'relational distance' between Eurocratic regulators and member-state bureaucrats, as discussed in Chapter 3. But this high degree of formality also seems to relate to the politicization of EU regulation. The Commission was under pressure from member states and other EU institutions, all of which routinely saw tables comparing member states' performance in transposing EU directives into national law,[24] the number of actions taken by the Commission against each member state for non-compliance (European Commission 1996a), and the number of frauds on the EU budget detected in each member state (European Commission 1997b). The political climate among the member states which such statistics created, and concern in each member state that others do not shirk, put pressure on the Commission to be seen to act in a way which showed up in the statistics.

One possible response to that outcome would be to separate the EU's regulatory functions into free-standing institutions, such as a competition office, a procurement agency, and an environment inspectorate (Williams 1995: 398–9). But there is considerable resistance to any such move. There has been some discussion of the establishment of a free-standing competition office (Riley 1997), but such a step would both remove a key source of power from the Commission and could weaken the member states' political influence over enforcement. And it is debatable how effective free-standing EC regulators could be in the absence of political

---

[24] e.g. DG XV's Single-Market Scoreboard published on the Commission Website at europa.eu.int/comm/dg15/en/update/score/score.htm.

commitment in member states to the programmes they were charged with enforcing.

Moreover, for member states EU obligations frequently clash with domestic political agendas; and formal sanctions applied by the Commission for non-compliance with EU norms may sometimes be less politically costly to national governments than immediate compliance—again working against the Braithwaite 'enforced self-regulation' doctrine. For example, the UK government's inability on political grounds to comply with EU fisheries rules has provoked considerable use by the Commission of formal enforcement powers, in a way inconsistent with the UK's more general good compliance record (Mendrinou 1996: 10). Hence the regulatory relationship was liable to reach the level of formal sanctions too frequently for the lower level responses to have the desired incentive effects. Moreover, the Council of Ministers might settle for stringent financial controls, applying equally to each member state, because each Minister imagined other member states would adopt excessively lax financial oversight systems in the absence of such controls (IEU1).

Thus the politicized nature of public-sector regulation at the EU level affected not only the quantity of enforcement but also the stringency of regulatory requirements. And far from a mirror-image process, in which increasing regulation at one level is accompanied by more managerial discretion at another as part of an overall New Public Management, EU regulation tends to enhance and formalize regulation inside government at national-government level. Clearly the mirror-image pattern discussed earlier in this book is far from 'the only game in town' in public-sector regulation, and the next chapter returns from sectoral case studies to a more general analysis of regulatory dynamics.

# PART THREE

The Overall Pattern

# 9

# Regulation in Government and the 'New Public Management'

I am not at all sure that Whitehall has fully recognized that diversity does increase the need for a strong central core.

Lord Nolan, quoted in *Financial Times*, 25 Feb. 1997

Having looked at some of the different domains of regulation in government in Part Two of the book, this chapter returns to a more general analysis. How do the developments described earlier in the book relate to the much discussed rise of 'New Public Management'? What changes have taken place in the forms of control and styles of operation that were discussed in Part One? Can any general conclusions be reached about the dynamics of regulation in government?

We argue that regulatory change is bound up with broader changes in public-service delivery, and when taken together the two elements constitute a major shift in the way many public bureaucracies are controlled in the UK. As noted earlier, many of the regulatory developments we observed seem to constitute a compensating movement for, or mirror image of, the changes in public-service delivery that have taken place in Britain over the past twenty years, and if there is any official view of regulatory growth in government it seems to be as a compensation for the removal of detailed controls. But (as noted in Part Two) we found several departures from the mirror-image pattern. More generally we argue Heclo and Wildavsky's classic picture of 'community' inside British government needs to be complemented by an understanding of the relational distance phenomenon, introduced in Chapter 3 and discussed in Part Two.

## 1. REGULATION IN GOVERNMENT—
## CHANGING PATTERNS OF CONTROL?

As noted in Chapter 3, many of the developments associated with the rise of New Public Management over recent years have consisted of systems that link oversight with competition (for example through quasi-markets and ratings competition in education, health, and local government). Two other common hybrids are peer-group review and peer-group competition used as means of putting more pressure to bear on previously autonomous public-sector professionals. Examples include NHS 'clinical audits', in which doctors, nurses, and other health-care professionals systematically review clinical practice (a process formalized and emphasized by the NHS Management Executive in the 1989 White Paper *Working with Patients*)[1] and the application of ratings competition to universities, which since 1988 have been obliged to compete for research ratings to be judged by committees of senior academics—ratings that in principle determine the level of universities' grant funding from government, on a modified 'best-to-best' allocation principle.[2]

Though New Public Management principles are often said to be spreading everywhere, these hybrids have not been uniformly applied. The oversight and competition hybrid in the form of league-table ratings rivalry that has developed in local government, health, and education (following Bentham's 'tabular-comparison' principle) has been much less applied to Whitehall, in accordance with what the relational distance hypothesis discussed in Chapter 3 would lead us to expect. With isolated exceptions such as the Parliamentary Commissioner for Administration's annual 'complaints league', league tables within Whitehall have mainly applied to executive agencies (which have been subjected to a mildly increasing degree of comparison on key indicators through the annual Next Steps reviews)[3] rather than to policy departments. Market testing came late to the civil service (a decade after the

---

[1] In England there were approximately 20,000 clinical review projects per year from 1992 to 1995, costing approximately £61m. per year (NAO 1995: 1–10).

[2] Since 1992, the system has been extended to teaching-quality assessments, to which universities were not subject before the ending of the 'binary divide' (between polytechnics and universities) by the Education Act 1992.

[3] See e.g. Cabinet Office (1994*b*): Annexe A, vi–viii.

introduction of compulsory competitive tendering in local government), and the experience of market testing contrasted sharply with
the runaway implementation of other reforms like Next Steps agencies or the Citizen's Charter.[4] And suggestions for a clinical-
audit-type method of assessing the quality of policy advice by
senior civil servants have been firmly resisted to date.

Nevertheless, regulatory developments during the New Public
Management era have commonly included new forms of oversight
and competition, oversight and mutuality, and mutuality and competition hybrids, the emergence of new forms of competition on top
of existing forms, and the advent of new forms of oversight. Such
general developments appeared to be weakening two traditional
mechanisms that had been important in controlling public-service
organizations in the UK, namely mutuality in its pure form and
contrived randomness. Decreased emphasis on pure mutuality as a
means of governing those public services formerly dominated by
professionals with an ideology of collegial control seems to have
been accompanied by the reintroduction of mutuality in hybrid
forms, and hybrids combining oversight and competition have been
prominent, but few have combined oversight with contrived
randomness.

### (a) *Mutuality*

Chapter 4 suggested that mutuality, traditionally important as a
regulator of public-service behaviour, remains a major feature for
the top ranks of the Whitehall village. Indeed, some developments,
like the creation of a Senior Civil Service for Grades 1–5 in 1996,
seem to have been intended to buttress cohesion at the top of
Whitehall, and in some ways team-working has been strengthened
in the top civil service, with a fashion for project teams and the
introduction of management boards in many departments. But for
the public service as a whole, much of the thrust of the managerial
reform movement for public services, which began to gather pace

---

[4] Market-testing lagged heavily behind its targets after its introduction in 1991,
and departmental market-testing targets were abandoned in 1994, being replaced by
an obligation for departments to produce 'efficiency plans', which did not need to
include any specific market-testing target. There is a sharp contrast with the degree
of compulsion to contract out in local government, even with the advent of the new
best-value regime announced in 1997.

only a few years after Heclo and Wildavsky's (1974) landmark study of mutuality was published, was intended to replace unwritten norms of professional reciprocity within relatively closed communities ('secret gardens'), or at least to supplement them by other forms of control. In particular, the introduction of market reforms in health care was widely interpreted as an attempt to weaken the traditional form of mutuality within the medical profession and enhance the position of general managers over hospital consultants. Even within the top civil service several forces in play seem likely to weaken the force of mutuality as a control process, such as a reduction in the number of formal committees in which top civil servants meet,[5] the increase in 'lateral entry' to the top ranks of the civil service discussed in Chapter 4, and possibly also the 'delayering' of senior civil servants which took place with Fundamental Expenditure Reviews in the mid-1990s, with approximately 25 per cent of the top three grades disappearing from many departments (Parry *et al.* 1997).[6]

### (b) *Contrived randomness*

It also seems likely that changes in the public service over the past two decades have weakened some of the conditions necessary for the operation of contrived randomness—that is, the deliberate use of chance as a way of helping to keep organizations under control by reducing predictability and so making control evasion more difficult. Again, not all of the traffic seems to be going in the same direction. Some aspects of the 'new public service' seem likely to increase random encounters. The creation of a more complex structure of public-sector organization may well increase the element of unpredictability in bureaucratic processes as those organizations combine in policy delivery. Recruitment of outsiders for senior positions, as noted in the last subsection, may decrease the predictability of working relationships over a career, and the same goes for increased outsourcing of public services, for example to ex-public

---

[5] In the form of official meetings within the Cabinet committee structure, which were cut substantially by Margaret Thatcher and further reduced by John Major and Tony Blair (Burch and Holliday 1996: 45).

[6] In principle, such a development might enhance mutuality (since it makes Whitehall's village world smaller still), but the net effect may well be the reverse, with increased responsibility for policy on the shoulders of hard-pressed individuals and less scope for mutual surveillance by top brass over policy as it develops.

servants turned consultants and multinational corporations which routinely post their managerial staff around the world.

What seems to have weakened, however, is the traditional form of random control in large public bureaucracies, as described in Chapters 1 and 3, which worked through 'dual-key' decision systems (meaning two or more officials needed to combine to achieve corrupt or anti-system outcomes in the handling of money, contracts, or staff) combined with unpredictable postings of staff around the structure. That approach to organizational control is standard practice in many multinational corporations, and therefore figures in outsourced services provided for government by such organizations. But within public bureaucracies an increasing stress on individual management responsibility reduces the dual-key element of contrived randomness. At the same time downsizing makes it less likely that any two or more individuals within the organization will be strangers to one another and reduces the scope for unpredictable postings. Delayering is likely to have a similar effect and reduces the likelihood of unpredictable surveillance interventions from higher grades, particularly when associated with a shift away from *ex ante* authorization systems.

Even in the form of regulatory hybrids combining an element of randomness with oversight, this type of control seems rare. There are exceptions, discussed elsewhere in this book, but many of the developments in regulation of bureaucracy associated with the era of New Public Management have made little conscious use of randomness. Over a period when New Right ideas were often said to have been highly influential over policy and institutional reform in the UK, Niskanen's (1971: 219–20) advocacy of the use of randomness in bureaucratic control has been left on the academic drawing-board (Hood 1998*a*: 237), while other features of his recipe (such as outsourcing and performance pay) have been enthusiastically adopted, albeit in a highly selective way.

### (c) *Competition*

For competition, however, a different pattern is detectable. Traditional forms of competition within bureaucracy—for recruitment and promotion, and for policy responsibilities—do not appear to have weakened. For example, in the civil service the numbers of applicants for each fast-stream vacancy rose slightly between 1980 and 1995[7] and the ratio of middle civil servants to every top position (an approximate indicator of competition for top civil-service jobs) seems to have slightly increased over the same period.[8] While traditional forms of bureaucratic competition seem to have remained strong, at least four other forms of competition have been added to them, some in the form of hybrids between competition and other types of control.

One, already discussed, was the attempt to step up competitive pressures in public services by the introduction of published rating systems or league tables of standards, such that the units being 'league-tabled' had increased incentives to outperform their rivals. A second was the introduction of competition for merit pay awards on top of (and to some degree in place of) competition for promotion between grades. Pay on performance is neither a new idea nor a new practice in the British public service (for instance, formula-linked performance pay was used to reward school-teachers until 1902 and tax collectors until well into the 1930s), but merit pay on the basis of discretionary judgements by super-ordinates was widely 'reinvented' as a formula for rewarding public servants since the 1980s.

A third new competitive element (discussed in Chapter 4) is the introduction of more 'lateral entry' for top jobs in parts of the public sector, meaning middle-level public servants aiming for the top faced more competition from outsiders, particularly for managerial positions like agency headships or senior positions in the NHS executive or regulatory Director-General roles. A fourth attempt to increase competition was the introduction of compulsory competitive tendering and 'market-testing' across the public service (introduced into local government and the NHS in the 1980s and in a less draconian and more short-lived form for central-government departments in 1991). As noted in Chapter 5, such measures in principle exposed bureaucrats to competition for

---

[7] Though there was a dip in the economic-boom years of the middle and late 1980s.

[8] Taking 'top' as the highest three grades (Grades 1–3) in the civil service and 'middle' as Grades 4–6, there were between 7 and 10 middle civil servants for every top position over 1980–95, with a slight increase in the competition ratio over the whole period.

their existing jobs (rather than competition for promotion with outsiders), since units within the public service were obliged to tender against other suppliers for the retention of their functions. In some cases, such as prisons (discussed in Chapter 6), contracting out created 'yardstick competition', enabling overseers like the NAO and Prison Inspectorate to use comparisons between contracted-out and publicly run prisons to seek performance improvements in the latter.

### (d)  *Oversight*

Along with these attempts to introduce greater competition came an expansion of oversight over the public service over the past twenty years, for which an aggregate picture was painted in Chapter 2 and some of the details in different regulatory domains discussed in Part Two. The growth in oversight comprised a population explosion in complaint-adjudicating bodies (accompanying a growth in judicial review), a major expansion and reshaping of public audit, and substantial growth in oversight through standard-setting and regulator-funder bodies. That went along with more formal specification of written codes of ethics for the conduct of civil servants, local-government officials and Ministers, and extension of formal regulation of 'merit' in public-service appointments from civil service to quango appointments. And the 1991 Citizen's Charter, which embraced the development of performance standards across the public service, was associated with a renewed (if perhaps short-lived) emphasis on independent inspection as a key to good government.

Moreover, not only has oversight grown in scale but it also appears to have changed in style. Over the twenty-year period taken for this study, several important regulators seemed to adopt a more confrontational approach towards their charges, mounting sharp challenges to policy and practice, often in a glare of publicity. The schools inspectorate, the prisons inspectorate, and the Audit Commission, whose activities were described in Part Two, developed into high-profile censors of service standards. Even the National Audit Office seemed to be moving in the same direction, with more attention being paid to issues in which top civil servants were directly involved, as discussed in Chapter 4.

## 2. REGULATION IN GOVERNMENT— A 'MIRROR IMAGE' OF DEBUREAUCRATIZED SERVICE DELIVERY IN NEW PUBLIC MANAGEMENT?

Viewing New Public Management in terms of changing forms of control over government thus reveals a pattern of some basic types of control becoming more salient, others less so, and a number of hybrid forms appearing or reappearing on the scene. At a more general level of analysis, Chapter 1 suggested the shift towards more oversight regulation in government, involving more formal procedures and in places increased confrontation between regulator and regulatee, is in some ways a mirror image or opposite-sign development of attempts to debureaucratize public-service delivery. The notion of the mirror image is that the scope, scale, and bureaucratic formality of arm's-length regulation over public bureaucracies increased at the same time that hands-on central direction diminished, with attempts to increase the scope of managerial discretion by relaxing uniform pay structures and procedural rules. In this mirror-image dynamic, increased 'freedom to manage' in public services at one level is accompanied by reregulation in the form of expanded arm's-length oversight, or a shift from one regulatory style to another, rather than the removal of regulation *simpliciter*.

To the extent that such a mirror-image development took place, it has attracted less attention than the much discussed attempts to boost managerial freedom. Even constitutional lawyers have paid little attention to these developments, as noted in Chapter 1, with commentary on managerial reforms from that quarter being concentrated on apparent reduction in accountability (Woodhouse 1997: 47). But that approach is premised on a worldview within which accountability to Parliament and the courts is normal, and to any other body pathological (cf. Loveland 1996: 371).

Some of the senior public servants we talked to saw an increase in arm's-length regulation as a 'natural' consequence of the increase in formal managerial discretion, just as social science often reveals movement in one direction by one element in a social system to be accompanied by movement in the opposite direction by another element, as part of social equilibrating processes (cf. McCloskey 1990: 27). But others saw it as a largely unintended development.

'We thought we were empowering people who manage things, but ended up empowering those who count things' was one senior civil servant's wry comment on the rise of internal regulation accompanying managerial reform. Some echoed Mark Freedland's (1994: 102) comment that: 'The transaction costs of devolved and fragmented management are apt to be very high, and it often turns out to be necessary to reintroduce new mechanisms of standardisation and control which are more elaborate than the centralised bureaucracies which it was thought to eliminate.'[9] But it is debatable whether the underlying problem is strictly one of transaction costs or simply lack of control.

However, the reregulatory mirror-image dynamic is neither the only logical possibility nor the only style that we observed. Table 9.1 identifies four possible directions of change in arm's-length regulation of public services relative to hands-on central direction. The mirror-image style discussed above belongs in cell 3 of the table, of arm's-length regulation increasing while central direction increases. But there are others. One is the double whammy pattern discussed for central–local government relations in Chapter 5, in which central direction and arm's-length oversight increase simultaneously.[10] That outcome is ironic, since (as noted in Chapter 5) the Layfield report of the 1970s explicitly envisaged and prescribed a reregulatory mirror-image pattern in its vision of the future of central–local government relations. The double whammy outcome may also appear elsewhere in spite of official claims about increased managerial discretion in government.

Apart from the reregulatory mirror image and the double whammy, two other possible dynamics are shown in Table 9.1. One is the opposite type of mirror-image development, of arm's-length regulation decreasing while central direction increases. There are historical instances which approximate to that development (such as the nationalization movements of the 1940s, which substituted Ministerial direction for independent regulation), but in the period under study the deregulatory mirror image dynamic

---

[9] See Schick (1996: 24), who makes a similar comment in an assessment of New Zealand's public-management reforms.

[10] Though as Ch. 5 suggested, when we turn from central–local government relations to relationships within local government, we see more evidence of a reregulatory mirror-image pattern, with local authorities substituting regulatory relationships with service providers for what had once been direct-management relationships across a range of services.

TABLE 9.1. *Changes in regulation and central direction of public services: four styles*

| Changes in hands-on central direction | Changes in arm's-length regulation | |
|---|---|---|
| | Increase | Decrease |
| Increase | (1)<br>Double whammy<br>*Example*: central–local government relations | (2)<br>Deregulatory mirror image<br>*Example*: *de facto* or formal de-agencification |
| Decrease | (3)<br>Reregulatory mirror image<br>*Example*: developments inside local government for service delivery | (4)<br>Double deliverance<br>*Example*: removal of central controls over CS hiring in early 1990s |

seemed rare. It appeared in cases of de-agencification (such as applied to some degree to the Prison Service Agency after 1997, in the wake of the Derek Lewis affair discussed in Chapter 6) and to other cases in which devices intended to entrench independence from day-to-day political control were found politically inconvenient (such as the scrapping of the 'policy guidance' arrangements for the Civil Aviation Authority in 1980, only nine years after its establishment (Baldwin 1985: 6 ff.).

The final possibility is 'double deliverance' (cell 4) in which arm's-length regulation and central direction simultaneously decline. At first sight, double deliverance might seem like every public manager's Nirvana, though in practice it is often convenient for such managers to have central regulators to blame for unpopular measures or bureaucratic restrictions for which they would otherwise have to assume sole responsibility (cf. Parry *et al.* 1997). Apart from relatively exotic examples (such as an apparent trend to deregulation of state Churches in England and Scotland), double deliverance seems to be rare and short-lived where it does occur (for example, in abandonment of central control over departmental hiring in the civil service in the early 1990s, discussed in Chapter 4, which led to a perceived free-for-all that quickly brought a reaction in the form of enhanced regulation by the Civil Service Commissioners). Finally, there are some cases where no major movement in any of the four directions identified in Table 9.1 seems to have taken place, such as the case of EU regulation of UK government, discussed in the last chapter. That exception to the mirror-image dynamic is scarcely surprising, since the EU's relationship with member states' public bureaucracies begins from an extreme point of 'regulatoriness', having never involved vertical integration of regulation and service provision, and EU oversight bodies work within fairly tightly drawn legal frameworks, as discussed in the last chapter.

The reregulatory mirror-image pattern is therefore not 'the only game in town' in contemporary UK public management. There are risks that what may be intended or presented as a deregulatory mirror-image development may unintendedly end up as a double whammy, just as some (like Foster 1992) argue that the intended deregulatory mirror-image pattern in some of the 1940s nationalizations in fact produced double deliverance for some of the nationalized industry boards. Nevertheless, the reregulatory mirror image seems to be a common and important development in UK public management, even if other patterns are also observable. And if we think of the four basic types of control discussed earlier as a saltire cross (like the Scottish flag) as depicted in Figure 9.1, the combined effect of regulatory and service-delivery changes has been to switch from the traditional emphasis on mutuality at the top and contrived randomness down the line (the north-west–south-east diagonal) to the opposite diagonal of control, with increasing emphasis on oversight and competition as the primary basis of control. That picture is oversimplified, but it gives a slightly different perspective on the rise of formal regulation accompanying managerial change in the public service.

## 3. A PATTERN OF REGULATORY CHANGE?

Another way of interpreting the reregulatory mirror-image style depicted above is to see it as a case of regulation in government going up-grid and up-group relative to its charges. The terms grid and group come from cultural theory (Douglas 1982) and refer, respectively, to the degree to which individuals are subject to specified rules and to the extent to which one social group stands out from others. Much of the thrust of New Public Management

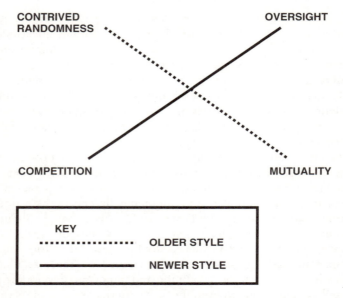

FIG. 9.1. A mirror-image process? Overall changes in public-service regulation

changes was designed to move public services down-group, in the sense of reducing the degree of distinctiveness between public and private management which was epitomized in Beatrice Webb's conception of public servants as a 'Jesuitical corps' (Barker 1984: 34). And those changes were also designed to move public services down-grid, at least by a process of breaking up formerly monolithic bureaucracies into their component 'businesses' and thereby reducing the degree to which common rules (for instance, about pay or grading) applied across the public sector.

However, in the reregulation mirror-image pattern, public-sector regulators have moved in the opposite direction relative to their regulatees: *up*-group and *up*-grid. They have moved up-group, in the sense of an *increase* in the extent to which they stand out from the public sector generally and from the organizations they regulate in particular (the relational distance phenomenon discussed in Chapter 3). At the same time, as the relational distance hypothesis would suggest, many seem to have moved up-grid at least in the formal sense of spelling out rules, standards, and procedures more explicitly than before. Going up-group for regulators means an increasing separation of oversight from other bureaucratic activities and a move towards more external regulation. Going up-grid means a pattern of oversight increasingly bound by explicit rules and standards.

### (a) *Compound and stand-alone regulation*

Regulation in government can vary according to how far the core regulatory activity—setting, monitoring, and enforcing of rules and standards—is separated from other bureaucratic functions, such as policy advice, consultancy, resource allocation, and line management. For instance, regulation is clearly separated from other functions for the 'regularity' work of public auditors (in contrast to auditors in the private sector and value-for-money audit in the public sector) and ombudsmen, but less so for central-agency regulators or funder-regulators, which combine regulation with other functions. A number of changes in regulation within UK government over the twenty years up to the late 1990s served to uncouple regulation from other roles in the bureaucracy. Privatization and outsourcing by its nature involved uncoupling previously hybrid regulatory functions, and not just in the much discussed case of the utilities (for which, during the era of public ownership, regulation was mixed with sponsorship, financial allocation, and ownership functions, notably the appointment and dismissal of chairmen and board members). We noted in Chapter 4 that the outsourcing of the handling of civil-service recruitment, together with delegation to departments and agencies, had shifted the Civil Service Commissioners from direct management of civil-service recruitment to a 'stand-alone' regulatory role of setting standards and auditing compliance. And in Chapter 5 we noted that outsourcing of services in local authorities had had a similar effect in detaching regulatory functions from direct management roles. In addition to privatization and outsourcing, 'corporatization' within government (the division of monolithic bureaucracies into separately managed operating units, like Next Steps executive agencies in the civil service and semi-independent operating trusts in the Health Service) also serves to detach regulation from other bureaucratic activities (and, as was suggested in Chapter 4, may create pressures for new types of regulation). But even apart from the reregulatory mirror-image

logic bound up with privatization and corporatization, a number of
important public-sector regulators became more 'stand alone' in
their activities over the New Public Management era: a leading
example is the case of schools inspection in England and Wales,
discussed in Chapter 7 and institutionally separated from policy
responsibility for education in 1992. In addition, new stand-alone
regulators were added (like the Public Appointments Commissioner
and the Magistrates' Courts Inspectorate) and some existing stand-
alone regulators attracted additional functions (notably the
Parliamentary Ombudsman whose role was extended in the 1990s
into reviewing compliance with Citizen's Charter principles and
the Code of Practice on Access to Government Information
(Woodhouse 1997: 89)). A trend for regulators of government to
move up-group relative to their charges seems to have been
bound up with a tripartite fragmentation of public bureaucracy
into policy, operations, and regulation, for example in the case of
prisons.

## (b) *In-group and out-group regulation*

As discussed in Chapter 3 and the chapters of Part Two, regulation
can vary according to whether those regulating and those being
regulated share a common professional or social background—the
central theme of relational distance. A number of key developments
in oversight in UK government over the two decades taken for this
study involved placing more emphasis on out-group regulation or
increasing RD. Corporatization within government might be expected to have such an effect insofar as it exchanged regulation
within a single organization for regulation by one organization over
another. But increased RD through out-group regulation developed
in other ways as well. In particular, as mentioned in Chapter 1,
a mood developed for recruiting outsiders to oversight organizations once confined to a single professional or occupational
group, to bring different experiences and values into regulation.
In a move formalized by the 1991 Citizen's Charter, 'lay' members
were added to many of the professional inspectorates, for example
for police, schools, fire services, and probation, in an attempt
to bring a different perspective into what were perceived as inbred
and excessively cosy relationships—as in the educational 'secret
garden' discussed in Chapter 7. In other cases, 'outsiders' were

appointed to head regulatory organizations, as with the Civil Service Commission (headed by an outsider for the first time in 1994, as discussed in Chapter 4), the Prisons Inspectorate under Stephen Tumim (as discussed in Chapter 7) and some of the new regulators, such as the Commissioner for the Security Services (headed by a judge rather than a spy or a soldier when the office was created in 1992) and the Public Appointments Commissioner in 1996. As we have noted, many of these appointments produced hybrid patterns of RD, in that outsiders were often complemented by insiders at other organizational levels or as part of a regulatory team. But to the extent that the net change amounted to an increase in RD of regulators relative to their charges, such developments involved a move up-group in regulators in terms of professional background.

## (c) *Partial and full regulation*

In Chapter 3, we distinguished the detector, director, and effector components of control systems. Few of the regulators in government we studied combined all of these three elements— standard-setting, monitoring, and enforcement—within a single organization, and that frequently applies to the regulation of business too. But some developments in public-sector regulation had the effect of moving regulators towards fuller regulation in the sense of including more of these features in a single unit. In some cases extra sanctions were added to the quiver of effector arrows, such as the Prison Inspectorate's adoption of 'inspection refusal' tactics (Chapter 6) and OFSTED's acquisition of 'nuclear weapons' in the form of powers to recommend closure of 'failing schools' (Chapter 7). In other cases additional monitoring capacity was added, as with the compliance audits developed by the Civil Service Commissioners and the teaching and research audits for universities developed by the Higher Education Funding Councils. For central-agency regulation of departments a traditional pattern of detection by detailed *ex ante* authorization regimes was partially swapped for a style of general standard-setting linked to monitoring or *ex post* audit. And in those services where patterns of public-bureaucracy provision were replaced by a mix of public and private providers (like prisons and some local-authority care services), regulation perhaps had to become 'fuller' since it could no longer borrow, or piggy-back on, other bureaucratic processes associated with direct service provision.

### (d) *Informal and formal regulation*

Finally, regulation can vary in formality. As noted earlier, 'formality' in regulation has more than one possible meaning, though the meanings tend to be related. It can mean a disposition to follow the rule-book rather than apply common sense or casual approaches to problem-solving. It can mean a disposition to write everything down, rather than working in an oral or 'off-the-record' mode. It can mean a reliance on official sanctions instead of other methods of securing compliance (such as the élite socialization often said to have been important in shaping the behaviour of the upper reaches of Whitehall (Dunsire 1988)) and a disposition to apply such sanctions in every case of infringement rather than apply discretion. In Chapter 3 we linked those elements of formality together, though they are in principle separable, and indeed the exploration of local-government and EU regulation in Chapters 5 and 8 showed that legalistic rule-mindedness and automatic sanctioning do not always go together. Chapter 3 suggested relational-distance factors would lead formality in those senses to be highest at the boundaries of public-administration cultures where trust might be expected to be lowest (notably the points at which central government meets local government, EU meets national bureaucracies, public bureaucracy meets private contractor). In general, that expectation fits the patterns of regulation described in Part Two.

However, a number of public-management developments seem to be combining to increase the formality of regulation in government in several of the senses of formality discussed earlier. Those developments include the increased stress on corporatization, contracts, outside appointments, and the generally 'low-trust' style of organization associated with what Michael Power (1997) terms 'the audit society'. The entry of private tenderers or contractors into areas formerly populated only by bureaucrats is also likely to be associated with a shift towards formal regulation driven by rising litigiousness and anxieties about avoidance of conflict of interest. Across a number of the domains of regulation in government we investigated—such as education, police and public-service conduct, public-service procedure—the formality of the process seems to have increased, consistent with the findings of Hoggett (1996) and Power (1997), and such a development might be expected to go further if public-service provision becomes more fragmented and less dependent on informal socialization.

## 4. TOWARDS 'JURIDIFICATION' OF REGULATION IN GOVERNMENT?

One index of formality of regulation is the degree to which decision-making approximates judicial procedure, with (*inter alia*) public hearings, highly developed rules of evidence and appeal processes, extensive written records, and independent legal representation (Mashaw 1983). Formality in this sense can be linked to more general discussions of 'juridification' of social relations. As noted in Chapter 1, one of the central hypotheses of the contemporary sociology of law is that the emphasis on regulation as a mode of governance has created the risk of 'the intrusion of law into fields that it is ill-fitted to regulate' (Teubner 1987: 4; Cotterrell 1992: 52). Such a process of juridification or legalization represents the displacement of non-legal governing values with legal rules, and the creeping involvement of lawyers and courts in determining outcomes, in a way that both tends to damage the activity being regulated and also to undermine the general claims of law to underpin public and private activity.

Pressures to juridify social relations in the public sector come from several sources. The redefinition of many relationships in contractual or quasi-contractual terms, for example in health care and education, have made more explicit the norms and expectations governing such relationships (Broadbent and Laughlin 1997; cf. Scott 1998). As noted earlier, judicial review of administrative decisions has assumed a higher profile, with widening jurisdiction and more cases being brought since the 1960s (Woodhouse 1997: 100–7).[11] Decisions are more likely to be challenged by those who are affected by them, whether individuals, companies, or other parts of the public sector (cf. Cabinet Office 1987, 1994*a*; Richardson and Sunkin 1996). While some regulators of

---

[11] Paradoxically, attempts by government to remove statutory appeal rights may also increase the pressure for growth of judicial review as an alternative mechanism of appeal (ibid. 108).

government appear to have been conceived as alternatives to orthodox judicial review processes (and the Parliamentary Ombudsman
in particular was hostile to his investigations being used to ground
judicial review actions (I23)), in many cases the regulators appear
in practice to facilitate and reinforce a culture of litigation against
public authorities. For example, the Prisons Ombudsman has supplied prisoners with information that has served to launch judicial
review of prison governors' decisions (I24); the success of a complainant with the Police Complaints Authority is commonly a preliminary to successful civil litigation against the police (I2); and
even the data provided by OFSTED over school quality have
prompted attempts to sue local authorities by parents (IEE10).

However, we found juridification had made much stronger ad-
vances in some domains of public-sector regulation than others.
Pressures for juridification seem to be greatest in those areas of
oversight of the public sector where funding is an important issue
or where the reputational consequences of grievance-adjudication
are important. Out of the seven types of regulator identified in
Chapter 2, it is the funder-regulators that are most routinely subject
to challenge by judicial review, and the grievance-handlers are also
subject to a greater degree of judicial review than other regulators.[12]
While inspectorates do not generally wield funding powers, where
their activities have become closely linked to funding regimes, and
where their activities have consequently moved from technical inspection to more political functions, juridification appears to be
more common.[13]

---

[12] e.g., judicial review is increasingly used to challenge decisions of the Police
Complaints Authority: e.g. *R* v. *Police Complaints Authority ex p. Wells* (1991)
COD 95; *R* v. *Police Complaints Authority ex p. Thompson* (1990) COD 205. The
courts have long been willing to judicially review the decisions of local ombudsmen:
e.g. *R* v. *Commissioner for Local Administration ex p. Croydon LBC* (1989) 1 All
ER 1033 (Jones 1988) and have recently relaxed their unwillingness to conduct
review of the Parliamentary Ombudsman: *R* v. *Parliamentary Commissioner for
Administration ex p. Dyer* (1994) 1 All ER 175; *R* v. *Parliamentary Commissioner
for Administration ex p. Balchin* (1996) EGCS 166. The Court of Appeal has held
that the Parliamentary Commissioner for Standards is not subject to judicial review,
as such action would lead the courts into the role of supervising the proceedings of
Parliament, contrary to s.1, Art. 9 of the Bill of Rights (1688): *R* v. *Parliamentary
Commissioner for Standards ex p. Al Fayed* (1998) 1 All ER 93.

[13] The importation of contractual relationships into service provision has not
automatically resulted in their being recast in judicial terms (cf. Broadbent and
Laughlin 1997). As noted in Ch. 6, contracts for prison provision seem to be rarely
referred to in contacts between the Prison Service and providers of contracted-out

Central–local government regulation, as discussed in Chapter 5, is one of the most notable areas where juridification has developed within a domain where funding is linked to regulation. Martin Loughlin (1996: 368) argues juridification of local-government regulation is linked to a process in which a previously facilitative regime of central-government oversight of local government was transformed into a tight regulatory regime. Three elements seem to be behind the development of juridification in this domain. First is the existence of a general statutory framework underlying the administrative relations between the two levels of government, linked with the separate legal personality of local authorities and central government providing the possibility for them to challenge each other's activities at law. Second is the attempt by central government over fifty years to tighten regulatory control over local authorities, as described in Chapter 5. Third is the existence in many cases of central–local government regulation of a link between oversight and funding, leading to pressures to redefine relations in juridical terms.[14]

To the extent that developments in other domains of public-sector oversight tend to produce administrative systems with those three characteristics, juridification may be expected to spread further. A case in point, already mentioned, is the emerging system of tighter regulation of university teaching and research, where decisions of the Higher Education Funding Councils over research quality are directly linked to funding and have given rise to litigation seeking to challenge the methods and outcomes of the research evaluation decision.[15] Another is the increasing presence of an EU aspect in public-sector regulation. For example, though it aims to avoid litigation (I8), the Treasury has been subject to litigation over its implementation of EU procurement

prisons. These relationships continue to be based more on hierarchical relationships than exchange or adversarial ones.

[14] Hence local authorities commonly sought to test the funding decisions of the Funding Agency for Schools in respect of grant-maintained schools through litigation (I30); local authorities commonly tested the jurisdiction of the Social Services Inspectorate through judicial review (I3); and oversight of standards by OFSTED created pressures to test the legality of OFSTED reports (IEE10), even in the form of threatened libel actions by criticized head teachers (IEE1). In contrast, where local services are still inspected in a low-profile 'technical' manner, typically with low relational distance (notably in fire services and police), juridification has not developed.

[15] *R* v. *HEFC ex p. Institute for Dental Surgery* (1994) 1 All ER 651.

rules,[16] and the UK government has also been the defendant in litigation for failure to implement EU legislation properly, brought both by the European Commission and by adversely affected EU citizens (Woodhouse 1997: 127–8). Accordingly, both the development of 'Europeanization' and domestic public-sector developments involving a fragmentation of organization, more formal regulation, and a link between resourcing and regulation, seem likely to bring further juridification in their train. Tackling the problems created by juridification in public-sector regulation may require more emphasis on reflexivity, in the sense of self-regulatory processes governed by law (Teubner 1987; Black 1996). We discuss that issue in the next chapter.

## 5. CONCLUSION

The reforms in public-service delivery introduced in the UK over recent decades have often been interpreted as ways of enabling service-delivery managers to 'add value' (Moore 1995) by relaxing stultifying top-down rules to allow a more entrepreneurial and consumer-driven approach to public management, and intensifying the pressure of competition relative to generalized oversight. The analysis above suggests that conventional interpretation captures only part of the picture. There is some evidence of new forms of competition supplementing traditional types as a method of controlling public-service provision (though whether second- and third-round competition for outsourced and franchised services will prove as effective as traditional bureaucratic competition for promotion as a control device remains to be seen). But along with attempts to managerialize and entrepreneurialize public services has gone a marked extension and development of oversight systems—the reregulatory mirror-image style discussed earlier, in the form of an aggrandizement of audit, inspection, grievance-handling, and judicial review which introduce copious new bodies of rules and standard operating requirements, imposed at one remove.

The reregulatory mirror-image style seems to involve some up-

---

[16] Case C-392/93 *R* v. *HM Treasury ex p. British Telecommunications plc* (1996) 3 WLR 203.

group/up-grid movement by regulators and to be linked to growing formality in the sense of juridification. It is not the only observable pattern of change in central direction and arm's-length regulation, and some of the other types were discussed earlier. But the double-whammy and reregulatory mirror-image styles seem to be the commonest dynamics during the New Public Management era, and the aggrandizement of audit, inspection, grievance-handling, and judicial review is increasingly coming into the centre of contemporary discussions of public-management reform.

Indeed some of the judgements about the role of bureaucratic regulatory agencies made in standard UK public-administration texts of earlier decades need to be reconsidered and, as noted in Chapter 1, the relative neglect of such agencies by constitutional lawyers may underplay the importance of such agencies in keeping public administration under control, given the limitations of judicial and direct parliamentary oversight. Contrary to what commentators of an earlier generation saw and expected (such as Normanton 1966: 274 and Rhodes 1981: 19–20, 204, and 221), audit and inspection were notably extended and emphasized across the public service in the last two decades of the century. Much of that development took place outside the confines of the top civil service in Whitehall, but Chapter 4 suggested that even there Heclo and Wildavsky's picture of mutuality as the dominant force controlling the village community of top civil servants may need to be qualified. There are more incomers relative to long-term residents in the village than there were a quarter of a century ago, and today's villagers have more regulators and regulation impacting on their own affairs than those of the early 1970s. And beyond the upper reaches of Whitehall there has been a much more dramatic advance of formal oversight to shape public services and keep them in check.

There are perhaps some historical precedents for this style. In the late eighteenth and early nineteenth century, regulation, rather than direct-line management, was much emphasized as a method of controlling a fragmented public service. In the centre of government, the Treasury established itself as the main regulator of the structure of departments and boards; public audit advanced in 1785 and 1866 (with the establishment of the Commissioners for Auditing the Public Accounts and the Exchequer and Audit Department respectively), and in 1855 the Civil Service Commissioners were created to oversee recruitment procedures. Oversight of locally produced services began in the eighteenth century with the establishment of Surveyors of Income Tax to oversee the local tax bureaucracy and from the 1830s a clutch of inspectorates were created to oversee prisons, poor law establishments, constabulary, and schools. For instance, five Inspectors of Prisons were appointed in 1835 to oversee locally provided prisons, and local Boards of Visitors were established as an additional regulator when the prisons were 'nationalized' in 1877, growing out of the earlier role of local magistrates in inspecting local private prisons.

Later, as a more inclusive and uniform 'public-bureaucracy state' (Hood 1990) developed, these regulators became less distinct from the rest of the public service. For example, the Surveyors of Income Tax, which were originally set up to regulate the local tax bureaucracy, increasingly took over the work of assessing tax liability directly, marginalizing the older structure of local tax officials, and in education the inspectors became part of a professional community of educators, working as consultants and policy advisers rather than quality checkers alone. In the late twentieth century a more fragmented and diverse public service has re-emerged (though the tide began to turn far earlier: cf. Hood 1978: 33). In these circumstances, it is perhaps not surprising that regulatory agencies have once again come into sharper relief, as operational activities have dropped away from central departments and agencies and contracting out, corporatization, and contractorization have moved the public service steadily away from late Victorian patterns of uniformity and inclusiveness.

Many explanations could be given of the causal processes behind these reregulatory mirror-image developments—including: 'self-interest' explanations such as 'bureau-shaping' (Dunleavy 1991); contextual explanations such as the development of a low-trust 'audit society' (Power 1997) or unstoppable forces of juridification in public services (see Jabbari 1994; Cooper 1995; Loughlin 1996); explanations stressing the persuasive force of particular recipes for better government, or functional explanations of a reregulatory mirror-image development in public management. For example, if it is true that the only fundamental way to control bureaucracy is through the balancing of opposed built-in pressures (Dunsire 1978), then any removal of contradictory forces at bureau or departmental level by substituting overall strategic targets for 'double-bind' structures (Hennestad 1990) may require a compensatory introduction of contradictory forces at another level through oversight structures. But our analysis here has been more concerned with *how* these developments occurred than *why* they occurred. And if the development of more extensive and formal oversight is part of a long-term change in UK public bureaucracy, these trends seem unlikely to be reversed in the near future, even if the rate of growth that bureaucratic overseers have exhibited in the last two decades seems unsustainable in the long run.[17] Hence in the final chapter we turn to broader issues of policy and institutional design raised by these developments.

[17] See Ch. 2.

# 10

# Regulating the Regulators: Policies for Reform

> A well-designed institution . . . is both internally consistent and externally in harmony with the rest of the social order in which it is set.
>
> R. Goodin, *The Theory of Institutional Design*

This chapter turns from analysis and description of regulation inside government to discussing policy and evaluation. What weaknesses need attention? How might regulation in government be improved? Drawing on the four-part analysis of types of control over bureaucracy, sketched out in Chapter 1 and applied in Chapters 3 and 9, this chapter explores issues of policy and institutional design under each of those four headings. The argument is in the form of an immanent or 'physician, heal thyself' critique. We claim that if any of the control techniques available to the regulators are of value in modifying the behaviour of public-sector bureaucracies, then those techniques must apply as much to the regulators of government as to the regulatees. Following this analysis, we identify four 'deficits' in the current institutionalization and behaviour of public-sector regulators. They are:

- A mutuality deficit
- A competition deficit
- An oversight deficit
- A randomness deficit

These four headings, and their subtypes, are used here more as a diagnostic and framing device (in the spirit of McKinsey's '7-s' formula (cf. Pascale and Athos 1981: 80–1)) than as a mechanical source of recommendations. Indeed, like Adam Smith's classic canons of taxation, many of these ideas pull against one another at the margin. But each merits closer attention than it has so far received.

## 1. A MUTUALITY DEFICIT?

Chapter 2 showed that regulation in government is a grouping, not a group. To the extent that regulators in government interact with one another at all, it is only within particular families, like the British and Irish Ombudsmen Association (which extends across the public and private sectors),[1] and the groupings of auditors, and, more recently, professional inspectorates. Much the same could be said about regulation of business, which also tended to be institutionally fragmented. For example, the 'Of-type' utility regulators recognized each other as part of a common family group and met periodically, but did not see themselves as part of a wider regulatory family which included all the other actors (like trading standards officers or health and safety regulators) attempting to influence business behaviour. In the same way there were no fora for regulators in government in which good practice or overall philosophy could be discussed across the various domains of regulation, or 'hot spots' examined (even though, as Chapter 3 showed, methods of operation cut across the different institutional families of regulators). In 1998 a step was taken in this direction by the creation of a Public Audit Forum, chaired by the Comptroller and Auditor-General, to ensure common standards and practice for public-sector audit across the UK. The Forum comprised the four main UK public audit bodies described as well as other stakeholders from central government, local authorities, and the health service, and its creation was prompted by the work of the Nolan Committee on Standards in Public Life.

The notion of a mutuality deficit, however, goes beyond a simple absence of rich (or in many cases, any) communication among bodies doing related work. It also means regulators in government did not for the most part seek to shape each other's behaviour or call one another to account in collegial fora. As will be noted later, the commonest response to jurisdictional overlaps among regulators was a search for *modi vivendi* through coexistence rather than collegial accountability. There were some exceptions to this

---

[1] See James (1997: ch. 9) for an extensive discussion of the Association. A meshing of public and private also applies to the audit family in so far as many public-sector audits are carried out by private accounting firms—in some cases, indirectly exercising state power via surcharge actions. We are indebted to Martin Loughlin for reminding us of this point.

pattern. For instance, as discussed in Chapter 6, the ombudsman club, the British and Irish Ombudsman Association, was reluctant to admit institutions not constituted in what it considered to be an acceptable form, notably the Prisons Ombudsman (to which it gave only Associate status), and there is no doubt the Audit Commission's approach of league-table performance ratings influenced the working of the professional inspectorates over local government.[2] But in general the relationship among regulators in government seemed neither fully collegial nor fully competitive, and this theme will be pursued further in the next subsection. There is a risk of a system that achieves the worst of all worlds, reaping neither the advantages of mutuality nor of competition and falling somewhere in the middle.

Given this cross-domain 'mutuality deficit', it is not surprising that coherent principles and practices tended to be conspicuously absent in regulation within government. Indeed, that mutuality deficit seems likely to be even worse than applies to business regulators, because in the absence of overseers concerned with synoptic regulatory impact analysis, there was little scope for mutuality-based self-regulation by the regulators of government in the shadow of formal oversight. At the time of writing, it was only the regulatees who had anything approaching a synoptic view of the system, since they were most aware of the various and contradictory demands being made of them.

Unless the mutuality deficit can be defended as inevitable and/or beneficent, how could it be reduced? Three possibilities (in roughly ascending order of the formal changes that would be required) include cross-domain fora for regulation in government, a more coherent career for those working in this domain, and restructuring of the organizations within it to bring disparate specialists together under broader 'umbrellas'. Cross-domain fora, the least radical way to tackle the mutuality deficit, would in principle require no formal changes from the present institutional set-up, simply more opportunities for regulators across the different domains to ex-

---

[2] e.g. since 1996 a joint Social Services Inspectorate and Audit Commission team has reviewed local-authority social-services provision and since 1994 the Housing Corporation has worked jointly with the Audit Commission to review the value for money of housing associations on the basis of the Commission's previous work (Audit Commission 1996: 14).

change ideas and develop common approaches and codes of practice. As noted in Chapter 2, a meeting we held for the various regulators of government in 1997 was the first opportunity many of them had ever had to discuss common issues, such as compliance costs and principles of sanctioning. If such exchanges were to move beyond first principles and develop cumulative common understanding among the players, a regular forum would be needed. Possible models include the fora for European regulators at the European University Institute at Florence, like the European Competition Forum and particularly the regular meetings of the heads of the new European agencies, which bring together regulators across different policy domains to discuss generic issues including institutional procedure, accountability, and financial control (see Kreher 1996; Ehlerman and Laudati 1997). More ambitiously, we could even conceive of an Institute of Public Sector Overseers, along the lines of the British and Irish Ombudsman Association, and such an institution could include prizes, fellowships, and distinctions as well as meetings.

Another way of achieving a similar result—which could be an addition rather than an alternative to the forum approach—would be to place more emphasis on the role of individuals carrying ideas from one domain to another through a career structure cutting across the 130-plus public-sector regulator organizations. The transfer of innovation and ideas in organizations often comes more from mobile individuals than summit meetings, and a career corps (along the lines of the French *grands corps*) is one well-established way of cementing a grouping into a group.[3] Indeed, as discussed in Chapter 4, such a notion lies behind the creation of the Senior Civil Service in 1996 for the top positions in central government (and the establishment of analogous systems in many other countries). Why not apply the same logic of a cohesive go-anywhere *grand corps* with a common *cursus honorum* to regulators inside government? Something of that sort seemed to be happening below the topmost (Director-General) level for the utility regulators, and a similar practice for regulators of government could bring the same pay-off. At the least a more general development of secondments and career

---

[3] Breyer (1993) argues for such an institutional approach to increase the coherence and consistency of risk regulation in US federal government.

exchanges, hitherto undertaken on a very limited basis (for example between NAO and the European Court of Auditors, and NAO and the Audit Commission) might help to carry over good practice from one domain of regulation to another.

A third and more radical way of tackling the mutuality deficit would be to restructure the boundaries of the multiple organizations operating in the field rather than simply promoting exchanges or developing a common career structure among the fragmented institutions regulating government. It would tackle the problem at source by reshaping the organizations themselves. In regulation of business and society, an umbrella approach to structuring regulatory organizations has developed, notably in the Health and Safety Executive (and Commission) and the Environment Agency.[4] These organizations combine particular specialized units at operating level (like the Railways Inspectorate or the Nuclear Installations Inspectorate) to reap the advantages of specialization and a 'common language' (low relational distance, as discussed elsewhere in this book) with a common cross-domain capacity for policy analysis, high-level sanctions, strategic direction, and clout in the higher reaches of government. Apart from combining the advantages of high and low relational distance simultaneously in a coherent organizational structure, such a structure obliges different specialists to work within a common overall policy framework. Applying a similar logic to regulation inside government would imply developing two-tier structures in which a super-regulator brought together a range of different regulatory specialists. There might well be a constitutional argument for developing different umbrella structures for regulation of central and local government, and for separating the parliamentary and executive umbrellas, but there seems no intrinsic reason why grievance-handling and other forms of regulation should always be located on different institutional planets. Again, in utility regulation we can find examples of grievance-handling combined with other forms of oversight under one roof, for instance in the case of OFTEL (since there is no separate telecommunications consumer council to share the grievance-handling aspect of regulation).

---

[4] The England and Wales authority which brought together several previously separate regulatory agencies such as the National Rivers Authority and HM Chief Inspectorate of Pollution.

## 2. A COMPETITION DEFICIT?

Earlier chapters of this book have shown that regulators in government frequently employed competition as a device to improve
performance among their charges, notably by fostering league-table
rivalry over performance indicators (Bentham's 'tabular-statement'
and 'comparison and selection' principles of public management
(Hume 1981: 161) dressed up for the information age). By contrast
the regulators themselves were exposed only to rather sporadic and
*ad hoc* competition, as noted earlier. Like all bureaucracies they
engaged in periodic 'turf wars' for policy responsibility (for example in the struggle between the Parliamentary Commissioner for
Administration and the Data Protection Registrar for oversight of
the provisions for 'open government' introduced in a 1993 White
Paper and a similar struggle that developed over responsibility for
Freedom of Information legislation four years later) or less overt
conflict (for example in the rivalry between the NAO and Audit
Commission over parts of NHS audit (Bowerman 1994)). And, as
shown in earlier chapters, they conflicted in the sort of pressure
they placed on the bureaucracies they oversaw (for example, in
the 'input-output' cost-based focus of the Audit Commission compared to the professional best-practice focus of the professional
inspectorates and the conflicting pressures put on prison governors
by different regulators, as described in Chapter 6). At first sight,
competition between rival administrative values entrenched in different regulatory institutions might seem to approximate to some of
the conditions for 'collibration' as identified by Andrew Dunsire
(1978: 1990), that is, the maintenance of contradictory pressures
within organizations as a condition of their effective control
from the top or outside). But there was rarely an obvious point at
which these contradictory pressures could be manipulated by 'selective inhibition' of the rival forces (a crucial part of Dunsire's analysis of how 'fingertip control' can operate in large bureaucratic
organizations). Much of the selective inhibition seemed to come
from climates of opinion, a changing *Zeitgeist*, or even from the
regulatees themselves rather than from identifiable high public
officeholders.

Whatever may be the truth of that, regulators of government
were not themselves systematically exposed to the sort of competition and rivalry they imposed on public-service organizations,

particularly in local government, education, and health. Indeed, the response of regulators to the considerable overlap among them was often to collaborate rather than compete, particularly over the debatable lands lying between audit, professional inspection, and funder-regulation. As noted in Chapter 5, the Audit Commission, originally instituted as a counterweight to the putative 'professional aggrandizement' focus of the specialized inspectorates, increasingly came to do joint work with them on social services, fire, police, and education (to the point of being formally brigaded with the Social Services Inspectorate after 1996 in the review of local-authority social-services provision) and joined with the Housing Corporation in 1994 to review the value for money of housing associations (Audit Commission 1996: 14).

In interviews and discussions, regulators were often sceptical about the value of competition applied to their own activities as opposed to those of the organizations they oversaw. Indeed, one member of an organization particularly noted for its zeal in publishing league-table lists of saints and sinners within its domain declared he was 'not sure it was a good idea for public-sector organizations to compete with one another' over regulatory tasks. But there were exceptions. For instance, we were told that competition between the NAO and Audit Commission was valuable for motivating middle-level staff and that the Audit Commission's techniques and in particular its style of presentation had been a major spur to the NAO (I42). Unless competition among regulators in government is to be dismissed as undesirable in principle (a doctrine which would be strikingly at odds with those applied elsewhere in the UK public service or in business regulation in the EU), the problem is to find forms of competition which do not involve excessive costs on the organizations being overseen. At least three forms of competition might be considered, namely more league-table comparisons among regulators as a group and between regulators and their charges, more systematic sunset- and market-testing of regulation in government, and more scope for an element of choice of regulator by public-service organizations.

More systematic league-table comparisons among regulators would simply extend the logic of publishing comparative performance indicators to regulators in government. Chapter 2 noted that performance standards for performance setters tended to be markedly less developed than those for the bodies the regulators oversaw. Regulators of government tended to measure their own performance in isolation from one another, and such performance standards as there were (in common with most public-sector organizations) tended to refer to economy and workflow rather than effectiveness. Regulators' response to this issue when we raised it in discussions tended to be that no meaningful comparative measures of performance could be developed for their activities, and to stress the uniqueness of each regulatory organization. Certainly, there are difficulties in measuring the performance of bodies whose objectives are multiple and conflicting and where it is hard to measure outcome as opposed to output. But those characteristics are shared by most public-sector bodies; they are not special to regulators of government. A possibly more distinctive feature of regulators of government that might make performance measurement problematic is that their effects are usually indirect, coming about at one remove through the improvement of other organizations' performance, which further complicates the identification of cause–effect links that besets any performance assessment. But even that problem is not unique to regulators (similar 'value-added' measurement problems arise in teaching, social work, and medicine, for example), and indeed many regulator organizations in government seem more like what James Q. Wilson (1990: 159) terms 'procedural' organizations (whose work can be observed but not the outcomes of that work) than 'coping' organizations (where neither work nor outcomes can be observed).

Moreover, even if there is something that makes for special problems in measuring the performance of regulators in government as opposed to other public-sector organizations, each regulator within government was by no means alone on the planet. As Chapter 2 showed, there were at least 130 'firms' in the business, and from the analysis in Chapter 3 of the methods they employed it is not clear that their activities were markedly more diverse than the differences within local government or the higher education sector (for instance, between All Souls College and a school of nursing), yet that diversity has not prevented attempts by the regulators to rank those organizations on a common scale. Indeed, given the dramatic growth of investment in regulation within government, it seems all the more important that comparative information on efficiency improvements, speed of communication, and quality-of-management indicators (such as clerical-grade absenteeism and turnover within the organization) should be routinely collected and published on a league-table basis for regulators as well as for service providers, and not confined to gnomic sentences in a set of separate annual reports. In addition, following European Union practice (by DG XIX) as described in Chapter 8, there is a case for regulators to include themselves in the league tables they publish of relative performance or practice among their charges.

A further step along the scale of competitiveness, more systematic exposure to sunset- and market-testing regulation in government, might also be expected to put regulators under more pressure to stay lean and achieve results. 'Sunset-testing' exposes regulation in government to competition with other policy priorities and claims on resources, yet none of the regulators we examined worked under an explicit 'sunset' regime. It might be argued that true sunset arrangements for public policies or institutions can hardly apply in the UK's constitutional context (in contrast to that of the US), since legislative or policy settings can always be reversed by the government of the day. But it is debatable how far this argument should be pressed. After all US sunset provisions typically stem from ordinary legislation, rather than from any constitutional entrenchment, which can also be overturned by any subsequent decision by the enacting or any subsequent legislature. The idea that there is some British constitutional reason why regulation in government should be an empire on which the sun never sets seems unconvincing, and indeed there are examples of sunset provisions (in all but name) in other policy domains. For instance the utilities-licensing regimes provided for price control to end after four or five years, requiring reformulation and licence modification if price control was to be retained.

In contrast to sunset provisions, market-testing exposes regulation to periodic competition with other providers of the service. The scope for systematic market-testing may be greatest for regulatory activities that involve multiple units doing the same thing and large-scale structures capable of mobilizing resources for setting up a market. Both are features which characterize schools inspection in England and may explain why OFSTED has developed the approach of franchising inspection activities to certified teams of inspectors, in a way that would not be so easily possible for small specialized inspectors. But it is not clear why the same approach could not be applied to social-services inspection, or to large areas of the work of the ombudsmen or public auditors.

A third and more radical application of competition to regulation in government would be to allow regulatees more scope than they currently have to choose their regulators. Such choice would need to be limited if it were not to lead to a 'race to the bottom' in regulatory standards (see McCahery *et al.* 1996) and earlier experience with the principle—as in the pre-District Audit days when local ratepayers elected their own auditors or the ability of local authorities to choose their own auditors up to 1982—shows up some of its limits.[5] But the principle has been established in some domains of regulation in government, notably in state-funded schools, where the opportunity to opt out of local-authority oversight and choose instead to be regulated by a central body was established in 1992. Similarly, the original bill which later became the Education (Schools) Act 1992 originally provided that school governors should be allowed to choose their own inspectors.[6] Likewise the Financial Services Act 1986 gave firms a limited choice on whether to be regulated directly by the Securities and Investment Board or by the appropriate self-regulatory organization.[7] It is possible at least to imagine a regime in which it was possible for central and local authorities to decide—within defined limits— which public-audit institutions they wished to be audited by or whether they wanted to be subject to efficiency scrutiny from Whitehall's Efficiency Unit or the Audit Commission.

## 3. AN OVERSIGHT DEFICIT?

Chapter 2 showed that regulation in government was a large and growing industry that was itself largely unregulated. In an era when codes of conduct in public service became commonplace, there was no code in this domain akin to the principles established for market-testing. No unit in government was responsible for

[5] In that case, the development of 'accountability conspiracies' (Dowding 1995: 70).
[6] Source: Education (Schools) Act 1992 in Current Statutes Annotated 1992, 38-2, Introduction and General Note.
[7] An arrangement which reflects Ogus's (1995) arguments for competition among self-regulator organizations.

comprehensive oversight or review of the field, and none of the top mandarins we spoke to in the higher reaches of Whitehall was in a position to take a balanced overview. External reviews were rare and such in-depth external reviews as there were tended to be on an isolated case-by-case basis, such as the review of the Audit Commission by an independent consultant (commissioned by the Commission itself) in 1995 or the review of the Commission for Local Administration by the Department of the Environment in 1995.[8] As Chapter 2 showed, a billion-pound-plus industry appears to have grown up in a relatively *ad hoc* way, with no systematic attempt to take stock. No one ever appeared to have compared the amount government invests in regulating itself with the amount it spends on regulating business and society, and asked if the balance made sense. It seems to be a dramatic case of 'no-one-in-charge-government' (Bryson and Crosby 1992: 4 ff.).

No-one-in-charge-government can have its virtues. But they are not advantages that the various regulators of government typically extolled for their own regulatee clients. If there was an oversight deficit in this case, there is an argument for a more systematic approach to overseeing the overseers, without arriving at the infinite regress of who oversees the overseers' overseer. At least three related elements could be included in a more coherent system of oversight: a common set of principles applying to regulators in government which included systematic logging of compliance costs, coherent principles of investment in regulation within government, and appraisal of the balance between external and reflexive regulation.

Chapter 2 commented on the absence of any general code of conduct and of any coherent system of logging compliance costs for regulation within government, in sharp contrast to the regulatory impact analysis routinely adopted for most business regulation. Reading across the notion of compliance costs from business to government can be problematic, but the narrow view of compliance costs taken in Chapter 2—the direct costs of interacting with the regulator in the process of scrutiny—is both measurable and important, given what many public-service practitioners said about the cost in expensive staff time of dealing with regulators. Regulators

---

[8] The review suggested that CLA was so ineffective it should be abolished, a finding rejected by the DOE, which had commissioned the review.

often tried to argue that there were in effect no compliance costs attached to their activities, since they were seeking only to generalize good practice. A typical regulator response was that 'We only ask for information that any well-run organizations should have for its own internal management.' We find this view disingenuous. Ratcheting all organizations up to the best-practice standards at the top will inevitably involve extra costs on those below best practice, which will often be the majority; repeated demands for multiple forms of information, coming from different regulators or even from the same regulator, are far from costless to respond to, and best-practice standards of management that may be easily achievable for large, well-resourced organizations may be much more costly for smaller organizations to achieve (cf. Hogwood *et al.* 1998).

The regulators' view of compliance costs as an issue only for business firms, not public-sector bodies, does not accord with what we learned from the selected regulatees we talked to about the costs of senior staff time in dealing with regulators (see Chapter 2). Indeed, the compliance-cost problem seems likely to be of increasing importance in regulation of government, since regulators can 'costlessly' (that is, at no cost to their own budgets) impose evergreater reporting requirements on their charges, and general changes in public management have tended to produce a more fragmented structure of service-delivery bodies facing increasing collective-action problems in protesting against compliance costs imposed on them by regulators. Since many aspects of compliance costs comprise a fixed-cost claim on resources regardless of organizational size, compliance costs in government regulation will tend to become relatively more burdensome as service-delivery units became smaller. The parallel with the regulatory 'squeeze' on small firms thus becomes closer, and the absence of any official effort to monitor regulatory impact and compliance costs more glaring.

There were isolated exceptions to the 'Nelson's-eye' vision of compliance costs among regulators in government, so different from the culture that has prevailed in the assessment of business regulation in recent years. And there were instances of best practice that could be built upon, albeit typically in the form of isolated *ad hoc* reviews rather than regular reporting. For instance, in the face of indignant protests from university Vice-Chancellors and

Principals about heavily increased regulatory compliance costs being imposed on their institutions with no additional public funding to cover those costs, the Higher Education Funding Councils assessed the costs of their surveys of academic standards in teaching and research.[9] In the regulation of Training and Enterprise Councils a 1995 efficiency scrutiny of the contract between TECs and the Department for Education and Employment focused on the costs of reporting on TECs and suggested that the regulatory burden from DfEE should be reduced to lower those costs (DfEE 1996: 132). Perhaps surprisingly, local-authority associations tended not to produce overall assessments of compliance costs imposed on local authorities by central-government regulators (as shown in Chapters 2 and 5), but they have been critical of the failure to extend deregulation effectively into this domain:

To date the results of this [deregulation] initiative have been very disappointing. Significant controls such as CCT, capping and capital . . . were excluded. The initiative has concentrated on controls by local authorities (e.g. control of dogs on roads, for which the rules have been simplified) rather than those imposed on local authorities by central government. . . . Departments other than the DOE appear to be less than committed to the initiative. (Select Committee on Relations Between Central and Local Government 1996: ii. 116)

Responsibility for coordinating the collection of information about compliance costs of regulation in government could either be brigaded with the central units responsible for orchestrating regulatory impact analyses for business regulation (the simplest and quickest solution), or assigned to some super-regulator unit, either in a central agency or free-standing, with responsibility for overall policy development and general overview of regulation within government.

More coherent principles of investment in regulation within government need to be developed along with a more systematic analysis of compliance costs and benefits. At the time of writing there seemed to be no general or clearly stated principles governing such investment. If small 'lean' organizations are the most effective way to regulate large, complex, and controversial privatized utilities, why did regulation of government need an investment that is so many times larger? If, as it repeatedly claimed, the NAO saved

---

[9] See e.g. Higher Education Funding Council for England (1998: 2).

seven times its own costs in any one year (compliance costs did not enter into this claim), why not massively increase it?[10] The stock assumption seemed to be that the bottleneck to expansion was the limited capacity of the Parliamentary Public Accounts Committee to process the NAO's value-for-money reports; but if those reports were as effective in saving costs as the NAO claimed, a random PAC scrutiny system or some form of franchising could be contemplated. In the absence of any coherent look at investment levels in regulation of government, resourcing will be wholly governed by happenstance and special pleading, and will not be justifiable by any coherent investment criteria—an approach which most regulators would roundly condemn if they found it in the organizations they oversee.

Reflexivity or responsiveness in public-sector regulation does not necessarily require a central-oversight regime, but it is closely bound up with compliance costs and investment in regulatory bureaucracy. By reflexivity is meant oversight practice which builds heavily on organizational self-regulation, aims to modify self-regulation at the margin (for instance by making regulatees write down the principles by which they work or by operating regimes of 'enforced self-regulation' (Ayres and Braithwaite 1992)), and only intervenes at the point where self-regulatory processes have clearly broken down. Reflexivity in that sense was far from unknown within government (it appeared for example in the Treasury's post-1994 system of general running-cost controls together with provision to put erring departments 'in the clinic' by exposing them to a full oversight system of control) but it appeared to be at best patchily applied, particularly outside Whitehall, and EU practice, as discussed in Chapter 8, might have valuable lessons to teach national-level regulators of government.

## 4. A RANDOMNESS DEFICIT?

This book has shown that regulators in government vary widely in the extent to which they consciously use random devices in their

---

[10] The Audit Commission also made dramatic claims for the potential savings achieved through its activities, which it put at £4.3bn. between 1983 and 1991 (Audit Commission 1991: 17). To the extent that savings on this scale were indeed directly related to the Commission's activity, there would also seem to be a case for massive expansion.

activities, like random tax audits. The Social Services Inspectorate used elements of randomness in planning its scrutiny programme and the Prisons Inspectorate followed a policy of unannounced snap inspections of prisons in addition to its programme of announced visits. As noted elsewhere in the book, while our research was in progress, OFSTED announced it planned to introduce a similar policy for school inspections. But randomness does not seem to be generally applied as a tool by regulators of government. We argued in the last chapter that many of the developments in public services in recent decades have the effect of displacing traditional elements of 'contrived randomness' in organizational control, and developments in regulation do not appear to be making up the deficit by sharply increased use of randomness allied with oversight.

Using lotteries in some form as a device of management or regulation is often controversial. It may be that the practice of public management has reached such an advanced level of development that the use of randomness can be relegated to the list of outmoded administrative devices along with wooden tally-sticks, sealing-wax, pipe-rolls, and red-tape itself. But we doubt it. More plausibly, it may be, as some Whitehall denizens commented when we raised this issue, that the environment of contemporary policy and bureaucracy, and the career paths of the people within it, is so widely perceived as turbulent and unpredictable that it is hardly necessary for further elements of randomness to be artificially contrived on top of the normal chaos. But if much of the village character of the central core of Whitehall remains (as claimed in Chapters 4 and 9), there may still be a randomness deficit at a personal level (where relational distance is low) while there is a randomness surplus in policy development. At least three devices could be used to ensure that the advantages of the use of chance were applied to regulation in government: random selection of regulatee units, random assignment of regulators to regulatees, and elements of randomness in managing regimes involving multiple performance indicators.

Random selection of regulatee units for scrutiny, where it was used at all, tended to be applied for the regulation of the lower-status organizations in public administration—prisons, schools, social-care institutions, and routine financial operations. But in some ways the greatest need for more randomness in oversight was at the top and the centre, where relational distance between regulator and regulatee tended to be lowest. There is accordingly a case for extending the random-selection principle to the scrutiny of central departments by public auditors or budget overseers rather than negotiating audits eighteen months in advance or relying on strategic overall targets and predictable review schedules.

A closely related principle is that of random assignment of regulators to regulatees. As was noted in Chapter 1, William Niskanen (1971) has advocated the application of such a system to legislative oversight of bureaux and policy programmes, as a means of avoiding 'capture' of the oversight process by legislators who are not representative of the majority of users. For regulation of bureaucrats by other bureaucrats, a similar principle can be invoked—and indeed the tradition of limited tenure in any particular position by top public servants (stretching back to the standard three-year term in post in the classical bureaucracy of imperial China) may help to bring it about. In fact, given the contradictory doctrines we noted at the outset of the book about best practice in regulation of government—whether regulation is best conducted by 'poachers turned gamekeepers' (low relational distance) or strangers and outsiders (high relational distance), or by some mixture of the two—a system of assignment of regulators to regulatees which made it unpredictable which of those principles will be invoked for any particular case could in principle achieve the advantages of both through the anticipated effects on the regulatee organization it is likely to generate.

Third, the same principle could be invoked for the design of the battery of performance indicators that so frequently figure in contemporary regulation of service-delivery bureaucracies (but markedly less so, as we have observed, for regulators themselves). Ever since Peter Blau's (1955) classic study of the way performance measurement of a welfare agency produced counter-productive outcomes (through caseload measures which led workers to encourage dependency rather than independence on the part of their clients) it has been well known that performance-indicator regimes tend to skew organizational behaviour in unintended ways through managerial activity to hit the targets, typically producing side- or even reverse-effects. Such behaviour is commonly discussed in the context of the contemporary vogue for quantitative performance measures in public bureaucracies. One way to counter the distorting effect that such performance measures can generate is deliberately to build elements of randomness into the weighting placed on any one out of a set of predeclared performance indicators. If managers are aware of a wide-ranging set of performance indicators by which they may be judged, but cannot predict what weight will be placed on each one, some of the grosser types of indicator-induced distortion will have a much more uncertain payoff. This effect often seems to come about by accident (by managers being unable to predict the weightings of indicators by which they will be judged because of the vagaries of the political and bureaucratic climate and the ubiquity of 'garbage can' processes (Cohen *et al.* 1972) in public policy). But if dense multi-indicator performance-assessment regimes are here to stay in public management, the time for more deliberate and self-conscious insertion of random terms into indicator weights may have arrived.

## 5. OVERALL

As explained at the outset, the argument above has been based on the assumption that 'what is sauce for the goose is sauce for the gander'—that is, the presumption that principles of regulation which are effective at one level or in one domain should normally be expected to be effective in other contexts unless the conditions can be shown to be radically different. From our analysis in Chapters 2 and 3, it is difficult to make a convincing case that regulators stand out from all other public-sector organizations in terms such as multiplicity of objectives, internal diversity, or the indirect character of the 'production' process. It consequently seems hard to argue that the organizational complex of regulators of government should itself remain largely unregulated, or that the design principles for regulating that complex should deviate radically from the design principles used to regulate other public-sector organizations.

In some cases, notably competition and oversight, we have found a marked instance of 'do as I say but not as I do' in the disparity between how regulators control and how they are controlled—a disparity which seems hard to justify. But the cases of mutuality and randomness seem different in two ways. First, mutuality and randomness applied at one level (control of clients by regulators) may also apply at the other level of control by regulators themselves. For example, random assignment of regulators to clients is as much a check on the regulator organization as the client organization, and mutuality can also be applied to face-to-face accountability of regulators to their clients. Second, the four deficits referred to earlier often seem to apply as much to regulation of their charges *by* the regulators as to regulation *of* the regulators. Even if mutuality remains strong (albeit supplemented by more formal paper-driven oversight) at the core of Whitehall, it tends to be weak in much of the rest of the public sector, and deliberate randomness is the exception, not the rule, in relationships between.

The methods discussed above for filling the four deficits are to some degree in tension, like the stays of a mast. But it has often been observed that most principles of institutional design tend to have a two-edged character (Goodin 1996: 40), and, as with the stays of mast, even though they pull against one another to some degree, they may achieve in combination what no single one could do on its own. A system of regulating the regulators which relied exclusively on any one of the four approaches sketched out above would be likely to have major and predictable limitations. And any formal institutional arrangement for manipulating the tensions among these approaches (following Dunsire's (1978) principle of collibration) is unlikely to be devisable. Apart from the sheer engineering difficulties of institutionalizing collibration on other than an opportunistic way (cf. Hood 1996*b*: 216–25), there is constitutional difficulty in assigning any single institution to regulate the regulators, given the aspiration to make many of them independent of 'politics'. Accordingly, any overall control of the four different approaches probably needs to be thought of as like the weather.[11] That is, the balance among these approaches might vary as political and social climates alter, but could not go beyond a certain point, like a masthead which bends to stress but is brought back by its opposing stays—at least up to the point where an extremity of stress brings the whole structure down. A system which built the four approaches discussed earlier into countervailing tensions could be a more balanced approach to institutional design for regulators of government.

---

[11] On some variant of the 'Gaia hypothesis' of self-regulating organisms in the biosphere (Tickell 1996: 40).

# APPENDIX I

## Interviews

The codes in the text denote interview types and sources: 'IPs' for pilot interviews, 'Is' for formal interviews with UK regulators, 'IEEs' for regulatee interviews, 'ITs' for telephone interviews, 'ISs' for interviews conducted jointly with another researcher in the ESRC Whitehall programme, and 'IEUs' for interviews with EU-level regulators and regulatees.

Pilot Interviews (IP)

| | |
|---|---|
| IP1 | Senior Official, NAO, 15 June 1995 |
| IP2 | Senior Official, DETR (then DOE), 21 June 1995 |
| IP3 | Senior Official, Housing Corporation, 18 July 1995 |
| IP4 | Former Senior Official, OFSTED, 8 Aug. 1995 |
| IP5 | Former Senior Official, LB Havering 1990/1995, 8 Aug. 1995 |
| IP6 | Senior Officials, Office of Passenger Rail Franchising, 15 Aug. 1995 |
| IP7 | Former Senior Official, HM Treasury, 18 July 1995 |
| IP8 | Former Senior Official, Audit Commission, 18 Aug. 1995 |
| IP9 | Senior Officials, Higher Education Funding Council, 29 Aug. 1995 |
| IP10 | Former Senior Official, OFTEL, 5 Sept. 1995 |

Regulator Interviews (I)

| | |
|---|---|
| I1 | Senior Officials, HM Inspectorate of Prisons, 6 Oct. 1995 |
| I2 | Senior Officials, Police Complaints Authority, 2 Nov. 1995 |
| I3 | Senior Official, Social Services Inspectorate, 13 Nov. 1995 |
| I4 | Senior Officials, Council on Tribunals, 22 Nov. 1995 |
| I5 | Senior Officials, The Commission for Local Administration in England, 6 Dec. 1995 |
| I6 | Senior Official, Cabinet Office, 11 Nov. 1995 |
| I7 | Senior Official, HM Treasury, 11 Jan. 1996 |
| I8 | Senior Officials, HM Treasury, 16 Jan. 1996 |
| I9 | Senior Officials, HM Treasury, 18 Jan. 1996 |
| I10 | Senior Officials, OFSTED, 19 Jan. 1996 |
| I11 | Senior Officials, HM Treasury, 6 Feb. 1996 |
| I12 | Senior Official, Data Protection Registrar, 7 Feb. 1996 |
| I13 | Senior Officials, HM Treasury, 12 Feb. 1996 |

| | |
|---|---|
| I14 | Senior Official, HM Treasury, 13 Feb. 1996 |
| I15 | Senior Officials, NAO, 20 Feb. 1996 |
| I16 | Senior Officials, Office of Public Service, 22 Feb. 1996 |
| I17 | Senior Official, HM Treasury, 26 Feb. 1996 |
| I18 | Senior Official, Office of Public Service, 1 Mar. 1996 |
| I19 | Senior Official, Magistrates' Courts Service Inspectorate, 21 Mar. 1996 |
| I20 | Senior Official, Cabinet Office, 29 Mar. 1996 |
| I21 | Senior Officials, Cabinet Office, 24 May 1996 |
| I22 | Senior Official, HM Inspectorate of Prisons, 18 June 1996 |
| I23 | Senior Official, Parliamentary Commissioner for Administration, 25 June 1996 |
| I24 | Senior Officials, Prisons Ombudsman, 27 June 1996 |
| I25 | Senior Official, NAO, 1 June 1996 |
| I26 | Senior Official, OFSTED, 22 July 1996 |
| I27 | Senior Official, Office of Public Service, 23 July 1996 |
| I28 | Senior Official, HM Prison Service, 29 July 1996 |
| I29 | Senior Officials, Cabinet Office, 30 July 1996 |
| I30 | Senior Official, Funding Agency for Schools, 6 Aug. 1996 |
| I31 | Senior Official, Department for Education and Employment, 12 Sept. 1996 |
| I32 | Senior Officials, HM Inspectorate of Railways, Health and Safety Executive, 4 Oct. 1996 |
| I33 | Senior Official, Northern Ireland Audit Office, 11 Oct. 1996 |
| I34 | Senior Officials, HM Inspectorate of Fire Services, 24 Oct. 1996 |
| I35 | Former Senior Official, Audit Commission, 30 Oct. 1996 |
| I36 | Senior Officials, NI Department of Finance and Personnel, 7 Apr. 1997 |
| I37 | Senior Official, Northern Ireland Ombudsman, 8 Apr. 1997 |
| I38 | Senior Official, Data Protection Registrar, 25 Apr. 1997 |
| I39 | Senior Official, Housing Corporation, 28 May 1997 |
| I40 | Senior Officials, Home Office, 16 July 1997 |
| I41 | Senior Official, Audit Commission, 28 Aug. 1997 |
| I42 | Senior Official, Audit Commission, 8 Sept. 1997 |

Regulatee Interviews (IEE)

| | |
|---|---|
| IEE1 | Headteacher and Chair of Governors, LEA Secondary School, London, 24 Nov. 1995 |
| IEE2 | Headteacher, GM Secondary School, London, 24 July 1996 |
| IEE3 | Director, Private Prison under contract to HM Prison |

Service, 29 July 1996

| | |
|---|---|
| IEE4 | Governor, HM Prison Service, 1 Aug. 1996 |
| IEE5 | Senior Official, LB Tower Hamlets, 30 Aug. 1996 |
| IEE6 | Senior Official, LB Tower Hamlets, 5 Sept. 1996 |
| IEE7 | Senior Official, HM Prison Service, 11 Sept. 1996 |
| IEE8 | Senior Official, LB Tower Hamlets, 28 Oct. 1996 |
| IEE9 | Senior Official, West Midlands Fire Service, 29 Nov. 1996 |
| IEE10 | Senior Official, LB of Lambeth, 13 Dec. 1996 |
| IEE11 | Senior Official, LB Islington, 23 Jan. 1997 |

Telephone Interviews (T)

| | |
|---|---|
| TI1 | Senior Official, HM Inspectorate of Prisons, 4 July 1996 |
| TI2 | Senior Official, Department for Education and Employment, 13 Sept. 1996 |
| TI3 | Senior Official Social Work Services Inspectorate, 9 Oct. 1996 |
| IT4 | Senior Official, West Midlands Fire Service, 22 Nov. 1996 |
| TI5 | Senior Official, Department for Education and Employment, 15 Jan. 1997 |
| IT6 | Former Senior Official, Audit Commission, 15 July 1997 |

Special Interviews (IS)

| | |
|---|---|
| IS1 | Senior Official, HM Treasury, 27 Mar. 1996 |
| IS2 | Senior Official, HM Treasury, 9 July 1996 |

Interviews with EU Regulators and Regulatees (IEU)

| | |
|---|---|
| IEU1 | Senior Official, DG V, 3 June 1997 |
| IEU2 | Senior Official, EU Inspectorate General, 3 June 1997 |
| IEU3 | Senior Official, DG XV, 3 June 1997 |
| IEU4 | Senior Official, DG V 4 June 1997 |
| IEU5 | Senior Official, European Court of Auditors, 4 June 1997 |
| IEU6 | Senior Official, European Court of Auditors, 4 June 1997 |
| IEU7 | Senior Official, European Court of Auditors, 4 June 1997 |
| IEU8 | Senior Official, DG XIX, 5 June 1997 |
| IEU9 | Senior Official, DG XX Financial Control, 5 June 1997 |
| IEU10 | Senior Official, UCLAF, Secretariat General of the Commission, 5 June 1997 |
| IEU11 | Senior Official, DG VI, 5 June 1997 |
| IEU12 | Senior MEP, Member of the Budgetary Control Committee, 11 July 1997 |
| IEU13 | Senior Official, EU Ombudsman (by email), 13 July and 27 July 1997 |

# APENDIX II

## Regulator Budgets and Staffing

TABLE AII.1. *Budgets and staff for 135 regulators, 1995*

| Regulators | Budget (£m.) | Staff |
|---|---|---|
| *Auditors* | | |
| Accounts Commission for Scotland | 4 | 87 |
| Audit Commission for Local Authorities and the NHS in England and Wales | 89 | 174 and 1,125 in District Audit |
| National Audit Office | 42.2 | 750 |
| Northern Ireland Audit Office | 3.8 | 92 |
| *Inspectorates* | | |
| HM Inspector of Anatomy, Department of Health | 0.08 | 1 |
| HM Inspectorate of Constabulary (England and Wales) | 5.1 | 91 |
| HM Inspectorate of Constabulary (Scotland) | 0.7 | 12 |
| Curriculum and Assessment Authority for Wales | 6.8 | 37 |
| Scottish Consultative Council on the Curriculum | 4.3 | 40 |
| Northern Ireland Council for Curriculum Examination and Assessment | 11.5 | 173 |
| Northern Ireland Education and Training Inspectorate | 3.3 | 66 |
| HM Inspectorate of Fire Services (England and Wales) | 3.9 | 89 |
| HM Inspectorate of Fire Services (Scotland) | 0.3 | 6 |
| HM Railways Inspectorate (HSE) | 3.2 | 82 |
| Higher Education Quality Council | 1.4 | 45 |
| Magistrates' Court Service Inspectorate | 1.2 | 27 |
| The Mental Health Act Commission | 2.6 | 36 |
| Mental Health Commission for Northern Ireland | 0.3 | 8 |
| Mental Welfare Commission for Scotland | 0.9 | 12 |

TABLE AII.1. *Continued*

| Regulators | Budget (£m.) | Staff |
| --- | --- | --- |
| Nuclear Installations Inspectorate Nuclear Safety Division (HSE) | 13 | 268 |
| HM Inspectorate of Prisons | 0.7 | 21 |
| HM Inspectorate of Prisons (Scotland) | 0.2 | 5 |
| HM Inspectorate of Probation | 1.1 | 24 |
| Office of HM Chief Inspector of Schools/ Office of Standards in Education | 64 | 549 |
| HM Inspectors of Schools The Scottish Office | 6.8 | 142 |
| Schools Curriculum and Assessment Authority | 30 | 203 |
| Office of HM Chief Inspector of Schools in Wales | 7.2 | 80 |
| Social Services Inspectorate | 9.2 | 248 |
| Social Services Inspectorate Northern Ireland | 0.9 | 26 |
| Social Services Inspectorate Wales | 0.6 | 16 |
| Social Work Services Inspectorate The Scottish Office | 1.1 | 31 |
| *Ombudsmen and Equivalents* | | |
| The Adjudicator's Office | 1 | 36 |
| Commission for Local Administration in England | 6.4 | 199 |
| Commission for Local Administration in Scotland | 0.4 | 12 |
| Commissioner for Local Administration in Wales | 0.4 | 15 |
| Interception of Communications Act Commissioner | 0.035 | 1 |
| Housing Association Tenants Ombudsman Service | 0.4 | 9 |
| The Housing Association Ombudsman for Scotland | 0.1 | 3 |
| Independent Assessor of Military Complaints Procedure in Northern Ireland | 0.05 | 3 |
| National Health Service Commissioner | 4.85 | 72 |
| Northern Ireland Commissioner for Complaints | 0.25 | 6 |
| Northern Ireland Parliamentary Commissioner for Administration | 0.25 | 6 |
| Parliamentary Commissioner for Administration | 4.85 | 82 |

TABLE AII.1. *Continued*

| Regulators | Budget (£m.) | Staff |
|---|---|---|
| Police Complaints Authority | 3.8 | 59 |
| Independent Commission for Police Complaints for Northern Ireland | 0.7 | 17 |
| Prisons Ombudsman | 0.5 | 13 |
| Scottish Prisons Complaints Commission | 0.08 | 2 |
| Security Services Act Commissioner | 0.035 | 1 |
| *Central Agency Regulators* | | |
| Council on Tribunals | 0.5 | 11 |
| Office of Public Service | | |
| Citizen's Charter Unit, OPS | 3.8 | 38 |
| Civil Service Employer Group, OPS | 1.7 | 147 |
| Deregulation Unit, OPS | 1.3 | 42 |
| Office of the Civil Service Commissioners | 1 | 23 |
| Civil Service Commissoners Northern Ireland | 0.15 | 5 |
| Office of the Commissioner for Public Appointments | 0.5 | 6 |
| Efficiency and Effectiveness Group, OPS | 1.7 | 35 |
| Machinery of Government and Standards Group, OPS | 0.5 | 52 |
| Senior Civil Service Group, OPS | 4.5 | 170 |
| Northern Ireland Department of Finance and Personnel | | |
| Central Personnel Group, NIDFP | 3.5 | 120 |
| Government Purchasing Service, NIDFP | 1 | 27 |
| Resource Control and Professional Service Group, NIDFP | 3.8 | 103 |
| Supply Group, NIDFP | 1 | 35 |
| HM Treasury | | |
| Budget and Public Finance Directorate, HMT | 5.2 | 178 |
| Procurement Policy Team and Procurement Practice Group, HMT | 0.9 | 18 |
| Financial Management Reporting and Audit Directorate, HMT | 0.3 | 26 |
| Spending Directorate, HMT | 5.6 | 169 |
| *Funder-Regulators* | | |
| Funding Agency for Schools | 10 | 218 |
| Further Education Funding Council for England | 23 | 393 |
| Further Education Funding Council for Wales | 2.3 | 41 |

TABLE AII.1. *Continued*

| Regulators | Budget (£m.) | Staff |
|---|---|---|
| Further Education Funding Division, The Scottish Office | 0.6 | 29 |
| Higher Education Funding Council for England | 12 | 180 |
| Higher Education Funding Council for Wales | 1.6 | 23 |
| Highlands and Islands Enterprise | 6.5 | 150 |
| The Housing Corporation | 30 | 658 |
| Northern Ireland Housing Executive | 3.2 | 289 |
| Tai Cymru Housing for Wales | 2.8 | 69 |
| Scottish Higher Education Funding Council | 3.4 | 68 |
| Scottish Homes | 39 | 1,154 |
| Scottish Enterprise | 16 | 367 |
| Teacher Training Agency | 1.6 | 70 |
| *Departmental Regulators of Agencies* | | |
| Sections of 26 central-government departments which regulate other parts of central government | 46 (estimate) | 1,000 (estimate) |
| *Central-Local Public Bodies Regulators and NHS Regulators* | | |
| Sections of 21 central-government departments regulating Local Government | 190 (estimate) | 3,900 (estimate) |
| 8 Central National Health Service Regulators | 112 (estimate) | 1,800 (estimate) |

# APPENDIX III

## Selected Regulator Profiles

TABLE AIII.1. *Origin, task, and accountability: twenty-eight selected regulators*

| Organization name and type | Origin and statutory basis of authority | Task | Accountability including publication of an annual report containing performance indicators |
|---|---|---|---|
| *Public Audit Bodies* | | | |
| Accounts Commission for Scotland | Established in 1974 under the Local Government (Scotland) Act 1973 and NHS (Scotland) Act 1973 as amended by the Local Government (Scotland) Act 1975 and NHS and Community Care Act 1995. | To secure the audit of local authorities, health and associated bodies in Scotland, to consider reports on these audits and to make recommendations to the Secretary of State. To carry out national value for money studies, to issues an annual direction to local authorities which sets out performance information. They are required to publish and to advise the Secretary of State on audit matters. | Commissioners are appointed by the Secretary of State for Scotland. Accounts are submitted to the Secretary of State, and a published annual report contains limited performance indicators. |
| Audit Commission for Local Authorities and the NHS in England and Wales | A statutory body established in its present form by the Local Government Finance Act 1982. The National Health Service and | Appoints auditors to all local authorities and health bodies in England and Wales and carries out national value for money studies. The | Reports to the Environment Minister who can issue directions to the Commission, although this power has never been used |

Table AIII.1. *Continued*

| Organization name and type | Origin and statutory basis of authority | Task | Accountability including publication of an annual report containing performance indicators |
|---|---|---|---|
| | Community Care Act 1990 extended its work to the NHS. The Local Government Act 1992 gave the Commission further powers relating to performance indicators. The post-1982 system replaced the District Audit Service and its central Audit Inspectors, arrangements which dated from 1844. | Commission defines comparative indicators of local authority performance that are published annually. The Commission is responsible for the District Audit Service which it operates as an arm's-length agency to provide local audit and other services. | except for the form of accounts. The Commission is required to consult audited bodies before exercising many functions and presents a published annual report to Parliament which contains some limited performance measures. |
| National Audit Office | The NAO is headed by the Comptroller and Auditor General (C & AG) whose statutory powers are laid out in the National Audit Act 1983. The first C & AG was appointed in 1314 but the post-1983 system replaced the Exchequer and Audit Department created by the Exchequer and Audit Department Act 1866, as amended in 1921. | To provide information, assurance and advice to Parliament about the use of taxpayers' money. The C & AG authorizes the issue of public funds to government departments and other public bodies, certifies the accounts, and reports on the value for money of bodies. The NAO also audits the accounts of some international bodies. | The C & AG is an officer of the House of Commons and NAO reports to Parliament, specifically to the Public Accounts Commission. An annual report is published containing some limited performance indicators. |
| Northern Ireland Audit Office | The C & AG for NI and the NIAO operate under statutory powers in the Audit (Northern Ireland) Order 1987. This system replaced | To provide assurance and advice to Parliament on the proper accounting for Northern Ireland departments and certain other public | Accountable to the Public Accounts Commission, and produces a published annual report to Parliament containing limited |

TABLE AIII.1. *Continued*

| Organization name and type | Origin and statutory basis of authority | Task | Accountability including publication of an annual report containing performance indicators |
|---|---|---|---|
| | the Exchequer and Audit Office NI set up under the Audit Act 1921 | bodies, to certify accounts, and report on value for money in the use of resources. | performance indicators. |
| *Inspectorates and Equivalents* | | | |
| HM Inspectorate of Constabulary for England and Wales | Statutory duties are set out in the Police Act 1964 as amended by the Police and Magistrates' Court Act 1994. It was originally established under the County and Borough Police Act 1856. | To certify the efficiency and effectiveness of the Police Service in England and Wales through inspection and direct advice and assistance and to provide advice to the Home Secretary on policing issues, maintaining independence of judgement and the highest professional standards. | Annual report submitted to the Home Secretary containing no performance indicators. The Inspectorate is part of the Home Office. |
| HM Inspectorate of Fire Service for England and Wales | Established under the Fire Services Act 1947. | To inspect and report on local authority fire brigades in England, Wales and Northern Ireland for operations, staffing and resources, fire prevention, fire research, and other activities. | Annual report submitted to the Home Secretary containing no performance indicators. Part of the Home Office. |
| HM Inspectorate of Railways, Health and Safety Executive | Part of the Health and Safety Executive enforcing the HSW Act 1974 on the railways. It was previously part of the Board of Trade 1840–1920 and the | To ensure safety on UK railways by issuing guidance for railway operation on the design, construction and operation of railways; prior | Annual report submitted to the Secretary of State for Transport and the Health and Safety Commission. There is a published annual report |

TABLE AIII.1. *Continued*

| Organization name and type | Origin and statutory basis of authority | Task | Accountability including publication of an annual report containing performance indicators |
| --- | --- | --- | --- |
| | Department of Transport 1920–90. | inspection of new lines, rolling stock and equipment; the monitoring of safety procedures on existing lines to ensure compliance with the HSW Act and relevant statutory provisions; and the investigation of selected incidents. | containing limited performance indicators. |
| HM Inspectorate of Prisons | Operates under the Criminal Justice Act 1982 which made it more independent than the previous body which operated under the Prisons Act 1952. | To examine and report on the treatment of prisoners and conditions in prisons. | Reports to the Home Secretary and submits an annual report containing no performance indicators. Part of the Home Office. |
| Magistrates' Courts Service Inspectorate | Established under the Police and Magistrates' Courts Act 1994. | To inspect and report to the Lord Chancellor on the administration and management of the Magistrates' Courts Service in order to improve performance and disseminate good practice. | An annual report is submitted to the Lord Chancellor and published, containing performance indicators for the Inspectorate. |
| Office of HM Chief Inspector of Schools (Office for Standards in Education, OFSTED) | Established in present form under the Education (Schools) Act 1992. The current system replaced HM Inspectorate of Schools for England and Wales which began in 1840. | To inspect and report upon every secondary, primary and special school in the state system every four years. To establish, monitor and regulate a new independent inspection system for grant-maintained | Submits an annual report to the Secretary of State for Education and Employment which is published and presented to Parliament. The report contains limited performance indicators. OFSTED |

TABLE AIII.1. *Continued*

| Organization name and type | Origin and statutory basis of authority | Task | Accountability including publication of an annual report containing performance indicators |
|---|---|---|---|
| | | schools in England. To keep the Education Secretary informed about standards of achievement, quality of education, efficiency of financial and other management, and the development of values in schools. | is a non-Ministerial government department. |
| Social Services Inspectorate | The SSI was formed in 1985. A General Board of Health was established in 1848 replaced by Ministry of Health in 1919. Personal Social Services and Children's Department were transferred to Department of Health in 1968. A Social Work Division of DHSS was created in 1971 from which the SSI was created in 1985. | To manage national inspection of the quality of service to users and carers; to contribute professional social work and personal social services knowledge and experience in advice to ministers and the Department of Health; to assist in putting policy in effect; to promote high standards for social services provision and value for money in the delivery of services through advice and guidance to local authorities and other agencies; to conduct Department of Health business on behalf of Ministers and to inspect local-authority inspection units. | Reports and presents an annual report to the Secretary of State for Health containing no performance indicators. SSI is part of the Department of Health. |

TABLE AIII.1. *Continued*

| Organization name and type | Origin and statutory basis of authority | Task | Accountability including publication of an annual report containing performance indicators |
|---|---|---|---|
| *Ombudsmen and Equivalents* | | | |
| Commission for Local Administration in England | Established by the Local Government Act 1974 | To provide independent, impartial and prompt investigation and resolution of complaints of injustice caused through maladministration and to promote fair and effective local government in district, borough, city and county councils, and various other local bodies, housing action trusts, police authorities, fire authorities, joint board of local authorities, the Norfolk and Suffolk Broads Authority, the National Rivers Authority, and the education appeals committee. | Annual published report containing some performance indicators. Accountable to DETR for use of resources. |
| National Health Service Commissioner for England, Scotland, and Wales | Statutory authority under the National Health Service Act 1973 and National Health Service (Scotland) Act 1978 and the Hospital Complaints Procedure Act 1985. | To investigate complaints against the NHS; to provide redress for justified complaints; and to contribute to improving the service. Some resources are shared with the PCA. | Annual report to Parliament containing performance indicators. |

TABLE AIII.1. *Continued*

| Organization name and type | Origin and statutory basis of authority | Task | Accountability including publication of an annual report containing performance indicators |
|---|---|---|---|
| Northern Ireland Parliamentary Commissioner for Administration and Northern Ireland Commissioner for Complaints | Parliamentary Commissioner Act (NI) 1969 and Commissioner for Complaints Act (NI) 1969 as modified by NI Act 1974. Independent statutory authority. | To investigate complaints made by persons who claim to have sustained injustice as a consequence of maladministration by government departments, local authorities, and certain other public bodies. | Annual report to Parliament containing performance indicators. |
| Parliamentary Commissioner for Administration | Parliamentary Commissioner Act 1967. | To investigate complaints from members of the public referred by an MP to the PCA who claim to have been subject to maladministration by action by or on behalf of government departments and certain non-departmental public bodies. | Annual report to Parliament containing performance indicators. |
| *Central Agency Regulators* Citizen's Charter Unit, Office of Public Service | Non-statutory, established in 1992. Part of the Office of Public Service. | To act as a central source of advice to public service organizations; to support the Prime Minister's Panel of Advisers, and to carry out specific projects. | Reports to the Permanent Secretary and Ministers in OPS; no separate annual report. |
| Office of the Civil Service Commissioners | Operates under the Civil Service Orders in Council 1991 and 1995. The first | To approve the selection of candidates for senior posts and fast-stream | An annual published report is submitted to the Crown. It contains no |

## TABLE AIII.1. *Continued*

| Organization name and type | Origin and statutory basis of authority | Task | Accountability including publication of an annual report containing performance indicators |
|---|---|---|---|
| | Civil Service Commissioners were appointed in 1855. The Civil Service Commission (which operated direct recruitment as well as regulating recruitment) was abolished in 1991 and replaced by the OCSC | feeder entries; to advise the Minister for the Civil Service and Foreign Secretary on the rules each lays down for the Home Civil Service and Diplomatic Service respectively, over selection procedures for appointments at grade levels below those directly approved by the Commissioners; to monitor the way departments apply the rules and comply with the Recruitment Code; and to hear and determine appeals under the Civil Service Code. | performance indicators. |
| Civil Service Commissioners Northern Ireland, NI Department of Finance and Personnel | Established in 1923 by the Northern Ireland Governors Order 1923. Updated by the Civil Service (NI) Order 1986. | To ensure that, apart from the exemptions listed in the Civil Service (NI) Order 1986, every candidate for appointment in the Northern Ireland Civil Service satisfies appropriate standards of suitability in such matters as knowledge, health, nationality, age, and character. | Annual published report submitted to the Crown. It contains no performance indicators. |

TABLE AIII.1. *Continued*

| Organization name and type | Origin and statutory basis of authority | Task | Accountability including publication of an annual report containing performance indicators |
|---|---|---|---|
| Deregulation Unit (in 1997 renamed the Better Regulation Unit), Office of Public Service | Non-statutory part of the Office of Public Service, which moved from DTI to OPS in 1995. | To secure deregulation and minimize the burden of new UK and EC regulations by working with departments and the Cabinet Office. | Reports to the Permanent Secretary and Ministers in OPS; no separate annual report. |
| Efficiency and Effectiveness Group, Office of Public Service | Non-statutory part of OPS. Created in 1995 containing the then separate Next Steps Project Team and the Efficiency Unit. | To help departments and agencies improve performance and value for money. | Reports to the Permanent Secretary, Ministers and the PM's adviser on efficiency; no separate annual report. |
| Procurement Policy Team and Procurement Practice Group | Non-statutory part of HM Treasury Finance Regulation and Industry Directorate. | To ensure UK government meets EU legal requirements on procurement and encourages best practice in procurement. | Reports to the Permanent Secretary and Ministers; no separate annual report. |
| Office of the Commissioner for Public Appointments | Created by and operates under Order in Council in 1995. The Commissioner for Public Appointments is also a Civil Service Commissioner. | To monitor, regulate, and provide advice on departmental appointment procedures for 2,754 executive NDPBs and 760 NHS bodies. The Commissioner has the right to investigate and deal with complaints. The Commissioner is also Commissioner for Public Appointments in Northern Ireland. | Publishes an annual report and is also accountable as a Civil Service Commissioner. |

TABLE AIII.1. *Continued*

| Organization name and type | Origin and statutory basis of authority | Task | Accountability including publication of an annual report containing performance indicators |
|---|---|---|---|
| Council on Tribunals | Operates under the Tribunals and Inquiries Act 1992. Originally established by the Tribunals and Inquiries Act 1958. | To keep under review the constitution and working of the tribunals and to report on their constitution and working; to consider and report on matters referred to the Council under the Act with respect to tribunals other than ordinary courts of law, whether or not specified in Schedule 1 to the Act; and to consider and report on these matters, or matters the Council may consider to be of special importance, with respect to administrative procedures which involve the holding of a statutory inquiry by or on behalf of a Minister. | Annual report submitted to the Lord Chancellor and Lord Advocate. |
| *Funding-cum-Regulatory Bodies* Funding Agency for Schools | Established under the Education Act 1993 | To fund grant-maintained schools; to monitor their financial situation; and to ensure that there is an adequate number of school places in certain LEAs. The Agency | Reports to the Secretary of State for Education and Employment and is an executive body of the department. Publishes an annual report containing performance |

## TABLE AIII.1. *Continued*

| Organization name and type | Origin and statutory basis of authority | Task | Accountability including publication of an annual report containing performance indicators |
|---|---|---|---|
| | | also has concern for educational quality and value for money in grant-maintained schools. | indicators. |
| Higher Education Funding Council for England | Established under the Higher Education Act 1992. | To administer funds made available by the Secretary of State for Education and Employment in support of the provision of higher education for teaching and research and associated activities; and to advise the Secretary of State for Education and Employment on the funding needs of these institutions. HEFCE regulates through conditions attached to funding, set out in financial memoranda; the audit of the management of public funds, the health of governance and compliance with guidance; intervention in individual cases of misconduct; and assessment of the quality of teaching in individual subjects. | Publishes an annual report and is responsible for resources to the Department for Education and Employment as a non-departmental public body. |

TABLE AIII.1. *Continued*

| Organization name and type | Origin and statutory basis of authority | Task | Accountability including publication of an annual report containing performance indicators |
| --- | --- | --- | --- |
| The Housing Corporation | Established by the Housing Act 1964, updated by Housing Acts of 1974 and 1988. | To register, promote, fund, supervise, and regulate housing associations in England; to safeguard housing association tenants' interests; to inform and assist local-authority and new town tenants interested in exercising their rights under Tenants' Choice; and responsibility for the approval and revocation of potential new landlords under this policy. | Annual report submitted to the Secretary of State for the Environment, Transport and the Regions, an executive non-departmental public body of the department. |
| *Departmental Regulators of Agencies* Home Office Prison Service Monitoring Unit (subsumed within Home Office Efficiency and Consultancy Unit in 1997) | Non-statutory part of the Home Office. | Responsible for overseeing HM Prison Service Agency and advising the Home Secretary. It is a more developed oversight section than those which exist in other departments for monitoring agencies and non-departmental public bodies. | Reports to the Permanent Secretary and Ministers; no separate annual report. |

TABLE AIII.1. *Continued*

| Organization name and type | Origin and statutory basis of authority | Task | Accountability including publication of an annual report containing performance indicators |
| --- | --- | --- | --- |
| *Central-Local Public Bodies, Regulators and NHS Regulators* Department of the Environment, Transport and the Regions, Local Government and Planning Sections | Non-statutory sections of the Department operating within legal frameworks associated with programmes and grant giving. | The local government and planning sections have a lead role in relation to local authorities and set and implement the legal and financial framework within which local authorities carry out their responsibilities; ensure adequate and affordable levels of service are provided by competition, the Citizen's Charter and by open government. | Reports to the Permanent Secretary and Ministers; no separate annual report |

# REFERENCES

Albert-Roulhac, C. (1998), 'The Influence of EU Membership on Methods and Processes of Budgeting in Britain and France 1970–1995', *Governance* 11 (2): 209–30.

Alchian, A. A. (1987), 'Property Rights', in J. Eatwell, M. Milgen, and P. Newman (eds.), *The New Palgrave: A Dictionary of Economics*, London, Macmillan.

Allison, G. T. (1984), 'Public and Private Management: Are They Fundamentally alike in All Unimportant Respects?', in R. J. Stillman (ed.), *Public Administration: Concepts and Cases*, 4th edn., Boston, Houghton Mifflin: 283–98.

Anechiarico, F., and Jacobs, J. B. (1996), *The Pursuit of Absolute Integrity*, Chicago, University of Chicago Press.

Armstrong, K., and Bulmer, S. (1998), *The Governance of the Single European Market*, Manchester, Manchester University Press.

Armstrong, M., Cowan, S., and Vickers, J. (1994), *Regulatory Reform*, Cambridge, Mass., MIT Press.

Audit Commission (1989), *Losing an Empire, Finding A Role: The LEA of the Future*, London, Audit Commission.

——(1991), *How Effective is the Audit Commission?* London, Audit Commission.

——(1996), *Annual Report and Accounts for the Year Ended 31 March 1996*, London, Audit Commission.

——(1997), *Reviewing Social Services: Annual Report 1997*, London, Audit Commission/Department of Health.

Ayres, I., and Braithwaite, J. (1992), *Responsive Regulation*, Oxford, OUP.

Bahmueller, C. F. (1981), *The National Charity Company*, Berkeley, University of Berkeley Press.

Baldwin, R. (1985), *Regulating the Airlines: Administrative and Agency Discretion*, Oxford, Clarendon Press.

——(1987), 'Health and Safety at Work: Consensus and Self Regulation', in R. Baldwin and C. McCrudden (eds.), *Regulation and Public Law*, London, Weidenfeld & Nicolson: 132–58.

Barker, A. (1998), 'Political Responsibility for UK Prison Security—Ministers Escape Again', *Public Administration* 76: 1–23.

Barker, R. (1984), 'The Fabian State', in B. Pimlott (ed.), *Fabian Essays in Socialist Thought*, London, Heinemann: 27–38.

Barrow, M. (1996), 'Public Services and the Theory of Regulation', *Policy and Politics* 24 (3): 263–76.

Becher, T. (1989), *Academic Tribes and Territories*, Milton Keynes, Open University Press.

Beck Jørgensen, T., and Larsen, B. (1987), 'Control—An Attempt at Forming a Theory', *Scandinavian Political Studies* 10 (4): 279–99.

Beer, S. H. (1965), *Modern British Politics*, London, Faber.

Bellamy, C. (1988), *Administering Central-Local Relations 1871–1919*, Manchester, Manchester University Press.

Bender, B. G. (1991), 'Whitehall, Central Government and 1992', *Public Policy and Administration* 6: 13–20.

Bentham, J. (1983), *Constitutional Code*, i, F. Rosen and J. H. Burns (eds.), Oxford, Clarendon Press.

Best, G. (1971), *Mid-Victorian Britain 1851–1875*, London, Weidenfeld & Nicolson.

Birkinshaw, P. (1994), *Grievances, Remedies and the State*, 2nd edn., London, Sweet & Maxwell.

Bishop, A. S. (1971), *The Rise of Central Authority for English Education*, Cambridge, Cambridge University Press.

Black, D. (1976), *The Behaviour of Law*, New York, Academic Press.

Black, J. (1995), ' "Which Arrow?" Rule Type and Regulatory Policy', *Public Law* (Spring): 94–117.

——(1996), 'Constitutionalizing Self-Regulation', *Modern Law Review* 57: 24–55.

Blackie, J. (1970), *Inspecting the Inspectorate*, London, Routledge & Kegan Paul.

Blau, P. M. (1955), *The Dynamics of Bureaucracy*, Chicago, Chicago University Press.

Bogdanor, V. (1987), *Evidence to House of Lords Select Committee on Public Services*.

Bourdieu, P. (1988), *Homo Academicus*, Cambridge, Polity Press.

Bowerman, M. (1994), 'The National Audit Office and the Audit Commission: Cooperation in Areas where Their VIM Responsibilities Interface', *Financial Accountability and Management* 10 (1): 47–63.

Brans, M., and Rossbach, S. (1997), 'The Autopoiesis of Administrative Systems: Niklas Luhmann on Public Administration and Public Policy', *Public Administration* 74 (3): 417–39.

Breyer, S. G. (1993), *Breaking the Vicious Cycle*, Cambridge, Mass., Harvard University Press.

Bridges, E. (1963), 'The Treasury as the Most Political of Departments', *Public Policy* 12: 1–20.

Broadbent, J., and Laughlin, R. (1997), 'Contracts, Competition and Accounting in Recent Legal Enactments for the Health and Education Sectors in the UK: An Example of Juridification at Work?', in S. Deakin and J. Michie (eds.), *Contracts, Cooperation, and Competition*, Oxford, OUP.

————(1998), 'Modes of Accountability in Schools: The Individualizing and Socializing Tendencies of Accountability Changes and Some Implications for Management Control', Paper presented at the Fourth International Management Control Systems Conference, 6–8 July 1998.

Bryson, J. M., and Crosby, B. C. (1992), *Leadership for the Common Good*, San Fransisco, Jossey-Bass.

Bulpitt, J. (1983), *Territory and Power in the United Kingdom*, Manchester, Manchester University Press.

Burch, M., and Holliday, I. (1996), *The British Cabinet System*, London, Prentice Hall/Harvester Wheatsheaf.

Burnheim, J. (1985), *Is Democracy Possible?*, Cambridge, Polity Press.

Butler, Sir R. (1997), 'The Changing Civil Service', Speech to ESRC 'Wither Whitehall' Conference, Church House, London, 24 Sept. 1997.

Buttery, R., Hurford, C., and Simpson, R. K. (1985), *Audit in the Public Sector*, 2nd edn., Hemel Hempstead, ICSA Publishing.

Cabinet Office (1987), *The Judge Over Your Shoulder*, 1st edn., London, Cabinet Office.

——(1993), *Career Management and Succession Planning Study*, London, HMSO.

——(1994a), *The Civil Service: Continuity and Change*, Cm. 262, London, HMSO.

——(1994b), *Next Steps Review*, Cm. 2750, London, HMSO.

——(1994c), *Judge over Your Shoulder. Judicial Review: Balancing the Scales*, 2nd edn., London, Cabinet Office.

——(1995), *Civil Service Statistics 1995*, London, HMSO.

——Office of Public Service (1995a), *The Ombudsman in Your Files*, London, Cabinet Office.

————(1995b), *Public Bodies*, London, HMSO.

————(1996a), *Next Steps Briefing Note*, London, Cabinet Office.

————(1996b), *Civil Service Fast Stream Recruitment Report 1995–96*, London, Cabinet Office.

————(1997), *Next Steps Briefing Note*, London, Cabinet Office.

——and HM Treasury (1996), *Spending Public Money: Governance and Audit Issues*, Cm. 3179, London, HMSO.

Carson, W. G. (1970), 'Some Sociological Aspects of Strict Liability and the Enforcement of Factory Legislation', *Modern Law Review* 33: 396–412.

Chapman, R. (1997), 'Civil Service Recruitment: the Civil Service Commissioners' Annual Report', *Public Policy and Administration* 12 (3): 1–5.

Chartered Institute of Public Finance and Accounting (CIPFA) (1996), *Local Government Comparative Statistics*, London, CIPFA.

Chester, N. (1951), *Central and Local Government: Financial and Administrative Relations*, London, Macmillan.

Civil Service Commission (1976), *Memorandum Submitted to Eleventh Report from the Expenditure Committee*: The Civil Service HC 535, iii, Session 1976–77, London, HMSO.

Civil Service Commissioners (1996), *Civil Service Commissioners' Annual Report 1995–6*, London, Office of the Civil Service Commissioners.

Citizen's Charter Complaints Task Force (1995), *Putting Things Right: Main Report*, London, HMSO.

Civil Service Department (1980), *The Integration of HM Treasury and the Civil Service Department Working Paper 2*, London, HMSO.

Clark, D., Wiseman, L., and Graven, I. (1994), *Responsibilities for Recruitment to the Civil Service*, Cabinet Office, Recruitment Studies Team, OPSS, London, HMSO.

Coase, R. H. (1960), 'The Problem of Social Cost', *Journal of Law and Economics* 3: 1–44.

Cohen, M., March, J., and Olsen, J. P. (1972), 'A Garbage Can Model of Organisational Choice', *Administrative Science Quarterly* 17: 1–25.

Collier, M. (1996), 'The Accountable Regulator', in *Public Finance Foundation Report: Adding Value?* London, Public Finance Foundation/CIPFA.

Commissioner for Public Appointments (1997), *Commissioner for Public Appointments Second Report 1996–97*, London, Office of the Commissioner for Public Appointments.

Committee of Public Accounts (1994), *The Proper Conduct of Public Business: Eighth Report from the Committee of Public Accounts*, HC 154, 1993–94, 154, London, HMSO.

Cooper, D. (1995), 'Local Government and Legal Consciousness in the Shadow of Juridification', *Journal of Law and Society* 22 (4): 506–26.

Cotterrell, R. (1992), *The Sociology of Law*, London, Butterworths.

Cranston, R. (1979), *Regulating Business: Law and Consumer Agencies*, London, Macmillan.

Creighton, S., and King, V. (1996), *Prisoners and the Law*, London, Butterworths.

Daintith, T. (1979), 'Regulation by Contract: The New Prerogative', *Current Legal Problems* [1979]: 41–64.

——(1995), 'Introduction: The Indirect Administration of Community Law', in T. Daintith (ed.), *Implementing EC Law in the United Kingdom*, Chichester, Wiley: 1–23.

——(1997) (ed.), *Constitutional Implications of Executive Self-Regulation: The New Administrative Law*, London, Institute for Advanced Legal Studies.

Day, P., and Klein, R. (1987), *Accountabilities: Five Public Services*, London, Tavistock.

————(1990), *Inspecting the Inspectorates*, York, Joseph Rowntree Memorial Trust.

————(1997), 'Steering but not Rowing? The Transformation of the Development of Health: A Case Study', University of Bath, Centre for the Analysis of Social Policy.

Department for Education (1992), *Choice and Diversity: A New Framework for Schools*, Cm. 2021, London, HMSO.

Department for Education and Employment (1996), *Departmental Annual Report, The Government's Expenditure Plans 1996–97 to 1998–99*, Cm. 3210, London, HMSO.

——(1997), *Excellence in Schools*, Cm. 3681, London, HMSO.

——and Ofsted (1998), *Departmental Report 1998*, Cm. 3910, London, HMSO.

Department of Education and Science and Welsh Office (1982), *Review of HM Inspectors of Education*, London, DES/WO.

Department of the Environment (1996), *Report of the Financial Management and Policy Review of the Commission for Local Administration in England: Stage Two*, London, DOE.

Douglas, M. (1982), *Natural Symbols*, New York, Pantheon.

——(1985), 'Introduction', in J. L. Gross and S. Rayner (eds.), *Measuring Culture: A Paradigm for the Analysis of Social Organization*, New York, Columbia University Press.

Dowding, K. (1995), *The Civil Service*, London: Routledge.

Drewry, G., and Butcher, T. (1984), *The Civil Service Today*, Oxford, Blackwell.

Dunleavy, P. (1991), *Democracy, Bureaucracy and Public Choice*, Hemel Hempstead, Harvester Wheatsheaf.

Dunsire, A. (1978), *The Execution Process*, ii, Oxford, Martin Robertson.

——(1988), 'Bureaucratic Morality in the UK', *International Political Science Review* 9 (3): 179–91.

——(1990), 'Holistic Governance', *Public Policy and Administration*, 5 (1): 3–18.

Edsberg, J. (1994), 'The European Community's Budget: Budget Discipline and Budget Accounting', *Financial Accountability and Management* 10: 1–16.

Ehlerman, C. D., and Laudati, L. L. (1997), *Proceedings of the European Competition Forum*, Chichester, Wiley.

European Commission (1996a), *13th Annual Report on Monitoring of the*

*Effectiveness of Community Law 1995*, Brussels, European Commission, Com (96) 600 (final).

European Commission (1996*b*), *Financial Report 1995*, Brussels, European Commission.

——(1996*c*), *Public Procurement in the European Union—Exploring the Way Forward*, Brussels, European Commission.

——(1997*a*), *8th Annual Report on the Structural Funds 1996*, Brussels, European Commission, Com (97): 525 (final).

——(1997*b*), *The Fight Against Fraud—Annual Report 1996*, Brussels, European Commission.

European Ombudsman (1997), *Annual Report*, Ombudsman of the European Union.

Evans, M., and Morgan, R. (1992), 'The European Convention for the Prevention of Torture: Operational Practice', *International and Comparative Law Quarterly* 41: 590–614.

Feintuck, M. (1994), *Accountability and Choice in Schooling*, Buckingham, Open University Press.

Ferlie, E., Pettigrew, A., Ashburner, L., and Fitzgerald, L. (1996), *The New Public Management in Action*, Oxford, OUP.

Fernandez-Martin, J. M. (1996), *The EC Procurement Rules*, Oxford, OUP.

Finer, S. E. (1952), *The Life and Times of Sir Edwin Chadwick*, London, Methuen.

Foster, C. (1992), *Privatisation, Public Ownership and the Regulation of Natural Monopoly*, Oxford, Blackwell.

——(1996), 'Reflections on the True Significance of the Scott Report for Government Accountability', *Public Administration*, 74 (4): 567–92.

——(1998), 'The Constitutional Role of the Civil Service: Would Legislation Help? Or The Haldane Relation: Can It, Should It Be Reclaimed?', Paper presented to seminar in Oxford, 16 Feb. 1998.

——and Plowden, F. J. (1996), *The State under Stress*, Buckingham, Open University Press.

Foucault, M. (1977), *Discipline and Punish*, Harmondsworth, Penguin.

Frazer, T. (1995), 'The New Structural Funds, State Aids and Interventions on the Single Market', *European Law Review* 20: 3–19.

Freedland, M. (1994), 'Government by Contract and Public Law', *Public Law* (Spring): 86–104.

Froud, J., Boden, R., Ogus, A., and Stubbs, P. (1998), *Controlling the Regulators*, London, Macmillan.

Gerber, D. J. (1994), 'The Transformation of European Community Competition Law', *Harvard International Law Journal* 35 (1): 97–147.

Glynn, J. J. (1985), *Auditing the Public Sector*, London, Prentice-Hall.

Golding, L. (1962), *A Dictionary of Local Government in England and Wales*, London, English University Press.

Goodin, R. (1996), 'Institutions and their Design', in R. Goodin (ed.), *The Theory of Institutional Design*, Cambridge, Cambridge University Press: 1–53.

Gosden, P. H. J. H. (1966), *The Development of Educational Administration in England and Wales*, Oxford, Blackwell.

Grabosky, P., and Braithwaite, J. (1986), *Of Manners Gentle*, Melbourne, OUP.

Graham, C., and Prosser, T. (1991), *Privatizing Public Enterprises*, Oxford, OUP.

Greenleaf, W. H. (1983), *The British Political Tradition*, i, London, Methuen.

——(1987), *The British Political Tradition*, iii, London, Methuen.

Griffith, J. A. G. (1966), *Central Departments and Local Authorities*, London, Allen & Unwin.

Hancher, L., and Moran, M. (1989) (eds.), *Capitalism, Culture, and Regulation*, Oxford, OUP.

Harden, I. (1995), 'Regulating Government', *Political Quarterly* 66 (4): 299–306.

——White, F., and Donnelly, K. (1995), 'The Court of Auditors and Financial Control and Accountability in the European Community', *European Public Law* 1: 599–632.

Harding, R. W. (1994), 'Models of Accountability for the Contract Management of Prisons', in P. Moyle (ed.), *Private Prisons and Police*, Sydney, Pluto Press: 63–90.

——(1997), *Private Prisons and Public Accountability*, Buckingham, Open University Press.

Harlow, C. (1996), 'Codification of EC Administrative Procedures: Fitting the Foot to the Shoe or the Shoe to the Foot', *European Law Journal* 2: 3–25.

——and Rawlings, R. (1997), *Law and Administration*, 2nd edn., London, Butterworths.

Harris, N. (1993), *Law and Education*, London, Sweet & Maxwell.

Hartley, O. (1972), 'Inspectorates in British Central Government', *Public Administration* 50 (4): 447–66.

Hawkins, K., and Thomas, J. (1984), *Enforcing Regulation*, Boston, Kluwer-Nijhoff.

Heclo, H. (1977), *Government of Strangers*, Washington, Brookings Institution.

——and Wildavsky, A. (1974), *The Private Government of Public Money*, London, Macmillan.

Hennestad, B. W. (1990), 'The Symbolic Impact of Double Bind Leadership: Double Bind and the Dynamics of Organisational Culture', *Journal of Management Studies* 27: 265–80.

Higher Education Funding Council for England (1998), *Research Assessment Consultation Paper*, Bristol, HEFC.

HM Chief Inspector of Prisons (1995), *Annual Report 1994–95*, London, HMSO.

——(1996), *Annual Report 1995–6*, London, HMSO.

Hoggett, P. (1996), 'New Modes of Control in the Public Service', *Public Administration*, 74: 9–32.

Hogwood, B. W., Judge, D., and McVicar, M. (1998), 'Too Much of a Good Thing? The Pathology of Accountability', Paper presented at the Political Studies Association Annual Conference, University of Keele, 7–9 Apr. 1998.

Hollingsworth, K., White, F., and Harden, I. (1998), 'Audit, Accountability and Independence: the Role of the Audit Commission', *Legal Studies* 18 (1): 78–100.

Hood, C. (1976), *The Limits of Administration*, London, Wiley.

——(1978), 'Keeping the Centre Small', *Political Studies* 26 (1): 30–46.

——(1983), *Tools of Government*, London, Macmillan.

——(1986), *Administrative Analysis*, Brighton, Wheatsheaf.

——(1990), 'Beyond the Public Bureaucracy State? Public Administration in the 1990s', Inaugural Lecture, London School of Economics, 16 Jan. 1990.

——(1995), ' "Deprivileging" the UK Civil Service in the 1980s: Dream or Reality?', in J. Pierre (ed.), *Bureaucracy in the Modern State*, Aldershot, Edward Elgar, 92–117.

——(1996*a*), 'Control Over Bureaucracy: Cultural Theory and Institutional Variety', *Journal of Public Policy* 15 (3): 207–30.

——(1996*b*), 'Where Extremes Meet: "SPRAT" versus "SHARK" in Public Risk Management', ch. 9 in C. Hood and D. K. C. Jones (eds.), *Accident and Design*, London, UCL Press: 208–70.

——(1998*a*), *The Art of the State*, Oxford, Clarendon Press.

——(1998*b*), 'Individualized Contracts for Top Public Servants: Copying Business, Path-Dependent Political Re-engineering or Trobriand Cricket', *Governance* 11 (4): 443–62.

——and Dunsire, A. (1981), *Bureaumetrics*, Farnborough, Gower.

——and Scott, C. (1996), 'Bureaucratic Regulation and New Public Management in the United Kingdom: Mirror-Image Developments?', *Journal of Law and Society* 23: 321–45.

Horn, M. (1995), *The Political Economy of Public Administration*, Cambridge, Cambridge University Press.

House of Commons Education Select Committee (1993), *School Inspections* HC 360 1992–93, London, HMSO.

Hughes, D., Griffiths, L., and McHale, J. (1997), 'Do Quasi-Markets Evolve? Institutional Analysis and the NHS', *Cambridge Journal of Economics* 21 (2): 259–76.

Hume, L. J. (1981), *Bentham and Bureaucracy*, Cambridge, Cambridge University Press.

Hustler, D., and Stone, V. (1996), 'Lay Inspectors: Insiders and Outsiders', in J. Ousten, P. Earley, and B. Fidler (eds.), *OFSTED Inspection: the Early Experience*, London, David Fulton Publishers: 61–72.

Hviid, M. (1995), 'Relational Contracts and Repeated Games', in D. Campbell and P. Vincent-Jones (eds.), *Contract and Economic Organisation*, Aldershot, Dartmouth.

Ignatieff, M. (1989), (orig. publ. 1978), *A Just Measure of Pain*, London, Pantheon.

Jabbari, D. (1994), 'Some Observations on Critical Theory in Administrative Law', *Oxford Journal of Legal Studies* 14: 189–215.

James, A. L., Bottomley, A. K., Liebling, A., and Clare, E. (1997), *Privatising Prisons*, London, Sage.

James, R. (1997), *Private Ombudsmen and Public Law*, Aldershot, Dartmouth.

Jennings, I. (1959), *The Law and the Constitution*, London, University of London Press.

Jones, G. (1993), *Local Government*, Hemel Hempstead, ICSA Publishing.

——(1997), *The New Local Government Agenda*, Hemel Hempstead, ICSA Publishing.

——and Stewart, J. (1985), *The Case for Local Government*, London, Allen & Unwin.

——and Travers, T. (1996), 'Central Government Perceptions of Local Government', in L. Pratchett and D. Wilson (eds.), *Local Democracy and Local Government*, Basingstoke, Macmillan.

Kagan, R. A., and Scholz, J. T. (1984), 'The Criminology of the Corporation' and 'Regulatory Enforcement Strategies', in K. Hawkins and J. M. Thomas, *Enforcing Regulation*, Boston, Kluwer.

King, R. D., and McDermott, K. (1995), *The State of Our Prisons*, Oxford, Clarendon Press.

Kreher, A. (1996), *The New European Agencies*, Florence, European University Institute.

Laffan, B. (1997), 'From Policy Entrepreneur to Policy Manager: The Challenge Facing the European Commission', *Journal for European Public Policy* 4 (3): 422–38.

Laudati, L. (1996), 'The European Commission as Regulator: The Uncertain Pursuit of the Competitive Market', in G. Majone (ed.), *Regulating Europe*, London, Routledge.

Laughlin, R., and Broadbent, J. (1993), 'Accounting and Law: Partners in the Juridification of the Public Sector in the UK?' *Critical Perspectives in Accounting* 4: 337–68.

————(1996), 'The New Public Management' Reforms in Schools and GP Practices: A Comparative Study of Professional Resistance and the

Role of Absorption and Absorbing Groups', *Working Paper*, University of Essex.

Laughlin, R., and Broadbent, J. (1997), 'Contracts and Competition? A Reflection on the Nature and Effects of Recent Legislation on Modes of Control in Schools', *Cambridge Journal of Economics* 21 (2): 277–90.

Layfield Committee (1976), *Reports of the Committee of Enquiry into Local Government Finance*, Cmnd 6543, London, HMSO.

Le Grand, J., and Bartlett, W. (1993), *Quasi-Markets and Social Policy*, Basingstoke, Macmillan.

Learmont, Sir J. (1995), *Review of Prison Service Security in England and Wales and the Escape from Parkhurst Prison on Tuesday 3rd January 1995*, London, Home Office.

Learmouth, J. (1996), 'OFSTED: A Registered Inspector's View', in J. Ouston, P. Earley, and B. Fidler, *OFSTED Inspection: the Early Experience*, London, David Fulton Publishers.

Lenaerts, K. (1993), 'Regulating the Regulatory Process: "Delegation of Powers" in the European Community', *European Law Review* 18 (1): 23–49.

Levy, R. P. (1994), 'Audit and Accountability in a Multi-Agency Environment: The Case of the Common Agriculutural Policy in the UK', *Financial Accountability and Management* 10: 65–75.

Lewis, D. (1997), *Hidden Agendas*, London, Hamish Hamilton.

Lewis, N., and Birkinshaw P. (1993), *When Citizens Complain*, Buckingham, Open University Press.

Light, P. (1993), *Monitoring Government*, Washington, Brookings Institute.

Livingstone, S., and Owen, T. (1993), *Prison Law*, Oxford, OUP.

Loughlin, M. (1992), *Administrative Accountability in Local Government*, York, Joseph Rowntree Foundation.

——(1996), *Legality and Locality*, Oxford, Clarendon Press.

——and Scott, C. (1997), 'The Regulatory State', in P. Dunleavy, A. Gamble, I. Holliday, and G. Peele (eds.), *Developments in British Politics 5*, Basingstoke, Macmillan: 205–19.

Loveland, I. (1996), *Constitutional Law*, London, Butterworths.

Lygo, R. (1991), *The Management of the Prison Service*, London, HMSO.

McCahery, J., Bratton, B., Picciotto, S., and Scott, C. (1996) (eds.), *International Regulatory Competition and Co-ordination*, Oxford, OUP.

McCloskey, D. (1990), *If You're So Smart*, London, University of Chicago Press.

McConville, S. (1981), *A History of English Prison Administration*, i, London, Routledge.

——(1995), *English Local Prisons*, London: Routledge.

McCubbins, M. D., and Schwartz, T. (1984), 'Congressional Oversight

Overlooked: Police Patrols versus Fire Alarms', *American Journal of Political Science* 28: 165–79.

McDonagh, O. (1977), *Early Victorian Government*, London, Weidenfeld & Nicolson.

McGowan, F., and Wallace, H. (1996), 'Towards a European Regulatory State', *Journal of European Public Policy* 3 (4): 560–76.

Mackenzie, W. J. M., and Grove, J. W. (1957), *Central Administration in Britain*, London, Longmans.

Maher, I. (1996), 'Limitations on Community Regulation in the UK: Legal Culture and Multi-Level Governance', *Journal of European Public Policy* 3: 577–93.

Majone, G. (1994), 'The Rise of the Regulatory State in Europe', *West European Politics* 17 (3): 77–101.

Makkai, T., and Braithwaite, J. (1995), 'In and Out of the Revolving Door: Making Sense of Regulatory Capture', *Journal of Public Policy* 12: 61–78.

Mandler, P. (1990), *Aristocratic Government in the Age of Reform*, Oxford, Clarendon Press.

Mashaw, J. (1983), *Bureaucratic Justice*, New Haven, Yale University Press.

Matthews, P., and Smith, G. (1995), 'OFSTED: Inspecting Schools and Improvement through Inspection', *Cambridge Journal of Education*, 25 (1): 23–34.

May, J. D. (1979), *Committee of Inquiry Into UK Prison Services*, Cm. 7673, London, HMSO.

Mendrinou, M. (1994), 'European Community Fraud and the Politics of Institutional Development', *European Journal of Political Research* 26: 81–101.

——(1996), 'Non-Compliance and the European Commission's Role in Integration', *Journal of European Public Policy* 3: 1–22.

Morgan, R. (1985), 'Her Majesty's Inspectorate of Prisons', in M. Maguire, J. Vagg, and R. Morgan (eds.), *Accountability of Prisons*, London, Tavistock: 106–23.

Moore, M. (1995), *Creating Public Value*, Cambridge, Mass., Harvard University Press.

Mulgan, G. (1995), 'Seven Maxims on the Future of Government', *Demos Quarterly*, 5, London, Demos.

National Audit Office (1993), 'Welsh Development Agency Accounts 1992–93', HC 827 1992–93, HMSO.

——(1995), *Clinical Audit in England*, HC 27 1995–6, London, HMSO.

——(1996), *The Work of the Directors General of Telecommunications, Gas Supply, Water Services and Electricity Supply* HC 645 1995–96, London, HMSO.

Niskanen, W. A. (1971), *Bureaucracy and Representative Government*, Chicago, Aldine-Atherton.

Nolan Committee (1995), *First Report of the Committee on Standards in Public Life*, Cm. 2850-I, London, HMSO.

Normanton, E. L. (1966), *The Accountability and Audit of Governments*, Manchester, Manchester University Press.

Office for National Statistics (1996), *Annual Employment Survey: Results for Great Britain*, London: ONS.

OFSTED (1995a), *The Annual Report of Her Majesty's Chief Inspector of Schools Part 2*, London, HMSO.

——(1995b), *Inspection Quality 1994/1995*, London, OFSTED.

——(1998a), *Annual Report of HM Chief Inspector 1996/7*, London: HMSO.

——(1998b), *News Release PN 98–23*, London, OFSTED.

Ogus, A. (1994), *Regulation*, Oxford, Clarendon Press.

——(1995), 'Rethinking Self Regulation', *Oxford Journal of Legal Studies* 15: 97–108.

Ouchi, W. (1979), 'A Conceptual Framework for the Design of Organizational Control Arrangements', *Management Science* 25 (9): 95–112.

Page, E. (1997), *People Who Run Europe*, Oxford, OUP.

Parkinson, C. N. (1961), *Parkinson's Law*, Harmondsworth, Penguin Books.

Parliamentary Commissioner for Administration (1996), *Parliamentary Commissioner for Administration Fourth Report Session 1995–96, Annual Report for 1995*, London, HMSO.

Parry, J. (1993), *The Rise and Fall of Liberal Government in Victorian Britain*, New Haven, Yale University Press.

Parry, R., Hood, C., and James, O. (1997), 'Reinventing the Treasury: Economic Rationalism or an Eurocrat's fallacy of control?' *Public Administration* 75 (3): 395–415.

Pascale, R. T., and Athos, A. G. (1981), *The Art of Japanese Management*, New York, Simon & Schuster.

Peterson, J. (1997), 'The European Union: Pooled Sovereignty, Divided Accountability', *Political Studies*, 559–78.

PM's Office (1994), *The Citizen's Charter: Second Report*, Cm. 2540, London, HMSO.

Pollitt, C., and Summa, H. (1997), 'Reflexive Watchdogs? How Supreme Audit Institutions Account for Themselves', *Public Administration* 75: 313–36.

Power, M. (1994), *The Audit Explosion*, London, Demos.

——(1997), *The Audit Society*, Oxford, OUP.

President's Committee on Administrative Management (1937), *Report of the Committee with Studies of Administrative Management in the Federal Government*, Washington, US Government Printing Office.

Prest, J. (1990), *Liberty and Locality*, Oxford, Clarendon Press.

Prison Service (1995), *Annual Report 1994–95*, London, HMSO.

Prisons Ombudsman (1995), *First Six Months Report*, London, Prisons Ombudsman.

——(1996), *Annual Report*, London, Prisons Ombudsman.

——(1997), *Annual Report 1996*, London, Prisons Ombudsman.

Prosser, T. (1997), *Law and the Regulators*, New York, Clarendon Press.

Public Accounts Committee (1996), *17th Report*, HC 234 1995–6.

Reiss, A. J. (1984), 'Selecting Strategies of Social Control over Organisational Life', in K. Hawkins and J. M. Thomas (eds.), *Enforcing Regulation*, Boston, Kluwer-Nijhoff.

Rhodes, G. (1981), *Inspectorates in British Government*, London, Allen & Unwin.

Rhodes, R. A. W. (1997), *Understanding Governance*, Buckingham, Open University Press.

Richardson, G. (1993), *Law, Process and Custody*, London, Weidenfeld & Nicolson.

——and Sunkin, M. (1996), 'Judicial Review: Questions of Impact', *Public Law* 79: 79–103.

Richardson, J. (1996), 'Eroding EU Policies; Implementation Gaps, Cheating and Re-Steering', in J. Richardson (ed.), *European Union: Power and Policy Making*, London, Routledge: 278–94.

Riley, A. J. (1997), 'The European Cartel Office: A Guardian without Weapons', *European Competition Law Review* 18: 3–16.

Rock, P. (1996), *Reconstructing a Women's Prison*, Oxford, OUP.

Rose-Ackerman, S. (1978), *Corruption*, New York, Academic Press.

Royal Sanitary Commission (1871), *2nd Report* C 281, i, London.

Ruimschotel, D. (1994), 'The EC Budget: Ten Per Cent Fraud? A Policy Analysis Approach', *Journal of Common Market Studies* 32: 319–42.

Rowan-Robinson, J., Watchman, P., and Barker, C. (1990), *Crime and Regulation*, Edinburgh, T. & T. Clark.

Rutherford, A. (1998), 'A Bold Vision of Decency', *New Law Journal* 148: 253.

Ryan, M. (1994), 'Private Prisons in the United Kingdom: Radical Change and Opposition', in P. Moyle (ed.), *Private Prisons and Police*, Sydney, Pluto Press: 235–56.

Schick, A. (1996), *The Spirit of Reform: A Report Prepared for the State Services Commission and the Treasury*, Wellington, New Zealand State Services Commission.

Schmid, A. A. (1978), *Property, Power and Public Choice*, New York, Praeger.

Scholz, J. T. (1991), 'Cooperative Regulatory Enforcement and the Politics of Administrative Effectiveness', *American Political Science Review* 85 (1): 115–36.

Scott, C. (1996*a*), 'The New Public Law', in C. Willet (ed.), *The Citizen's Charter and Public Sector Reform*, London, Blackstone Press: 43–64.

——(1996*b*), 'Changing Patterns of European Community Utilities Law and Policy: An Institutional Hypothesis', in J. Shaw and G. More (eds.), *New Legal Dynamics of European Union*, Oxford, OUP: 193–215.

——(1998), 'The Juridification of Regulatory Relations in the UK Utilities Sectors', in J. Black, P. Muchlinski, and P. Walker (eds.), *Commercial Regulation and Judicial Review*, Oxford, Hart Publishing.

Scottish Office (1997), *Scotland's Parliament*, Cm. 3658, London, HMSO.

Selby-Bigge, L. A. (1927), *The Board of Education*, London, G. P. Putnam & Sons.

Select Committee on Relations Between Central and Local Government (1996), *Report vol. II, Rebuilding Trust HL Paper 97-I*, London, HMSO.

Seneviratne, M. (1994), *Ombudsmen in the Public Sector*, Buckingham, Open University Press.

Sherlock, A., and Harding, C. (1991), 'Controlling Fraud within the European Community', *European Law Review* 16: 20–36.

Shichor, D. (1991), *Punishment for Profit*, London, Sage.

Sieber, S. (1981), *Fatal Remedies: The Ironies of Social Intervention*, New York, Plenum.

Smellie, K. B. (1946), *A History of Local Government*, London, Allen & Unwin.

Snyder, F. (1995), 'The Effectiveness of European Community Law: Institutions, Processes, Tools and Techniques', in T. Daintith (ed.), *Implementing EC Law in the United Kingdom*, Chichester, Wiley: 51–87.

Symons, E. (1996), 'Accountability', in *Government Accountability: Beyond the Scott Report*, London, Public Finance Foundation/CIPFA.

Teubner, G. (1987), 'Juridification', in G. Teubner (ed.), *Juridification of Social Spheres*, Berlin, De Gruyter: 3–48.

Thain, C., and Wright, M. (1995), *The Treasury and Whitehall*, Oxford, Clarendon Press.

Thompson, M., Ellis, R., and Wildavsky, A. (1990), *Cultural Theory*, Boulder, Colo., Westview.

Tickell, O. (1996), 'Healing the Rift', *Independent on Sunday*, 4 Aug. 1996: 40–1.

Treasury, HM (1991), *Competing for Quality*, Cm. 1730, London, HMSO.

——(1996*a*), *Public Expenditure: Statistical Analyses 1996–97*, Cm. 3201, London, HMSO.

——(1996*b*), *Government Procurement—Progress Report to the Prime Minister*, London, HMSO.

Trosa, S. (1994), *Next Steps: Moving On*, London, Office of Public Service and Science.

Tumim, S. (1992), 'The Inspector as Critic: The Job of the HM Chief Inspector of Prisons', *Political Quarterly* 63: 5–11.

Vagg, J. (1994), *Prison Systems*, Oxford, Clarendon Press.

Veljanovski, C. (1991) (ed.), *Regulators and Markets*, London Institute of Economic Affairs.

——(1993), *The Future of Industry Regulation in the UK*, London, European Policy Forum.

Vincent-Jones, P. (1998), 'Governance of and by Contract: Reflexivity and Responsiveness in the Bureaucratic Regulation of UK Local Authority Public Service Provision', Paper presented to the Law and Society Annual Conference, 4–7 June 1998, Aspen, Colo.

——and Harries, A. (1996), 'Conflict and Cooperation in Local Authority Quasi-Markets: The Hybrid Organisation of Internal Contracting Under CCT', *Local Government Studies* 22: 214–37.

Voltaire (1965/orig. publ. 1759), *Candide*, Oxford, Basil Blackwell.

Webb, S., and Webb, B. (1920), *Constitution of a Socialist Commonwealth of Great Britain*, London, Longmans.

————(1922), *English Prisons under Local Government*, London, Frank Cass.

Wessels, W., and Dietrich Rometsch, D. (1996), 'Conclusion: European Union and National Institutions', in D. Rometsch and W. Wessels (eds.), *The European Union and Member States*, Manchester, Manchester University Press: 328–65.

Wheare, K. (1955), *Government by Committee*, Oxford, Clarendon Press.

Wilby, P. (1989), 'Why Heads are Right to be Wimps', *The Independent*, 28 Sept. 1989.

Wilcox, B., and Gray, J. (1996), *Inspecting Schools*, Buckingham, Open University Press.

Wilks, S. (1996), 'Regulatory Compliance and Capitalist Diversity in Europe', *Journal of European Public Policy* 3: 536–59.

——and McGowan, L. (1996), 'Competition in the European Union: Creating a Federal Agency', in G. B. Doern and S. Wilks (eds.), *Comparative Competition Policy*, Oxford, OUP.

Williams, R. (1995), 'The European Commission and the Enforcement of

Environmental Law: An Invidious Position', *Yearbook of European Law* 14: 351–99.

Wilson, J. Q. (1990), *American Government: Brief Version*, Lexington, Mass., D. C. Heath.

——and Rachal, P. (1977), 'Can the Government Regulate Itself?', *The Public Interest* 46 (Winter): 3–14.

Woodhouse, D. (1997), *In Pursuit of Good Administration*, Oxford, OUP.

Woolf, Lord, and Tumim, S. (1991), *Prison Disturbances, April 1990: Report of an Inquiry by the Rt. Hon. Lord Justice Woolf (Parts 1 and 2), and His Honour Judge Stephen Tumim (Part 2)*, Cm. 1456, London, HMSO.

# INDEX